Housewife or Harlot

Housewife or Harlot:

The Place of Women in French Society 1870–1940

JAMES F. McMILLAN
Lecturer in History, University of York

ST. MARTIN'S PRESS · New York

All rights reserved. For information, write:
St Martin's Press, Inc., 175 Fifth Avenue, New York, NY 10010
Printed in Great Britain
First published in the United States of America in 1981

ISBN 0-312-39347-4

Library of Congress Cataloging in Publication Data

McMillan, James F., 1948–
Housewife or harlot
Bibliography: p.
Includes index.
1. Women – France – Social conditions 2. Women – France – History.
3. Housewives – France – History. 4. Women – Employment – France –
History. 5. Feminism – France – History. 6. France – History – Third
Republic, 1870–1940. I. Title.
HQ1617.M26   1980   305.4'2'0944   80-18675

ISBN 0-312-39347-7

To my Mother and Father

Contents

Preface

THIS book has been a long time in the making. Its origins go back to the research which I did at Oxford and Paris between 1969 and 1972 while a graduate student at Balliol College. After further research carried out in time stolen from teaching or preparing new courses, a first draft was delivered to Harvester Press in the Autumn of 1978. While the manuscript was with the publisher, however, a number of major contributions to the literature on the subject appeared which necessitated substantial rewriting. A work which failed to mention Louise Tilly and Joan Scott's, *Woman, Work and Family*, Alain Corbin's *Les filles de noce* or Christiane Dufrancatel and Michelle Perrot's essays in the collection *Histoire sans qualité* would have been out-of-date before it appeared. The present work dates from a spell of frantic activity in the Spring and early Summer of 1980. In a field which is expanding so rapidly, any book runs the risk of being overtaken by the most recent research. It is nevertheless the author's hope that the present volume will establish the wider context against which more specialised studies may be better understood, and that it will be some considerable time before a second edition is required.

I would like to record my gratitude to all those institutions which over the past decade have provided the financial assistance so essential for the insolvent British historian who embarks upon research in France. It was thanks to a generous grant from the Social Science Research Council, in conjunction with the Centre Nationale de la Recherche Scientifique, that I was able to spend the summer of 1977 working in Paris. Smaller, but no less appreciated, sums were awarded at various times by the Carnegie Trust for the Universities of Scotland, the University of Glasgow, Balliol College, Oxford and the University of York.

My intellectual debts are even more numerous. While at Oxford, I had the great good fortune to be supervised by Professor Richard Cobb. His unrivalled gifts as a social historian and his unique insights into French society remain a constant source of inspiration. At Oxford, too, I benefited from the discussions which took place at the seminar of Dr Theodore Zeldin. In 1977 in Paris, Mme Michelle Perrot gave good advice, while Dr Charles Sowerwine, the historian of French socialist women, generously shared his formidable knowledge and stimulating ideas.

Among the librarians and archivists who readily responded to my copious demands, Mme Léautey, librarian of the Bibliothèque Marguerite Durand, deserves special mention for putting all the resources of her remarkable collection at my disposal. During my time at York, I have learnt a great deal from colleagues and students involved in our Comparative Special Subject on 'The Condition of Women in Society'. Dr Jane Rendall, in particular, must take most of the credit for making this course a notable success. Finally, I must thank Joanna Woodall for compelling me to formulate some of my ideas more precisely and, above all, for giving moral support with what seemed at times to be a labour of Sisyphus.

York, July 1980

Introduction

I first became interested in the history of women as a postgraduate student at the University of Oxford. At that time (1969-1972) the subject was far from the fashionable field of study that it has since become. I well recall that, on research trips to France, I was one of only a handful of clients who regularly patronised the Bibliothèque Marguerite Durand, the delightful feminist library situated in the *mairie* of the 5e *arrondissement* in Paris. Now, the librarian requires an assistant to help her cope with the endless queue of researchers into the feminine condition past and present. Women, until recently hidden from history, are currently faced more with over-exposure than with neglect.

Nevertheless, much remains to be done. In spite of the general upsurge of interest in women's history, we still lack a serious academic study devoted to an analysis of women's place in modern French society. Reading the standard histories of the Third Republic, one would never know that, for instance, women outnumbered men in the French population: that their experience of life differed radically from that of men even within the same social class: and that in the France of *la belle époque*, as in other countries, the 'woman question' was a matter for extensive comment and debate. With the exception of Theodore Zeldin,[1] historians have largely excluded women from their histories of nineteenth- and twentieth-century France, and the primary objective of the present work is to rescue them from the obscurity in which, for too long, they have languished.

The most fundamental question which confronts any historian interested in the condition of women is the extent to which they have been relegated to a position of social inferiority on account of their sex. How far, we must ask, has women's social status been determined by their gender? Secondly, we must address ourselves to that other constant preoccupation of the historian, the question of change and continuity: how far, in other words, can we see any significant evolution in the position of women over time? In this book, I attempt to answer these general questions with reference to a particular case study, that of French women during the period of the Third Republic (1870-1940).

1

'Status', it goes almost without saying, is a somewhat nebulous concept. Rather than make a futile attempt at defining it 'scientifically', (which would only outrage sociologists) I have preferred to assume that in common sense and in common parlance, 'status' is deemed to involve a mixture of subjective and objective considerations. Partly, it is a matter of looking at attitudes and cultural values: hence the opening chapter on the ideology of domesticity. Partly, it requires investigation of social realities. Factors of particular relevance to the condition of women include demographic data, the law, family structure, educational opportunities, and, certainly not least, female participation in the labour force. All of these serve both to influence and to reflect the place which women occupy in society and therefore constitute themes with which this book will be much concerned in looking at the condition of women in France under the Third Republic.

Almost inevitably, the starting point for our analysis of the more 'subjective' elements which affected women's status is the hoary maxim, affirmed by moralists throughout the ages, that women's proper place is in the home. As Chapter I will explain, the cult of domesticity was widely diffused in nineteenth-century France. Among its champions, none was more outspoken than Pierre-Joseph Proudhon, the father of European anarchism, whose celebrated phrase *'courtisane ou ménagère'* I have borrowed for the title of this book. According to Proudhon, women had a choice between only two possible roles: that of housewife *(ménagère)* or harlot *(courtisane)*.[2] As a statement of historical fact, Proudhon's *dictum* is patently absurd. Quite apart from the very considerable number of women engaged in the world's oldest profession, some 2,768,000 women were employed in the non-agricultural labour force in 1866.[3] Yet, however worthless from the point of view of employment statistics, Proudhon's stark dichotomy is not without value as a brief, if brutal, enunciation of the doctrine of *la femme au foyer* ('woman by the hearth'). The nature, extent and practical relevance of this ideology of domesticity (together with its close relation, the double standard of morality) are matters central to the task of trying to evaluate women's status in French society. So, too, is the degree to which the doctrine of separate spheres was challenged by the rise of feminism. The existence of an organised feminist movement has been almost entirely overlooked by historians of the Third Republic and it is hoped that one of the virtues of this book will be to make some contribution towards remedying this deficiency.

When we turn to the more 'objective' determinants of women's status, to establish the facts is one thing, interpreting them is quite another. Thus the law, for example, is in itself no sure guide to the real social position of French women under the Third Republic. Without doubt, the Civil Code, drawn up by Napoleon and his lawyers, provided explicitly for the subordination of women to men, and more particularly of married women to their husbands, while the Penal Code wrote the double standard of morality into the law by its unequal treatment of male and female adulterers. Yet, the letter of the law notwithstanding, observers of post-revolutionary France have frequently alleged that women enjoyed at least equal, if not superior, social status. In the days of the July Monarchy, Mrs Trollope gained the impression that women dominated French society.[4] In the early twentieth century, this view was reiterated by another interested English commentator, Mrs Emmeline Pankhurst, who explained the absence of a militant suffragette movement in France by alleging that women there already enjoyed power and influence behind the scenes.[5] Native French observers, too, emphasised this indirect control: a contributor to a special issue of *Le Crapouillot* claimed that political issues were not infrequently resolved in the *boudoir*.[6] The historian of French women thus has to recognise at least the possibility of a discrepancy between the law and social mores, between women's theoretical legal position and their ordinary everyday situation. Simply to portray them as victims of a 'masculinist system' of which the Napoleonic Code was one of the twin pillars (the other being the Catholic Church) is not enough.[7]

Similarly, the ideal 'angel of the hearth' extolled by moralists should not be assumed to represent an accurate description of real-life wives and mothers without further analysis of women's position in the French family. Alongside the ideology of domesticity, one must set the evidence to be derived from demography as to, say, nuptiality and fertility patterns. Even if one should conclude with the moralists that women's place was primarily in the home, one then has to confront the sensitive question of whether motherhood was the instrument of women's oppression or of their progressive emancipation. This latter issue, raised by the work of historians such as Edward Shorter and Patricia Branca, will be discussed extensively in Chapter II.[8] At present, I need only declare my position with regard to the concept of 'modernisation' which features prominently in this debate. Like Tony Judt,[9] I regard this word as a substitute for genuine historical analysis, and a fraudulent organisational device which perverts the notion of *la longue durée*: it is a term which can have no place in the vocabulary of any self-respecting social historian. Certainly, we will be concerned to determine whether women's position improved over time, but we will not in consequence seek to locate the history of French women under the Third Republic within the bogus conceptual framework of 'modernisation'.

No treatment of women's place in French society in this period would be complete without considering their relationship with the world beyond the home, in the wider spheres of politics, education and employment. In the twentieth century, the denial of women's right to vote and to run for public office clearly marked them out as second-class citizens. Some of the factors which explain this anomaly are discussed in Chapter IX. Discrimination against women in the field of education, especially in secondary and higher education, not only limited their cultural horizons but also deprived them of the opportunity to obtain the qualifications necessary for access to professional life. Conversely, enhanced educational opportunities may be regarded as an important index of progress towards sex equality and are discussed as such in Chapters III and VI.

Entry into the world of paid employment outside the home, on the other hand, is an ambiguous criterion of women's status. In both the Marxist and feminist schools of thought, the exclusion of women from the labour force (or their underprivileged position within it) amounts to the most intolerable sexual injustice of all, in that women are thereby reduced to economic dependence upon men, whether husbands or lovers.[10] Such a view of the sexual division of labour in a capitalist economy, however, was by no means unanimous among those French women of the Third Republic, working-class as well as middle-class in origin, who opted for a life of domesticity. The social historian faces a very real problem in trying to interpret how women's economic activity (or inactivity) relates to their status. My own feeling is that it would be both arrogant and anachronistic to assume *a priori* that those women who remained by the hearth, in preference to the factory, workshop or office, chose for themselves, either consciously or subconsciously, a subordinate role in society. Certainly, crude employment statistics in themselves provide no reliable key to women's status: attitudes to work and the actual experience of work are of much greater significance, as I hope will be evident from discussion of women's work in Chapters III and VII.

In Part One of this book, then I consider the various factors which in their different ways served to determine the status of women in French society, and I also try to establish the extent to which their position was undergoing change in the late nineteenth and early twentieth centuries. In Part Two it is the latter theme which is accorded priority since both contemporary observers and more recent historians have advanced the view that, as a consequence of the impact of the First World War, a transformation, tantamount to a social revolution, took place in women's position. Struck by the scale on which women successfully took over jobs vacated by the men who had departed for the Front, contemporaries of all shades of opinion depicted the war as the harbinger of women's emancipation, as we shall see in Chapters VI and VII. Later commentators likewise attribute to the war the shattering of the ideal of domesticity. In the words of one author:

> The economic upheaval, which the war of 1914–1918 provoked, entailed a change of values, and the middle classes saw themselves constrained, on behalf of their daughters, to look for a guarantee for the future in employment and no longer exclusively through marriage.[11]

Michel Collinet, too, has argued that in depriving girls of the petty and middle bourgeoisie of their dowries, the war pushed them towards a career.[12] According to Pierre Grimal, the editor of a *World History of Women*, it was 'the crisis of the Great War which precipitated reforms, by making brutally clear the urgency of a general participation of women in the responsibilities and combats of the nation'.[13] John Williams, who has made a comparative study of the domestic fronts in Britain, France and Germany during the First World War, identifies 'perhaps the most far-reaching social change caused by the war' as being 'the emancipation of women from their traditional status of inferiority'.[14] Finally, Arthur Marwick, who has been perhaps the most persistent advocate of the view that the First World War benefited underprivileged status groups, points to two significant ways in which women were rewarded for their participation in the war effort. One was 'the increased sense of their own capacity and an increased self-confidence on the part of women themselves'. The other was 'the total destruction of all the old arguments about women's proper place in the community, which both men and women had previously raised against any moves towards physical and social equality for women'.[15] Part Two challenges all of these claims and argues rather that the First World War had little effect on the status of French women. Continuity rather than change will be the theme.

Several points remain to be clarified before we proceed to a detailed analysis of women's place in French society in the period 1870–1914. First, it should be stressed that while I shall refer to women *qua* women (for it was on the basis of gender that both the law and social custom sought to prescribe their status) in practice, when we come to look at specific women in their ordinary everyday, real-life situations, case studies will be taken from women who lived in an urban rather than a rural environment, that is to say from middle-class and working-class women. The reason for the exclusion of peasant women is not simply the author's predilection for city life but rather the fact that one of this book's major themes is the sexual division of labour created by industrial capitalism – a factor of little relevance to the *paysannes* who remained in the countryside and carried on with the domestic and labouring duties allotted to them by tradition.[16] A further limitation is that, in geographical terms, most of the evidence comes from the Paris region: the treatment of the provinces is somewhat random and unsystematic, although where possible I have tried to include provincial case studies in order to fill out the picture. Perhaps future studies will bring out more clearly the significance of regional differences. Finally, the present work makes no claims to be a definitive social history of even Parisian middle-class and working-class women over the entire period of the Third Republic's duration: the 1930s, for instance, receive particularly scant attention. Nevertheless, despite all its shortcomings, it is hoped that the book will justify its existence by going at least part of the way towards putting women back into modern French history.

PART ONE

*THE POSITION OF WOMEN
IN FRENCH SOCIETY
1870-1914*

Chapter I
THE FRAMEWORK OF SEX DISCRIMINATION: IDEOLOGY, SOCIAL MORES AND THE LAW

The doctrine of separate spheres

THE view expressed by Proudhon, that women's place was primarily in the home, was peculiar neither to the nineteenth century nor to France. Moralists throughout the ages have held that gender should be the central consideration in determining the role of women in society. The Romans venerated the woman who lived chastely and served the hearth.[1] Medieval didactic treatises such as *The Goodman of Paris* (c. 1393) exhorted women to cultivate the home as a shelter (for both men and women) from the turbulence and strife of the outside world.[2] The seventeenth century French writer, Pierre Le Moyne, although quite prepared to concede women's moral equality with men and their equal aptitude for learning, repudiated the call for the extension of women's public education on the grounds that 'I respect too much the boundaries that separate us'.[3] The doctrine of separate spheres has been preached down the centuries and should in no way be regarded as a comparatively recent innovation. What was new in the nineteenth century was not the ideal of the 'woman by the hearth' in itself, but the unprecedented scale on which it was propagated and diffused.

Moreover, the actual inspiration behind the ideology of domesticity has varied considerably over time and place. In Victorian England, for instance, it would appear that the roots of this ideology can be located in Evangelicalism.[4] But the same explanation can hardly be applied to France, where Evangelical influence was non-existent and where the Catholic Church continued to be the principal representative of organised religion. Catholic apologists, of course, were among the most prominent champions of *la femme au foyer*. As one priest put it in a series of sermons on *The Duties of Men Towards Women*:

> man and woman will be to each other as the head and the heart. To man intelligence, reason, reflection, wisdom, majesty, strength, energy, resolution, authority. To woman delicacy, sensibility, grace, sweetness, goodness, tenderness, discreet attention, devotion, enthusiasm, communicative warmth.[5]

In part, the Catholic attitude had to do with the perpetuation of a misogynous strain in Christianity which can be traced back to St Paul and the writings of the Early Fathers.[6] It was in keeping with this misogynous tradition that as well as enumerating the feminine virtues, the abbé de Gibergues also observed that 'the devil makes use of women to ruin men by seducing them'.[7] More specifically, in late nineteenth- and early twentieth-century France, at a time when the Church was on the defensive against the attacks of the anti-clerical masters of the Third Republic, its leaders saw in women their best hope for the preservation of the religious, social and political values which, since 1789, the Church had set against those of the Revolution. Aware that it was women rather than men who sought the consolations of religion in an increasingly 'dechristianised' society, churchmen looked to women to transmit clerical ideals to subsequent generations through the process of the socialisation of children, in which mothers, by tradition, had the predominant part.

French conservatives had long understood the influence wielded by women through motherhood. Joseph de Maistre, the luminary of counter-revolutionary theory, taught that morality had to be inculcated at a mother's knee.[8] *Education maternelle*, the education of children by mothers themselves, was widely advocated in the first half of the nineteenth century, in manuals such as Mme de Rémusat's *Essay on the Education of Women* and Pauline Guizot's *Family Letter on Education*.[9] Far and away the outstanding bestseller of this type of literature, however, was Aimé Martin's *The Education of Mothers of Families or the Civilisation of the Human Race by Women*. Published in 1834, it went through at least ten French editions and was translated into English and Spanish.[10] Martin's thesis was really little more than an elaboration of de Maistre's point, namely that a mother's role in bringing up her children was so important that it made her the potential redemptress of mankind, as it was through her that children early in their lives could acquire salutary notions of goodness, morality and religion.

It would, however, be a serious mistake to associate the prevalence of the domestic ideology in France exclusively with the defence of traditionalism on the part of the Catholic Church. Anti-clericals and republicans, likewise, appreciated the powers inherent in motherhood, and consequently were equally strong protagonists of *La femme au foyer*. Proudhon, himself one of the nineteenth century's most notorious priest-haters, is obviously a case in point.[11] So too is Michelet, the great republican historian, who eulogised motherhood in the most extravagant terms. His book *L'Amour* was a veritable hymn to domesticity, lauding women's 'poetry' and 'intuition': even the most vulgar woman, he claimed, possessed these qualities. Marriage was, in his view, the natural destiny of a woman, preferably to a man aged about ten years older than herself, so that her moral ideas could be moulded by the one she loved. She had no need to work outside the home 'since it is the paradise of marriage that man works for woman'.[12]

The doctrine of separate spheres was an article of faith for clericals and anti-clericals alike.

Indeed, one might reasonably argue that, in the first instance, the ideal of 'woman by the hearth' in nineteenth-century France gained ground as a result of the ideological and political conflict between the Catholic Church and its anti-clerical opponents, as both sides sought to extend their influence through the medium of motherhood. The intensity of this conflict perhaps explains why French moralists laid even more stress on women's role as wives and mothers than is to be found elsewhere. Anti-clericals did not dispute that the true place of women was in the home but objected only to the claims of the Church to be uniquely qualified as guardians of female morality and educators of women themselves. Hence Michelet's violent diatribe against the alleged hold of priests over women, realised through the confessional and the convent school, which, he claimed, had the effect of dividing the family and diminishing the authority of the husband and father.[13] Jules Ferry, principal author of the Third Republic's 'laic laws', before coming to power had decried the barriers erected between husbands and wives as a result of the Church's excessive control of girls' education.[14] In general, positivism, the creed to which most of the new régime's rulers subscribed, taught that women were made for the home, where their role was first and foremost to exercise a moral influence over the rest of the family.[15] Given the degree to which motherhood was thus identified as a crucial battleground in the struggle between republican anti-clericals and the Catholic Church from the days of the French Revolution, it is hardly surprising that the ideology of domesticity loomed so large in discussions of women's role in French society in the nineteenth century.

The French version of the doctrine of separate spheres was, however, not simply a by-product of the clash between the revolutionary and counter-revolutionary traditions, for its elaboration also owed a great deal to the development of a deepening sense of class consciousness. The period after 1848 has been called 'the era of the triumphant bourgeois'[16] and in the milieu of the French bourgeoisie, despite the considerable differences of wealth, status and interests which frequently divided the members of this large and variegated class, it is possible to distinguish a code of cultural values, a 'bourgeois ethic', adherence to which was a means of delineating the boundaries between the bourgeois world and that of other social groups. True, as Theodore Zeldin has reminded us, many so-called 'bourgeois' ideals sprang originally from the values of the aristocracy, and were also shared by many members of the working classes.[17] This, however, does not invalidate the point that the bourgeoisie had its own distinct sense of awareness and identity. Indeed, to the extent that bourgeois values were consciously or subconsciously embraced by other social groups, they may be thought of as constituting a hegemonic culture. At the very centre of the bourgeois conception of the social order was the institution of the family, headed by its lord and master, the *paterfamilias*, husband, father, and representative of patriarchal authority, upon whom wife and children alike depended. Within the bourgeois world, the social roles of men and women were allocated strictly on the basis of gender. Man's destiny was to work and to participate in public affairs: woman's place was to organise the household and to raise children. As the moderate republican politician Jules Simon put it:

> What is man's vocation? It is to be a good citizen. And woman's? To be a good wife and a good mother. One is in some way called to the outside world: the other is retained for the interior. [18]

As will become evident when we look at the debates on women's education, women's employment and the female suffrage, Simon's view may be regarded as wholly typical of the outlook of the political leadership of the Third Republic.

The spread of bourgeois values, then, was a powerful force behind the development of an ideology of separate spheres in nineteenth-century France. Evidence of the assumptions which governed bourgeois thinking on women's role may be sought in a variety of treatises, etiquette books and manuals written for the purpose of laying down the correct forms of behaviour in the bourgeois milieu. Invariably, marriage is depicted as woman's 'natural' goal. Any woman not attached to a hearth, as Proudhon had so bluntly pointed out, was regarded as a kind of social misfit. Mme Romieu, one of the self-appointed authorities on bourgeois morality, suggested that in France the position of the single woman was even more difficult than in other countries: custom demanded that the *vieille fille* cling to her family of origin and feign ignorance of love and marriage, no matter her age or experience of the world. [19] In 1912, the same prejudice against 'old maids' could be documented from a savage issue of the satirical magazine *L'Assiette au Beurre*, which represented them as shrivelled, sterile, emotionally barren and obnoxious creatures who spied on their neighbours, spread malicious gossip, hypocritically pretended to be pious and, who, with no human being to turn to, focused their limited affections on some pet – a cat, a dog or a parrot. [20] In bourgeois ideology a woman had to marry before she could enjoy either status or happiness. As another moralist, Mme Louise d'Alq, explained, the problems facing a woman who wanted to make her way independently in the world were so great that even a mediocre husband was preferable to none. [21] The Baronne Staffe, author of a phenomenally bestselling work, *Usages du monde* (1887), likewise warned women against the perils of attempting to abandon their separate sphere.[22] In 1900, the novelist Daniel Lesueur succinctly stated the grounds of bourgeois opposition to female participation in the labour force: '*le travail de la femme la déclasse*'.[23] A bourgeois woman had to be a lady, and by definition a lady did not work. Her exclusive devotion to the hearth was a touchstone of respectability, one important symbol of the family's bourgeois status.

And yet the doctrine of 'woman by the hearth' was by no means confined to bourgeois circles, for it was also fervently championed by leaders of the French labour movement. Why, asked Auguste Chirac in *La Revue Socialiste* (March 1888), should not the wife of the proletarian, the wife of the *déclassé*, remain at home just as much as the wife of the aristocrat?[24] Commemorating the anniversary of Proudhon in 1909 in an article in *Le Mouvement Socialiste*, Edmond Berth maintained that the master's views on the woman question were of continuing relevance. After admitting that capitalism had served to bring women into the labour force, he insisted nevertheless that Proudhon was right to see no valid role for women outside of the *ménage*.[25] The theoretician of revolutionary syndicalism and defender of women's right to work, Alfred Rosmer, was saddened by the frequency with which such views were to be encountered among French labour leaders. As he noted ruefully, when Paul Bourget could no longer find disciples among the bourgeoisie, he would always be able to discover new ones among trade unionists.[26]

Much of the syndical opposition to female labour was based on narrow corporatist considerations. To the minds of many male trade unionists, women were dangerous rivals in the labour market and, because of their willingness to accept lower wages than men, a threat to the living standards of the working-class family. This was particularly the case in printing, where the male workers were virulently hostile to female competition. The first conflicts dated back to the early 1860s when on several occasions male workers struck and were consequently arrested (at this time strikes were still illegal) because employers had brought in women workers prepared to work at below the going syndical rate. Inability to stop the spread of female labour in the printing works (by 1901 women accounted for 26% of the labour force) served only to increase the bitterness of the male workers. Whereas many other corporations tried to salvage the situation by saying that they would accept women working on the principle of equal pay for equal work, the printers, after momentarily adopting this line, repudiated the idea of women in their industry even if they were to receive equal pay (this was their verdict at the Congress of Lyons in 1905).[27] In 1910, however, most reluctantly, the leaders of the

Fédération du Livre agreed at their congress in Bordeaux to defend the line of equal pay for equal work – though Keufer, the General Secretary, hoped that in practice this would lead to the exclusion of women, since employers would not want to hire them at men's rates. But despite the Bordeaux resolution many rank and file members remained attached to the old policy, most notably in the local branch at Lyons. There, in 1912, the *syndicat* not only rejected the application of a woman printer called Emma Couriau who was paid full union rates, but also expelled her husband Louis because he would not use his marital authority to make her give up her job. Worse still, the Central Committee of the Federation upheld the local decision against Couriau's appeal. Significantly, the defence of the Couriaus was undertaken, in the first instance, not by the labour movement but by the Feminist Federation of the South-East, although it is also possibly true that the rumpus created by the Couriau affair ultimately led to a change in attitudes towards women workers on the part of male trade unionists. The most prominent figures of the new generation of syndicalist leaders – men such as Pierre Monatte, Alfred Rosmer and George Dumoulin – all sided with the Couriaus against the Lyons printers. Rosmer, in particular, as the author of a series of penetrating articles on the affair in the *Bataille Syndicaliste*, concluded by denouncing the 'antediluvian mentality' of the corporatists and went on to advocate the syndical organisation of women.[28]

Corporatism, however, is far from being the sole explanation for the French labour movement's commitment to the ideal of 'woman by the hearth'. A genuine attachment to the virtues of domesticity is also apparent in the consistency with which syndicalist militants demanded the right to a family wage in the late nineteenth and early twentieth centuries.[29] At the Socialist Workers Congress held at Marseilles in 1879, the subject of women's work generated extensive debate. Very few delegates supported the pursuit of sex equality through an extension of the female labour force. On the contrary, most of the male trade unionists argued that men should be paid a living family wage, which would allow their wives to remain in the home. Some admitted that women might be forced to work in order to supplement the family income, but in this event they should not take jobs in factories (described by one delegate as 'industrial hells') but rather find some kind of domestic employment. The idea that work in itself could emancipate women was dismissed as ludicrous. It is true that the Congress eventually passed a resolution proclaiming women's right to work and calling for the suppression of work in institutions such as convents and prisons which provided unfair competition to women workers. This resolution, however, was adopted largely as a result of the successful lobbying of Hubertine Auclert, not a working woman at all, but a middle-class feminist. (We shall meet her again in Chapter IV.)

In the years following the Marseilles Congress, male syndicalists remained slow to evolve new ideas about the proper role of women in society. At the fourth congress of the CGT, held at Rennes in 1898, a motion was carried that 'man must provide for woman'. In the unfortunate case of a widow or single woman, obliged to minister to her own needs, the formula of equal pay for equal work was to be applied. Men should be prevented from taking up jobs which by rights belonged to women, while women should be kept out of jobs which 'naturally' fell to men. It was likewise in the name of domestic harmony that the CGT, from 1912 onwards, began a vociferous campaign for the 'English Week' (Saturday afternoon and Sunday free). The working-class woman, as much as her bourgeois counterpart, required time to devote herself to the needs of her family and household.

Two important developments underlay the rhetoric about domestic bliss in French working-class circles. One was acquiescence in the sexual division of labour created by the advance of industrial capitalism. As will be explained more fully in the next chapter, the nineteenth century witnessed a physical separation between home and work which had not existed in the proto-industrial family economy.[30] The new situation meant that, on the whole, men went out to work for wages while married women stayed at home, unless compelled by poverty to seek additional income for the family. This trend, which coincided with the rise of the labour movement, tended to be reflected in socialist iconography. Man came to be represented as 'the worker' – the brawny, muscular proletarian who had to undertake heavy physical labour to earn his daily bread. Woman, on the other hand, was typically depicted as man's companion, the epitome of the suffering proletarian and the most exploited victim of the capitalist system.[31] In defending the ideology of domesticity, therefore, French labour leaders both accepted the inevitability of a sexual division of labour and at the same time sought to use it for propaganda purposes.

The second factor which lay behind the labour movement's adherence to the doctrine of separate spheres was its increasing dissatisfaction with the position of the working class under a régime which was patently biased in favour of the peasantry and the different sections of the bourgeoisie. Whether revolutionary or reformist, French socialists believed in the reality of the class struggle and therefore seized every opportunity to highlight the iniquities of the present social order. Here, once again, the image of the hapless proletarian woman had enormous potential as propaganda. Thus, for example, it could be alleged that it was 'bourgeois justice' which allowed the rich to seduce working-class girls with impunity (before 1912 affiliation suits were prohibited by law). Bourgeois vice and corruption could be poignantly exposed in the image of the seduced and abandoned female and a contrast thus established with the working man's fidelity to his companion, whom he loved and cherished in return for her devotion to him. From the point of view of socialist and syndicalist propaganda, concentration on the plight of the proletarian woman was ultimately a way of affirming the moral superiority of the working class over the bourgeoisie.[32] By raising the 'woman question', bourgeois militant labour leaders could not only refute bourgeois accusations that working men were uncouth, even bestial, towards their women, but also give the lie to that equation of the labouring classes and the 'dangerous classes' which had persisted in reactionary circles since the days of the July Monarchy.[33] It was for this reason that some militants argued that women should be prevented from working not just in factories but also in bars and cafés, where their morals might be all too easily undermined.[34] It was likewise in the interests of demonstrating the respectability of the proletariat that socialist leaders, on the whole, were strong opponents of birth control. In their view, the 'population question' served only to divert attention from the class struggle and, even worse, made a virtue of a highly individualistic and anti-social act which perverted women's natural destiny and made sexual pleasure the fundamental criterion of human happiness.[35] Once more, socialist rhetoric could assert the moral superiority of the working class over the 'Malthusian' bourgeoisie. In all these different ways, then, as a logical consequence of the language of class struggle and social reform, the French Left developed its own version of the doctrine of separate spheres.

The double standard of morality

When considered in the context of sexual mores, the doctrine of separate spheres is indistinguishable from the notion of a double standard of morality. The precepts of the double standard discriminated against all women, but in different ways according to social class. It was perhaps most explicit in the bourgeois ethic, where social convention prescribed chastity for daughters and fidelity for wives, whereas boys and men were assumed to indulge in both pre- and extra-marital sexual relations. Balzac claimed that a man who was still a virgin at the age of, say, twenty-eight would be a laughing stock in the salons.[36] Confirming this view, Dr Louis Fiaux observed that it was highly exceptional to find boys who remained sexually inexperienced by the age of seventeen or eighteen, for on school half-holidays schoolboys were among the most regular patrons of brothels.[37] The eve of departure for military service was another recognised occasion for the *rite de passage* of male sexual initiation.[38]

Bourgeois adherence to the double standard had deep economic and ideological roots. Largely, it derived from the concept of marriage as a property arrangement, which some historians have connected with the rise of capitalism but which in fact seems to have had a much longer history, evident in the dynastic and familial considerations which characterised marriage transactions in both the Middle Ages and in the Ancient World.[39] In the arranged marriage – and certainly, as we shall see, this was the norm among the nineteenth-century bourgeoisie – it may well be that the virginity of the bride symbolised the inviolability of the 'property' being exchanged between the two families. Of course, no such economic thesis was put forward by the moralists who championed the double standard. These preferred to dwell, rather, on women's 'femininity', or on that process of cultural conditioning which gave rise to the view that women were inherently more pure and more moral than men. Any reference to the ignoble subject of sexual activity, it was understood, would damage women's delicate, 'ladylike', sensibilities. That such a mentality was common throughout the ranks of the French bourgeoisie in the nineteenth century may be appreciated from the efforts on the part of the medical profession to lend scientific respectability to theories about cultural differences between the sexes. Thus a number of doctors boldly insisted that the sexual urges of women were much less imperious than those of men. William Acton, the most celebrated exponent of this view in the United Kingdom, had his counterpart in France in Dr Louis Fiaux, who held that a major reason for male recourse to prostitution and adultery was the relative sexual passivity of women.[40]

The operation of the double standard discriminated against women in at least three important respects. Its fundamental premise – that the purity of the family had to be preserved at all costs – implied that the adultery of women should be treated as a much more serious offence than the adultery of men, for a woman could infiltrate the child of an outsider into the *foyer*. All women were victims of this assumption, in that it had the sanction not merely of bourgeois mores but of the law itself. The Penal Code prescribed that a husband's adultery could be punished only when the act had taken place within the marital home, and even then only by a light fine. In the case of women, by contrast, the offence was punishable no matter where it took place, and she could be imprisoned as well as fined. If the husband discovered his wife and her lover *in flagrante delicto*, he had the right to kill them both on the spot. No affiliation suit was permitted to establish if a child had been fathered by a particular man, whereas no such veto applied to attempts to discover maternity.[41] In the nineteenth century these legal provisions were far from being dead letters, but were sternly enforced in the courts. In 1847 a poor woman called Mesnager admitted her adultery before the *Police Correctionnelle*, explaining how she had been forced to leave her brutal, drunken husband who never gave her enough money to keep herself and her children. Their ex-lodger, a M Soubret, had befriended her and taken her in permanently. The Tribunal graciously admitted that there were 'very extenuating circumstances' in the case, but the President told Mme Mesnager that while her gratitude was understandable, she ought not to have shown it to the point where she forgot her familial duties: he then proceeded to sentence her and her companion to a week's imprisonment 'only'.[42]

Unworthy husbands were still exacting justice from the courts for the adultery of their wives in 1880. One, Eugène-Julien Hamelin, deported for life for his part in a murder, was later reprieved, and was outraged to find on his return home that his wife now lived with another man, and was pregnant by him. In vain the poor woman protested that she had never expected to see her husband again and considered herself a widow: likewise, no attention was paid to the fact that he was 'a brute and a drunkard'. The verdict was six days imprisonment for her and a fifty franc fine for her lover.[43] In another case, a M Bourlier brought charges against his thirty-three year old wife and M André Rigaud, an elderly gentleman who was a distiller and a municipal counseller at Levallois-Perret. Having seen the couple enter a hotel, Bourlier had sent for the police, who burst in to discover the lovers in a state of undress. At the trial, Rigaud admitted that they had had relations over the previous six years, but only at rare intervals, an allegation which the court admitted seemed very plausible in view of M Rigaud's advanced years. Nevertheless, each was sentenced to three months imprisonment.[44]

Cases of the *crime passionnel* are even more revealing of the way in which the double standard of morality was written into the law: witness the instance of the cabaret singer, Maria Béraldi (real name Marie Bière) who tried to kill her lover M Robert Gentien, a rich landowner from Bordeaux, after the breakup of their affair on her becoming pregnant. Gentien's parting advice to her had been to have an abortion, for he wanted nothing to do with the child. Having, to her immense credit, rejected this counsel, Maria was torn with grief when the baby died naturally soon after birth. Her first thought was to kill herself at Gentien's feet, but, having failed, she tried to kill Gentien instead. The jury, taking all the circumstances into account, acquitted her, instead of passing the death sentence as the law could have required. At the same time, however, the President of the court went out of his way to show sympathy for Gentien's position. As a man with important family commitments, he said, M Gentien naturally wanted to keep his liaison secret to avoid all taint of scandal.[45] In other words, it was implied, the family name of an upper-class gentleman was not to be impugned on account of his passing infatuation with a mere *artiste*.

In the years before 1914, the courts seem to have softened their line towards women guilty of adultery. The penalty imposed became purely nominal, as in the case of a Mme Martinelli, who was fined sixteen francs for receiving regularly one Bonneton in the absence of her husband.[46] The fact remains, however, that the principle of a double standard continued to enjoy the sanction of the law. Husbands were thus still able to shoot their adulterous wives with impunity, even when the crime was premeditated. Henri Fougère, seeing his wife become intimate with his supposed friend Rivet, rented a room opposite Rivet's place to watch them: at the same time he bought a revolver and started to put in some target practice. One day, having pretended to go to work, he observed that Rivet came round to spend the morning with his wife. When they came out, Fougère followed them and shot Rivet dead as he tried to run away. The court acquitted him of murder.[47] Another husband, abandoned by his wife after seven years of marriage, pleaded with her to come back when he met her in the street. She refused. He shot her, and was duly acquitted by the court.[48]

Apart from its legal manifestations, the double standard was evident in the sheltered upbringing given to young girls of the bourgeoisie. Whereas the daughters of working-class parents enjoyed a good deal of freedom of movement and of sexual opportunities, middle-class girls were deliberately kept in ignorance of the world outside the home and treated as decorative ornaments who might on occasion help their mothers in the running of the household. According to the self-appointed expert on bourgeois morality, Mme Romieu, 'in poor families the young girl makes deprivation seem less unbearable by the attention she gives to the household. In comfortably-off families she is an invaluable asset to her mother whom she helps out with supervising and giving orders. She embellishes the life of the interior by a thousand charming details: she is the poetry of the hearth'.[49] The writer Emile Faguet took a less charitable view of this genteel existence, sarcastically dismissing it as a life of idleness in which flicking through a glossy magazine or going to mass were regarded as strenuous activities.[50]

The essential purpose of this sheltered upbringing was to keep the marriage market well stocked with virgin brides.[51] At every turn, the young girl of good family was cosseted from the world. She was never allowed out unaccompanied and her conduct was scrutinised at dances and other social gatherings by her mother or chaperone.[52] Her reading material was likewise the object of strict surveillance. Marcel Prévost, even though a successful novelist, warned against the perils of allowing girls to read novels, since in his view they were likely to wound their delicate sensibility.[53] Another advice book addressed to the 'model' girl of the early twentieth century claimed that reading novels led only to an over-worked imagination, a distaste for duty and a preoccupation with the frivolous.[54] Both these would-be moral experts advocated only safe, traditional writings for the female youth – the tales of Mme de Genlis, the proverbs of Mme de Maintenon, the moralising stories of the comtesse de Ségur. The *Journal des demoiselles*, also standard reading for the bourgeois girl, never tired of making the point that marriage was the proper goal of a woman's existence, and that even young ladies of no fortune could hope to be rewarded in the end by a happy match, provided they remained virtuous.[55]

In the years before the First World War, there seems every reason to suppose that the aim of preserving the chastity of the bourgeois girl was successfully accomplished. True, Marcel Prévost alerted his readers to the appearance of a female type which he classified as *demi-vièrges*, reputedly young women in fashionable Parisian society who shamelessly flouted all the genteel conventions to which modest, well-brought up young girls were expected to adhere.[56] Another moralist was also convinced that some 'turn of the century girls' took liberties which could 'compromise their future'.[57] Such fears seem to have been baseless if manuals of sex education of the day are anything to go by. In a climate of opinion where reading novels was regarded as dangerous, instruction on the subject of sex was hardly likely to be enlightened. Despite advances in medicine and a decline in religious practice over the course of the nineteenth century, secular attitudes towards sexual behaviour continued to reflect traditional Christian teaching.[58] Doctors and moralists, many of them obsessed with the problem of depopulation, persisted in regarding masturbation and contraception as acts contrary to natural law and noxious to society. The famous Swiss doctor, Tissot, whose book on onanism went through thirty-nine editions between 1760 and 1905, described in lurid detail the appalling disorders likely to ensue from habitual masturbation, as did Dr Rozier in his *Secret Habits or Masturbation by Women*.[59] Without adequate sex education, young girls might discover their wedding night to be something of a trauma, as Caroline Rémy (later to be famous as the radical journalist Séverine) has related.[60] That vitriolic critic of bourgeois morality, the *Assiette au Beurre*, was not slow to point out this sordid side to the much vaunted ideal of marriage. In two cartoons entitled 'Wedding Night', the first has a bride weeping by the bedside, while her husband remarks: 'So your mother didn't warn you what to expect?' In the other, the couple are shown sitting up in bed, with the husband saying philosophically: 'And there you have the reason why we troubled 1500 people this morning.'[61]

If working-class girls were not subject to the same constraints and controls as those imposed on the daughters of the bourgeoisie, they, too, suffered from the double standard in a way that was unique to their class. Given that bourgeois men were expected to acquire sexual experience while women of their class were required to retain their virginity until marriage, it followed that male debauchery could not take place in the beds of decent, well-brought up young ladies. Prostitutes, recruited essentially from the ranks of the urban poor, were the necessary guardians of the bourgeois woman's virtue. If bourgeois men idealised the chastity of their own womenfolk, they frequently regarded other, less fortunate women as fair game. As Fernando Henriques has observed, the constant references to whores and visits to bordels in a work like the *Journal* of the Goncourts would appear to indicate that such activities were part of the normal life of men.[62] Most prostitutes were not full-time professionals, but rather comprised a heterogeneous collection of barmaids, waitresses, singers, dancers, actresses, unemployed work-girls and the like.[63] In this way, clandestine prostitution was the main buttress of the double standard in France.

Much more indicative of official tolerance of the double standard, however, and rightly regarded by the feminists as its most redoubtable bastion, was the state's own system of regulated prostitution.[64] The unspoken assumption of such a system could only be that male extra-marital sexual activity was acceptable, provided it was carried on in conformity with certain legal requirements. Indeed, Dr Parent-Duchâtelet said as much in his famous defence of regulation by the state. According to him, prostitution was endemic in society, on the one hand because of the permanent nature of the demand and on the other because of the existence of a morally defective class of women whose propensities for idleness, luxury and debauchery ensured a permanent supply of prostitutes. Prostitutes, in Parent-Duchâtelet's view, were born rather than made. Since prostitution could never be eliminated, it therefore followed that the authorities had a duty to control it, in order to prevent the spread of disease and infection throughout society.[65]

Parent-Duchâtelet's theories on the need to control prostitution were widely shared by the French governing class. Hence the elaboration of a regulatory system over the course of the nineteenth century. In Paris, control was in the hands of the Prefect of Police, with whom all prostitutes were obliged to enrol: in the provinces, the municipal authorities carried on the necessary supervision. Initially it was the intention of the regulationists that prostitution should be strictly confined to a *milieu clos*, to prevent it from impinging upon the sensibilities of children and 'honest' women. In other words, business should be transacted only in certain 'tolerated houses' (*maisons tolérées*) preferably in specified 'red light' areas, the better to facilitate surveillance. Prostitutes should be inmates of their brothels, allowed out only at extremely rare intervals. Even the compulsory medical inspection of prostitutes should take place at the brothel. Likewise, when treatment for venereal disease was necessary, they should be assigned to special hospitals, and again, when they flouted the regulations, they should be incarcerated in special prisons (in Paris, the sinister prison-hospital of Saint-Lazare combined this dual function).

By the early years of the twentieth century, however, the operation of the *milieu clos* system on the 'classic' model was in decline. The number of brothels had diminished notably. Prefect of Police Lecour claimed that out of 204 Parisian tolerated houses in existence in 1855, only 152 remained in 1869.[66] By 1888 this figure was down to sixty-nine. The same trend was even more pronounced in the provinces: for example, Amiens had thirteen brothels in 1880 but none at all by 1895, while in Marseilles the 125 brothels of 1873 had dwindled to thirteen in 1895.[67] The number of enrolled prostitutes continued to rise, however, but increasingly they preferred to work as *filles isolées*, living out of the brothel and only coming to work there, as they would to a factory. The *maison close* thus gave way to the *maison de rendez-vous*, except for the high-class, luxury establishments which survived in the large urban centres and which catered not for the needs of the *homme moyen sensuel* but for the sexual perversions of cosmopolitan plutocrats.

Alain Corbin has suggested that the conversion of the French authorities to the virtues of the *maison de rendez-vous* rather than the *maison close* can be attributed to heightened awareness of the extent to which bourgeois society was open to contamination from venereal diseases.[68] Already shaken by the social upheaval of the Commune and troubled by the prospect of further political and social change, the conservative bourgeoisie of the Third Republic increasingly saw in the spread of syphilis yet another peril to the maintenance of the social order. Writers such as Maxime du Camp painted a lurid picture of how indulgence in clandestine prostitution in France could transmit the dreaded disease of the 'dangerous classes' to solid middle-class homes, with appalling consequences for the birth rate and the future of the race itself. Paranoia at this prospect was rife throughout the medical profession. Doctors such as Homo and Mireur took the lead in denouncing the dire results of the bourgeois male's indulgence in extra-marital sexual activity and in calling for the strictest possible surveillance of clandestine prostitution.[69] The researches of Dr Commenge produced frightening statistics which revealed that of 6842 known non-registered prostitutes arrested in Paris between 1878 and 1887, 2681 (31.18%) were domestic servants.[70] The dangers of infection in the midst of the bourgeois household were only too obvious. Fears aroused by the findings of medical science can hardly have been allayed by the publication of a novel such as Zola's *Nana*, with its horrifying portrayal of how a prostitute could be the instrument of class vengeance by her ability to ruin her upper-class lovers.[71] George Darien, a lesser novelist but perhaps a more virulent polemicist than Zola, likewise developed the theme of the prostitute as the corrupter of the bourgeoisie and the avenger of exploited working-class women. His novel *Le Voleur* (1898) was a particularly savage attack on the hypocrisy and depravity of bourgeois morality at the time of *la belle époque*.[72]

Profiting from the mounting concern about the venereal peril, a neo-regulationist lobby began to agitate for reform of the *milieu clos* approach to the problem of controlling prostitution.[73] In the late nineteenth and early twentieth centuries, under the leadership of medical men such as Dr Alfred Fournier (himself a specialist in the treatment of syphilis), propagandists of the neo-regulationist school taught that the mission of medical science was to organise '*la prophylaxie sanitaire et sociale*'. The existing regulationary measures were criticised not on the grounds that they were immoral or unjust, but rather because they were inefficient. Doctors rather than bureaucrats thus ought to take over the running of the system to ensure that surveillance was effective. These ideas, current in medical circles from the late 1880s, were readily absorbed by the exponents of nationalist doctrines who came to enjoy a prominent position in the French political forum at the beginning of the twentieth century. A group of prominent parliamentarians, headed by Senator Béranger, sounded the alarm at the danger which syphilis posed not just to the family but to the *patrie* itself. Pressure groups such as the *Société française de prophylaxie sanitaire et morale*, founded in 1901, came into existence. The administration, succumbing to the arguments of these neo-regulationist bodies, ended by incorporating their essential ideas into new provisions for the state supervision of prostitution. Thus Prefect of Police Lépine conceded that the *maison de rendez-vous* offered better opportunities for surveillance than did the old *maison close*. Better facilities were made available for the treatment of venereal disease to encourage infected women to come forward for medical care, while, on the eve of the First World War, with widespread support in public opinion, the police began to crack down harder upon those who sollicited and pimped in the streets. In 1914, the double standard seemed to be more entrenched than ever.

Yet the concept of two moralities did not go completely unchallenged in the period before 1914. If the classic regulated system of prostitution came under fire from doctors, politicians and moralists on the grounds of its inefficiency, other more hostile critics advocated its entire abolition on account of its flagrant exploitation of women. The example of Josephine Butler's crusade against the Contagious

Diseases Acts in England inspired kindred spirits in France to launch a similar campaign against state control of prostitution in the 1870s.[74] Significantly, the most sympathetic French response to the Butler initiative was to be found among Protestants like the Monod family and the economist Frédéric Passy. Moreover, quite distinct from this moral assault on the double standard, another, more obviously politically motivated, attack on the *police des moeurs* was mounted in the mid-1870s by Parisian radicals and progressives, led by the liberal economist Yves Guyot. Acting in the name of the rights of the individual and of the common law, the Guyot lobby denounced the abuses of bureaucratic authority, all too evident in the conduct of the Vice Squad, with a view, first of all, to embarrassing the 'Moral Order' régime of Marshal MacMahon and his Prime Minister Dufaure, and secondly, in the longer term, to dismantling the powers of the Prefecture of Police and placing this body under the jurisdiction of the Paris Municipal Council. Under the stimulus of the Guyot lobby's propaganda and a second visit to France on the part of Mrs Butler, the *Association française pour l'abolition de la prostitution officielle* was founded in 1878. Meantime, on the Municipal Council itself, Guyot engineered the setting up of a commission to examine the workings of the regulationary system. The latter campaign reached its climax between 1879 and 1881 in fierce criticism of Prefect of Police Andrieux, who vividly recalls the episode in his colourful memoirs. But as Guyot himself was later forced to admit, this first wave of abolitionism in France soon fizzled out for lack of general support.[75]

Mrs Butler's final triumph in England in 1884–6, however, breathed new life into the cause of abolitionism in France. For the nascent feminist movement in particular, abolitionism became a primary objective, and, making good use of the arguments already formulated by Guyot and his friends, the feminists concentrated their propaganda on the excesses committed by the Vice Squad and on the appalling conditions of women prisoners detained at Saint-Lazare.[76] In time, press coverage of arbitrary and high-handed behaviour on the part of the *police des moeurs* (especially after a number of unsavoury incidents, the most serious of which involved the wrongful arrest of two respectable women for solliciting) led to the creation of a *commission extra-parlementaire du régime des moeurs* in 1903. Among its seventy-seven members the commission numbered the first woman ever to be appointed to such a body in the person of the feminist leader Mme Avril de Sainte-Croix, who as a journalist writing under the pen-name 'Savioz' had been one of the most outspoken critics of the state regulation of prostitution. Deliberating over a period of three years, the Commission encouraged abolitionists to believe that the end of the regulated system was in sight, especially when its recommendations were incorporated into a parliamentary bill tabled by the deputy Paul Meunier in June 1907.[77]

But unfortunately for the abolitionists, their hopes were speedily dashed by effective lobbying on the part of the *Société de prophylaxie* and the Medical Academy, which prevented Meunier's bill from making any headway in the Chamber. In the end, its only provisions to reach the statute books were those relating to minors, covered by a law of April 1908. Indeed, by focusing attention on the question of the prostitution of minors, Senator Béranger and his fellow neo-regulationists strengthened their case for greater and more effective regulationary controls. Deliberately exaggerating the perils of the 'white slave trade' (by which they meant the international traffic in under-age virgins) they successfully headed off abolitionist attacks on the *maisons tolérées*. Instead, with powerful backing in the press, they set out to persuade public opinion that young girls stood in need of protection against the ever present menace of sexual assault and that ultimately such protection depended on their own vigilance over their chastity. The state, of course, would do its utmost to see to the rigorous supervision of all extra-marital sexual activity.[78] As in Augustinian theology, so in the code of bourgeois morality in the France of the *belle époque*, the brothel justified its existence to the extent that it preserved the virtue of respectable young ladies. The fact that it degraded and marginalised the prostitutes themselves seems to have mattered little.

The legal position of women

In the early years of the Third Republic the institution of marriage may have been extolled by the moralists but, looked at from the point of view of the law, it foisted nothing less than legal servitude upon the married woman. According to the Civil Code, wives were required to obey their husbands, to reside wherever their husbands chose to live, to obtain their permission when seeking employment and to recognise their full parental control over the children. Under the various types of marriage contract, the husband invariably had the right to administer his wife's property. As far as the law was concerned, women had the status of minors.[79]

In practice, the legal situation of women was not quite as bad as it might seem at first sight.[80] To begin with, the theoretical powers of a husband over his wife were nothing like as great as they had been under the *ancien régime*, when he could – though not always easily – have her locked up for life in a convent by the expedient of a *lettre de cachet*. No longer could he chastise her with impunity: only a single case is recorded by nineteenth-century jurisprudence and the accepted position was that the husband himself was liable to prosecution if, in beating his wife, he created a public disturbance. Likewise, his marital authority did not permit him to interfere with the practice of her religion, or stop her visiting relatives and friends. Nor were marriage contracts necessarily a licence for a husband to squander his wife's fortune. On the contrary, these complicated arrangements were devised primarily to safeguard the property of married women and there is evidence, in the commercial bourgeoisie at least, that in the event of business failure wives preferred to salvage their money rather than their husband's good name.[81] In any case, the legal incapacity of women was in good part overcome by the doctrine of the 'tacit consent', whereby a woman could act independently, taking decisions or perhaps buying goods on behalf of the family, on the assumption that all was done with her husband's unspoken authorisation. Some lawyers indeed, feared that discretion under this convention was so great that the whole spirit, let alone the letter, of the Code was being violated. One case, decided by the *Cour de Cassation* on 8 November 1908, made a husband responsible for his wife's operations on the Stock Exchange, despite their having lived apart for ten years. As one indignant legal commentator pointed out, it was hardly likely that the unfortunate husband had given his tacit consent, and such judgements therefore rendered the wife 'the absolute mistress of the conjugal partnership'.[82]

Even if this claim is somewhat exaggerated, it is true that the years after 1880 saw some improvement in the legal position of French women.[83] In 1881 women for the first time obtained the right to open a savings bank account without the assistance of their husbands, while a law of 1886 extended this right to make the husband's consent unnecessary. A major step forward came for single or separated women in 1893 when they were granted full legal capacity. In 1897, all women became eligible as witnesses in a civil action. The law of 13 July 1907 allowed married women to dispose freely of their own salaries, earnings and also to seize part of their husbands' salaries if they did not contribute enough of their income to the upkeep of the household – an improvement on a situation where previously the lord and master could squander his wife's wages with impunity. In 1909, women got the right to initiate an action concerned with family property and to be consulted before the alienation of family property by their husbands. Inroads on the omnipotence of the *paterfamilias* were also made by legislation on compulsory schooling and the law of 1889 on delinquent children, which for the first time challenged a father's exclusive right to discipline his offspring. Another law of 1912 carried this process a stage further by instituting a régime of 'liberty under surveillance' for delinquents who would duly be handed back to their families if they proved cooperative.

By far the most significant legal change affecting the position of women in French society in this period was the law of 27 July 1884 which reintroduced divorce. Divorce legislation was first enacted in France in 1792, although the Napoleonic Code considerably reduced the grounds on which a divorce could be obtained. The restored Bourbon régime abolished divorce altogether and it took Alfred Naquet, the main sponsor of the 1884 law, eight years to get his bill through Parliament (in a greatly amended form).[84] Four grounds were envisaged in which a divorce might be permitted: adultery; *excès et sévices*, that is physical violence on the part of one spouse against another; *injures graves*, a very flexible category which amounted to virtually any kind of moral cruelty; and finally *condemnation afflictive et infamante*, which would apply in the case of, say, a spouse sentenced to life imprisonment. The actual procedure by which one obtained a divorce was deliberately made as complicated as possible, though it was simplified slightly by a law of 18 April 1886.

It should be stressed that the Republican legislators who passed the divorce law did so, for the most part, reluctantly. Hence the exclusion of divorce by mutual consent, which had been permitted by the earlier divorce law of 1792. Advocates of easy divorce were few, though further liberalisation of the law did take place in 1904, when the partner guilty of adultery was allowed to marry his or her accomplice.[85] From the constant rise in the number of divorces, it would appear that the law met a real need: just as women had been the main beneficiaries of the original divorce legislation of the Revolution, so, too, women outnumbered men in submitting divorce petitions under the terms of the 1884 Act. (According to one study, six out of ten divorces were demanded by women.)[86] It may well be true, however, that the law sometimes made it harder for a wife than for a husband to obtain a divorce, especially on the grounds of adultery, where it was first of all more difficult for her to establish the guilt of her husband, and when secondly the prevailing climate of opinion, as we have seen, accepted a double standard of morality. Thus a decision of the *Cour de Cassation* in February 1914 allowed that the bad conduct of a wife mitigated the offence of her husband and rejected her plea for a divorce.[87] Yet if the husband's culpability was notorious, a wife could certainly have her divorce – as was well illustrated by perhaps the most celebrated divorce case of the *belle époque*, that of Anna Gould, daughter of American tycoon Jay Gould, who eventually tired of seeing her fortune squandered by her husband, the spendthrift, playboy aristocrat, Boni de Castellane.[88]

In any event, the mere existence of a divorce law obviously undermined the absolute authority of the husband in the household. Many instances can be found in jurisprudence which show that the law was often well disposed to the many and varied actions bought by women under the heading of *injures graves*. An offence against public decency was sufficient, for example, as was the seizure of her property for no good reason.[89] Equally, the law prevented unworthy husbands from ridding themselves of their wives when they became inconvenient. A wife's obligation to live with her husband was not absolute: one man who deliberately moved to a place where his wife would be unable to follow him in order to file a divorce suit had his plea rejected.[90] Another husband who brought his wife from Algeria and abandoned her in Paris was unable to obtain a divorce on the grounds that his wife would not return to the conjugal home.[91]

Undeniably, then, the law was more favourable to women in 1914 than it had been in 1870. Whether these changes correspond to a rise in the prestige of the married woman in the family, as Patricia Branca maintains, is a matter for the next chapter to examine.[92] For the moment, it should be remembered that, apart from the reintroduction of divorce, which in any case affected only a small minority of women, the legal reforms which we have noted did not contribute much to women's emancipation. Some laws made little impact on everyday life, as in the case of the law of 1907 allowing working women to dispose freely of their own wages. A survey carried out in the Lyons area discovered that very few husbands were aware of their theoretical right to avail themselves of their wives' earnings, and still fewer exercised it in practice.[93] Some legal experts argued that the abolition of the notorious article 213 of the Civil Code was unnecessary, since no woman was likely to obey her husband all the time.[94] On the other hand, the same article allowed a husband to open his wife's correspondence and to use in evidence against her letters he may have come across by chance. Wives had neither of these rights.[95] Even a simple social activity like a visit to the theatre could, in law, require the husband's authorisation.[96] French feminists, therefore, were not wrong to see the law as one of the most powerful agents of discrimination against women, at once a source and a sign of their inferior status in French society.

Chapter II
THE DOMESTIC SPHERE: MARRIAGE, SEX AND THE FAMILY

Marriage and motherhood in the bourgeoisie

IN the nineteenth century, the notion of woman as wife and mother represented not merely a moral ideal but also an important social reality. How women's place in marriage and the family affected their status in society, however, is a matter on which present-day commentators are far from agreed. Thus in contemporary feminist literature, women's domestic role is invariably portrayed as a major factor behind their underprivileged position in society at large. Likewise, works influenced by Marxist ideology allege that capitalism, in cutting women off from the productive process and creating a well-defined sexual division of labour, reduced women to economic dependence upon men. On the other hand, a number of American social historians incline to the view that, as a consequence of the 'modernisation' of the family from the late eighteenth century onwards, significant improvements are to be observed in women's position both within the home and in society generally. This novel thesis, deriving essentially from the rebarbative but influential work of Edward Shorter, *The Making of the Modern Family*, requires further scrutiny.[1]

According to Shorter, in the 'traditional' society of the sixteenth and seventeenth centuries, the manifold constraints of the community prevented the individual from experiencing self-fulfilment. Marriage was based on property considerations and lacked any emotional content – sex being purely 'instrumental' in contrast to the 'affective' relations characteristic of our own day. Thankfully, this grim state of affairs was transformed by the rise of romantic love, itself the product of the advent of capitalism, which laid a new emphasis on the importance of the individual as against the claims of the community. From the late eighteenth century onwards, Shorter tell us, couples began to marry for love rather than for money, and to have sex for pleasure rather than for the simple purpose of procreation – a veritable sexual revolution. At the same time, we learn, a sentimental revolution was taking place in the relations between mother and child. Maternal love entered human history for the first time, accompanied by a new cult of domesticity which was championed initially by the urban bourgeoisie but which

29

had spread by the middle of the ninteenth century to the ranks of the proletariat.

Despite its breath-taking crudeness of both analysis and style, Shorter's argument has encouraged others – most notably Patricia Branca – to advance the idea that in the course of the nineteenth century the position of women, and especially of married women, was upgraded. For Branca, the critical breakthrough was made by women of the middle classes, who 'modernised' by achieving a new 'concomitant relationship' within marriage which increasingly approximated to the sharing, caring, understanding and sexually fulfilled unions supposedly typical of twentieth-century America. Motherhood, she informs us, was the key, not the barrier, to progress. In her words, 'far from being a major stumbling block, the family has been the stepping-stone toward female emancipation'.[2] Whether either this view or the other pessimistic line taken by feminists and Marxists corresponds to the social realities of women's place in family life at the time of the Third Republic forms the subject matter of the present chapter.

As far as marriage formation is concerned, very little evidence can be adduced to support Branca's contention that 'increasingly marriages were founded on that elusive emotional tie which we call love'.[3] On the contrary, under the Second Empire, if the contemporary stage can be regarded as any guide to social values, for the middle classes marriage amounted to little more than a financial transaction.[4] But it was not only the dramatists who pointed out the mercenary aspect of marriage. Moralists like Mme Romieu also complained that the wedding day was 'only too often the result of a calculation of interests and convenience, the first step along the road to unhappiness'.[5] Maria Deraismes, one of the founders of the modern feminist movement in France, noted that marriage lacked any special esteem because it was thought of primarily as a lucrative investment (she herself was to remain unmarried).[6] Such lamentations were to continue right up to the First World War, with the satirical journal, *Assiette au Beurre*, mercilessly flaying the venal side of bourgeois marriage.[7] As another commentator noted at a slightly later period, marriage was the most important financial decision a bourgeois would make in his life.[8]

The essentially mercenary character of bourgeois marriage is also apparent in the notion of *mésalliance*, or an undesirable union between two persons of different social rank. A recurring theme in French literature is how such an imprudent match will eventually lead to disaster.[9] (Perhaps the classic version of this moral is located in Proust's *Du côté de chez Swann*, published in 1913, in which Swann, the gifted and superior man is cheapened and degraded by Odette, his inferior and unworthy wife.) To be a success, marriage in the bourgeois ethic had to take place in accordance with very definite rules, readily available in various etiquette manuals such as the *Mémento Larousse*. All of these stress careful attention to the financial aspects of marriage as well as outlining the correct behaviour to be observed by the couple during courtship. The close consultations which took place between the families of the two partners (and of course their lawyers) do not suggest that the romantic attachment of the spouses was the chief criterion of their suitability.[10]

Bourgeois marriage formation, then, retained many 'traditional' features, and had more in common with the aristocratic ideals of past centuries than with 'the capacity for spontaneity and empathy in an erotic relationship', Shorter's definition of romantic love, which is supposedly the hallmark of 'modern' marriage. In the sixteenth and seventeenth centuries, moralists had strongly warned against the dangers of marrying for love or of showing excessive emotion to one's partner within marriage. Montaigne, for example, counselled that one should marry not for one's own personal happiness but for the good of one's family or line.[11] That such a view long continued to represent aristocratic thinking on marriage may be seen from the *Livre de famille* of Antoine de Courtois (1762-1828), in which the author maintains that arranged marriages were best because parents had a better understanding of their children's real interests than they had themselves. As for love, this was of less importance than mutual respect and trust.[12] Obviously, the very fact that Montaigne or de Courtois bothered to attack the love match is in itself evidence that the concept of romantic love was known in pre-industrial Europe. Shorter's thesis that it only came into existence as a by-product of the Industrial Revolution is one of the most extravagant absurdities ever to have found its way onto the printed page, rivalled only by Lawrence Stone's callous and patronising remarks about the emotional deficiencies of men and women who lived before about 1750, particularly if they belonged to the poorer classes.[13] In general, however, it seems clear that neither the aristocracy of the *ancien régime* nor the bourgeoisie of the nineteenth century attached much weight to the romantic inclinations of their daughters when it came to choosing husbands for them. As Mme George Renard complained in 1898, girls still had too little say in the choice of their marriage partners, and therefore ought to have the right to take the initiative in proposing – an idea which seems not to have commended itself to the bourgeoisie of the *belle époque*.[14]

Yet, if the model of 'the modern life-style' is, to put it mildly, of little help when considering the position of married women of the French middle classes in the late nineteenth century, so too is the feminist stereotype of the enslaved and oppressed housewife. Even if a woman did have to marry in order to have any status at all, and even if she did have minimal control over the choice of her spouse, once she actually was married, she acquired a position of dignity and influence. The bourgeois wife and mother of the early Third Republic was not necessarily a victim of exploitation or even a sad case of insufficiently raised consciousness. In the eyes of contemporaries, both male and female, the domestic role was neither passive nor degrading. Within marriage, it was the primary duty of women to keep an orderly home, a haven of routine and regularity away from the chaos and threats of the outside world. In this private milieu, treasured by men and women alike, wives enjoyed immense prestige and authority, for they took charge of the running of the household in all its aspects. As a busy household manager, the 'angel of the hearth' had little time to sit on a pedestal. She was valued not for adorning the home but for making it an attractive place in which to live.

Only in the upper classes did the daily life of the married woman look like a vapid round of receptions, social calls, first nights at the theatre and occasional charitable activity on behalf of the deserving poor.[15] Critics of this way of life could see no difference betweeen idle married women and courtesans, on the grounds that both were parasites maintained by the men in their lives.[16] Yet even this apparently empty existence served a purpose in the bourgeois ethic, namely that of emphasising class distinctions, by defining the boundaries between the upper stratum of society and those outside its orbit.[17] Women of this background had an integral part to play in the preservation of social exclusiveness: their idleness was a symbol of the family's status. Even in the upper classes, however, it was not possible for a woman to be completely idle and carefree. Central to her role as manager of the household was the task of controlling the servants, which in the nineteenth century seems to have become an increasingly demanding job.[18] In the lower reaches of the middle class housewives had no opportunity to be idle ladies of leisure. Commonly, they employed only one servant and, after 1870, they often made do with the services of only a daily help.[19] To judge by the household manuals which were produced to assist the housewife plan her day, she had to cope with a crowded schedule. For instance, the guide prepared for the *petite ménagère* by Aline Valette, who was to become both a socialist and a feminist, left little time for leisure at the end of an exhausting day.[20] By the early twentieth century, household management was being elevated into a science, with courses established in domestic education.[21]

Moralists who extolled the virtues of motherhood were hardly exaggerating when they pointed out women's paramount importance in the sphere of child-raising. A mother's charge over the infant and very small child was complete. Ministering to all his needs, teaching him the basic notions of morality and dealing out punishments when necessary, the mother was a much more immediate and powerful figure of authority than the father. The ideology of motherhood as preached by clericals or anti-clericals, feminists or anti-feminists, corresponded to an important social reality. As one contemporary put it:

> The woman of high enough education, with a clear conscience, an enlightened mind and a generous heart, is the veritable master-key for the whole of society. It is she who, in the home, gives the children their earliest education, it is she who is the real moral bastion, often the consoler of father, brothers and husband: it is she who is the soul of the house and it is on her sense of order and on her worth that, very often, the happiness of the whole family depends.[22]

In the nineteenth century, the condition of motherhood benefited from advances in medicine and technology. Doctors devoted more attention to pre- and post-natal care. By the 1830s they could examine the uterus by means of the vaginal speculum, and could also use the stethoscope to listen to the foetal heartbeat. French doctors were also among the first to realise the importance of urine tests for pregnancy, and in France, unlike America, advances in the field of obstetrics led to the elevation of the status of midwives as professionals rather than their elimination. In the matter of after-care French doctors were particularly sympathetic to the use of anaesthetics, but surprisingly, in view of the pioneering experiments of Pasteur, they neglected to institute the types of sanitary measure common in England and America by the beginning of the twentieth century: the result was a higher rate of infant mortality. The contribution of medicine to the development of a closer relationship between mother and child is not to be doubted, however, and medical progress also played a part in ending the practice of sending infants out to wet-nurses, simultaneously encouraging maternal breast-feeding. As far as the doctors were concerned, motherhood can only have boosted rather than lowered the prestige of women in the late nineteenth century.[23]

To agree with Patricia Branca's positive evaluation of the role of women as wives and mothers is one thing; to accept her claim that within the family wives came to enjoy a *new* concomitant relationship with their husbands is quite another. In the bourgeois milieu, a man married only after the completion of his education and once his position in society had been securely established. In practice, a lawyer, say, would be over thirty when he married, whereas his bride might be fresh out of a convent school.[24] In view of their greater maturity and experience of the world, bourgeois husbands can be assumed to have exercised considerable authority over their wives. Moreover, as regards the sexual side of the marital relationship, it seems rash to represent women as the beneficiaries of a 'sexual revolution'. The debate on this issue, started by Shorter and continued by Stone, Branca and Phayer,[25] is a spectacular example of the depths to which contemporary social history is capable of sinking. According to Shorter, in the late eighteenth and early nineteenth centuries European women achieved the removal of 'outside controls upon personal freedom of action' and established their 'rights to sexual gratification and emotional autonomy'.[26] Relying principally upon statistical evidence provided by increases in marital fertility and in the incidence of illegitimacy, Shorter argues that it was the women of the urban and rural poor who first mapped out the road to sexual emancipation, though their example was soon followed by women of the middle classes. Branca, too, hails the advent of a sexual revolution pioneered by 'the lower classes, those without property in city or countryside',[27] despite the fact that she thereby contradicts her general thesis that it was middle-class women who acted as the dynamic force behind the drive towards 'the modern mentality' and who alone attained the felicity of the new concomitant relationship within marriage in the course of the nineteenth century. Theories of a sexual revolution, at the end of the day, serve only to reveal how ill-informed are its exponents about the sexual experience of married women both in the nineteenth century and earlier. One can only be grateful that there is no nineteenth-century French Kinsey Report to confuse the issue further by quantifying that most meaningless of all statistics, the female orgasm.

Given the inadequacy of historical writing on the subject of sexuality – and it may well be that this is an area where historians are faced with questions which they cannot possibly hope to answer – only the most tentative remarks can be made about the sentimental lives of married women in nineteenth-century France. Against the theory of the sexual revolution one might cite the influence of the pervasive double standard, which taught that sexual pleasure was for men and to be sought not within marriage but with prostitutes. One might also suppose that the shortcomings of the sex education given to young bourgeois girls can hardly have prepared them for the pleasures of the marriage bed. Furthermore, insofar as they remained pious daughters of the Catholic Church, nineteenth-century middle-class women in France were exposed to the constant instruction of clerics who insisted that the primary purpose of marriage was procreation.[28] As Jean-Louis Flandrin reminds us, from the sixteenth century Tridentine Catholicism, especially in France, had embarked upon a largescale enterprise of sexual repression.[29] By the nineteenth century, its development may have been arrested among the popular classes, and its severity tempered by the more liberal moral theology of Alphonse Liguori (1697-1787), but equally it may well have been responsible for continued sexual inhibitions on the part of more religiously inclined bourgeois women.

Finally, quite apart from psychological factors, various female gynaecological problems may frequently have induced women to abstain from sexual activity, which would further contribute to a sense of frustration and lack of sexual fulfilment within bourgeois marriage.[30]

On the other hand, the idea that the joys of sex were unknown before the 'sexual revolution' of 'modern' times is inherently absurd, as is obvious to anyone who has read of the sexual adventures of the priest Pierre Clergue, the Don Juan of fourteenth century Montaillou, or who has made even the most cursory examination of literary evidence such as Boccaccio's *Decameron*, or of medieval and early modern theological writings and confessors' manuals, in which the subjects of concupiscence and the rendering of the marriage debt constitute perennial themes for discussion.[31] In the nineteenth century, alongside the precepts of the double standard and the teachings of the Catholic Church there existed a body of contemporary literature which not only suggested that married women were entitled to sexual fulfilment but also discussed how best they could attain it. Gustave Droz, a journalist on the *Revue des Deux-Mondes*, wrote a best-selling book, *Monsieur, Madame et Bébé*, in 1866 which by 1884 had gone through 121 editions. His purpose was to advocate love within marriage and to recommend wives to show the same type of coquetry as mistresses.[32] A number of doctors wrote marriage and sex manuals which stressed the duty of husbands to satisfy the sexual needs of their wives.[33] Just as the views of the too celebrated William Acton have been shown to be something less than an infallible guide to the intensity of the sexual desires of women in the Anglo-Saxon world,[34] so too we would be wrong to conclude that the only French women to confer and enjoy sexual pleasure were the professional courtesans.

Thus generalisations about either a sexual revolution or the sexual deprivation of the middle-class married woman are not particularly illuminating when one tries to understand nineteenth-century sexuality. As Eric Hobsbawm has very properly reminded us, 'it is entirely illegitimate to read post-Freudian standards into a pre-Freudian world or to assume that sexual behaviour then must have been like ours'.[35] Social historians who fondly imagine that marital relations have been evolving from the emotionally barren unions of 'pre-modern' times to the sexually-fulfilled partnerships of 'modern' society must stand convicted of a naïve, vulgar and ultimately ridiculous whiggery.

Similar criticisms may be levelled at the equation of birth control and modernity (for Branca, the practice of contraception represents 'the most dramatic expression of the new outlook of the middle-class woman').[36] In reality, birth control was not merely known in the Middle Ages but also extensively practised by married couples, much to the dismay of the clergy. Medieval confessors' manuals, in citing *coitus interruptus* as a grave sin, supply evidence that the withdrawal method was not exactly novel in the nineteenth century. The author of one of these manuals, Pierre de la Patu, a Savoyard writing in Paris in the early fourteenth century, put forward the suggestion that the motive for regulating births was to avoid producing children which the family could not feed – testimony to the existence of what Philippe Ariès calls the 'Malthusian mentality' long before 'modern' times.[37] In the nineteenth and early twentieth centuries, bourgeois couples undoubtedly resorted to contraceptive devices in order to limit the size of their families (the average marriage produced only two children) but few right-thinking and respectable people were prepared to be identified with the open advocacy of birth control.[38] On the contrary, neo-Malthusians such as Paul Robin and his collaborators in the League of Human Regeneration (founded in 1896) were vilified by the nationalist press and branded as dangerous subversives by the state, which classified their propaganda as obscene literature.[39] The pro-natality lobby, by contrast, enjoyed official approval. To speak of birth control as 'the characteristically innovative and prompt' response of bourgeois women to the process of women's modernisation'[40] (Branca) or as 'the second stage of the sexual revolution'[41] (Shorter) is to misrepresent the ambivalent, not to say hypocritical, attitude towards contraception shown by the French bourgeoisie.

Yet despite the reluctance of French middle-class women to admit that they both favoured and practised contraception, there seems little reason to doubt that the material conditions of their lives were transformed by the general adoption of birth control during the nineteenth century. Above all, it released women from the horrific dangers to which mother and child are exposed where multiple pregnancies are the social norm. Even if the most common methods of contraception (*coitus interruptus* and the condom – the latter improved by the vulcanisation of rubber) left the initiative to the male, it seems safe to assume that nineteenth-century women were willing to cooperate in the general strategy of frustrating pregnancy. Significantly, by the late nineteenth century, devices such as sponges, douches, pessaries and diaphragms were increasingly available to women who wished to control their own fertility.[42] Whether or not the practice of contraception heightened women's appreciation of the pleasures of the marriage bed it is not for this historian – or possibly any other – to say. What might be less contentious to suggest is that, though bourgeois marriage may have begun as a financial transaction, over the years of life together it may well have developed into an intimate union in which both partners could be regarded as emotional equals. In this sense, then, the concomitant relationship may have been a reality but it can hardly be described as a novelty. Not only had it long been an ideal of intellectuals, advocated, for example, by medieval theologians such as John Major and spiritual leaders of the seventeenth century such as St François de Sales, but in addition, and more importantly, it can be shown to have existed among couples in medieval Montaillou and in many marriages of the early modern period. In any case, it should be remembered that the concomitant relationship within marriage was founded upon the acceptance of well-defined masculine and feminine roles, in accordance with the doctrine of separate spheres. It may have tempered, but it did not transform, the fundamentally patriarchal structure of society.

Work, home and the working-class woman
When we turn to look at the position of women in the working-class family, at first sight it might appear that the ideal of *la femme au foyer* bore little relation to social realities. Unlike their middle-class counterparts, few, if any, working-class girls grew up in the expectation that they would never have to seek paid employment. By 1906, excluding women employed in agriculture, some 4,356,000 women were employed in the labour force (forming 36.6% of all non-agricultural workers). [43] As early as the first half of the nineteenth century social investigators such as Villermé, Buret and Blanqui had drawn attention to the appalling conditions of labouring women in the new textile factories in the north and east of France. [44] Outraged by their findings, which he saw as a profanation of the feminine ideal of the wife and mother, Michelet denounced the very term *ouvrière* as an 'impious and sordid word, which no language has ever, and no epoch could ever, have understood before this iron age'. [45] If, as Jules Simon suggested, a woman who worked ceased to be a woman, [46] millions of working-class women seem to have failed to live up to the standards of bourgeois domestic ideology.

This verdict, also reached by other contemporary commentators, has been endorsed by more recent social historians. Thus A Audiganne, writing of working-class women in Rouen, observed that they were treated less as companions than as servants – a subjection which he attributed largely to their work in the textile factories, which took them away from their 'natural mission' and turned them into cogs in the mechanism of industrial production. [47] In addition, Audiganne reckoned that the way in which young working-class girls early acquired loose morals caused them to forfeit the respect normally accorded to an honest wife. [48] Perhaps more surprisingly even an advanced socialist and radical feminist like Madeleine Pelletier (of whom we shall learn more in a later chapter) also deplored the backwardness of social relations between the sexes in the working-class milieu and predicted gloomily that the working-class woman would be the last to achieve emancipation.[49] Agreeing with these assessments, Patricia Branca notes with regret the failure of the working-class woman to 'modernise'. Not for her the new concomitant relationship of the middle-class couple. Deriving little prestige from her domestic duties and obliged to improvise on a day-to-day basis, a victim of frequent pregnancies and economic hardship, the working-class woman, according to Branca, 'was doomed to fail'.[50]

Despite the massive presence of women in the non-agricultural labour force, however, we have already had occasion to notice that the domestic ideology was widely advocated by French proletarian leaders in the late nineteenth century. The point which must now be emphasised is that it would be a very great mistake to assume that this ideal remained a pipe-dream of working-class males and was flouted in practice by working-class women. A closer inspection of female employment patterns reveals, in the first place, that the typical working woman was by no means to be found among the factory proletariat. Only in textiles did women enter large-scale industry in any significant numbers (in 1906 they constituted 55.2% of the total labour force in this sector). In metal-work, by contrast, the comparable figure was only 5.8%.[51] Textiles, moreover, accounted for only 14% of the total female non-agricultural labour force in 1896, whereas domestic service contributed 19% and the clothing industry 26%.[52] Secondly, within the female factory proletariat, the typical worker was not a married woman but a young single girl. Whereas youths under the age of twenty comprised only 19.33% of the male labour force in factories, girls under twenty accounted for 39.13% of female workers.[53] Male factory workers were most numerous in the age group 25–29, while women were most heavily represented in the category of those under twenty.[54] Thus the existence of the *ouvrière, pace* Simon and Michelet, did not necessarily mean that working-class women rejected the domestic ideology.

To understand the attitude of working-class women towards work and the home, it is necessary to appreciate the developments which took place over the course of the nineteenth century in the relationship between the mode of production and the organisation of the family. Whatever nineteenth-century moralists may have asserted, the working woman was no new phenomenon. In what has been called the 'proto-industrial family economy' – that is, the phase between the decomposition of the medieval peasant economy and modern industrial-capitalist society – the wives and daughters of rural artisans made vital contributions to the household budget. Men were far from being the sole breadwinners, for it was the family as a whole which formed the basic unit of labour.[55] Without women's work the family could not have hoped to survive as a viable economic concern. Indeed in the poor families of petty artisans and casual labourers, where the joint income of husband and wife failed to maintain the household above subsistence level, it was the mother who organised an 'economy of expedients' by engaging in begging, petty crime or prostitution in order to keep the family solvent.[56] It was only after 1830 that domestic and craft industry in France began to be replaced by large-scale industry to any significant extent, and even then the textile industry retained many connections with isolated, home-based production, as in the weaving of cotton, tulle and silk. As late as 1906, it was still possible to find the family as the basic unit of production under the factory system, as was the case among the power loom weavers in the linen industry, where the women and girls prepared the looms while the men and apprentices wove the cloth.[57]

Under the family economy, it was possible for a woman to reconcile three distinct functions: to earn a wage or to produce for the market, to manage her household, and to bear and rear children. The destruction of the domestic system under the impact of industrialisation (a slow and gradual process in France) created a new type of economy – what Scott and Tilly call the 'family wage economy' – and this in turn brought about a new relationship between home and work.[58] As work increasingly came to signify wage labour outside the home, there arose a new sexual division of labour whereby men went out to work in return for a wage, while women concentrated upon their maternal, as opposed to their economic, role. As the nineteenth century wore on, a further shift towards a 'family consumer economy' (that is a wage-based economy in which expectations were higher than mere basic subsistence) served only to emphasise the dichotomy between home and work, and to underline the role of wife, mother and household manager as the essential preoccupation of women. In other words, in the working class as in the middle class, women increasingly came to define their role primarily in terms of their family responsibilities.

Of course, it would be wrong to suggest that in France married working-class women did not form a significant proportion of the non-agricultural female labour force. At around 20% of the total, they provided twice the number to be found in Britain.[59] The percentage of French married women in manufacturing industry was particularly high (about 32%).[60] Such figures, however, do not necessarily refute the contention that, on the whole, married working-class women in France regarded themselves more as housewives and mothers than as workers. Scott and Tilly make out a convincing case that married women's work was sporadic, and varied according to the needs of the family. Their wage-earning capacity was 'a reserve resource', to be called upon when the family found itself in straightened circumstances. As in pre-industrial times, this contribution to the family budget should not be under-estimated, since it was vital to the family's economic survival. An invaluable study carried out by the Board of Trade into the conditions of working-class life in the early twentieth century discovered that women contributed 8.6–14.5% of total family income.[61] The wage-labour of married women should therefore be interpreted not as a sign of the French working-class woman's failure to conform to the ideology of domesticity but as her immense dedication to the most basic needs of her family.

The reason why France had a large proportion of married women among the non-agricultural labour force was in the first instance demographic. Quite simply, the French population contained a higher proportion of married women that was to be found in, say, Britain. In 1901, some 42% of French women aged between 20–24 were married, whereas in Britain the figure was only 25%.[62] Moreover, the decline in the French birthrate was more marked than in other countries, with a fall from 25 per 1000 in 1851–5 to 20.7 in 1901–05.[63] Among the working classes, it is true, the decline was less steep than the national average, but it was perceptible nevertheless. In the mining town of Anzin, the figure for 1861 was 37.2: in 1906 it was 26.5. Similarly, in Roubaix, one of the principal centres of the textiles industry, the equivalent figures were 42.8 and 27.[64] Like middle-class women, working-class women also increasingly sought to control their own fertility. Their techniques may have been crude, and certainly included abortion as a 'back-up' method.[65] The point still remains that working-class women did not have to wait to hear the 'good news' (as Shorter calls it) about contraception from middle-class proselytisers but quite independently began to provide their own Malthusian solutions, very often with a view to allowing married women the opportunity to continue to bring in an additional wage to the family. Despite the hostility of socialist leaders towards the neo-Malthusians, many working-class women welcomed advice about birth control, which could both shorten their reproductive lives and enhance their prospects of employment.[66]

The demographic circumstances which rendered married working-class women in France more available for work than in a country like Britain were complemented by economic factors which had the same effect. As Scott and Tilly point out, married women tended to find paid employment in the least industrialised sectors of the labour force, that is 'in those areas where the least separation existed between home and workplace and where women could control the rhythm of their own work'.[67] Hence the type of labour they engaged in depended largely on the occupational structure of a particular town, but on the whole they did unskilled and casual jobs (as laundresses, charwomen, street-hawkers, bread-carriers and so on). Alternatively, where the opportunity was open to them, they worked for wages at home as domestic workers, an option available to many women in late nineteenth-century France because the Industrial Revolution was slow to spread to the clothing industry in its entirety, with the consequence that in many towns it was still organised on the basis of the pre-industrial putting-out system.[68] At the same time, the expansion of the large department stores created the possibility of mass sales to the urban market, so that recourse to domestic labour was necessary to keep pace with demand. The invention of the sewing machine, too, acted as a stimulus to domestic manufacture, while the passing of protective legislation on behalf of women factory workers in the 1890s may have decided some employers to hire domestic workers. For all these reasons, domestic industry was very far from extinct in France at the turn of the century; it is reckoned that there were some 250,000 in the Paris region and another 750,000 in the provinces.[69] Many of these women were married with families. A survey of Parisian seamstresses carried out by the Office du Travail discovered that 50% of the sample consisted of married women while another 33% were either widows or divorcees.[70] Another study of artificial flower makers showed that 52% were married and 22% either widowed or divorced.[71] As in pre-industrial times, the economic activity of married women under the Third Republic testifies not to the breakdown of the working-class family but rather to the crucial and continuing importance of the family in working-class culture.

If bourgeois observers of the working-class condition in the nineteenth century failed to appreciate the centrality of family life to the experience of the working-class woman, this was because, in addition to their obsession with women's work outside the home, they were even more shocked by the degree to which the working classes ignored the basic canons of bourgeois morality. To the bourgeois mind the sexual freedom of young working-class girls and the widespread existence of *union libre* were incontrovertible signs of the 'immorality' of the working class and of the disintegration of the family in their milieu.[72] So great, indeed, was bourgeois concern at the practice of cohabitation among working-class men and women that a special charity, the Society of St François-Régis was established as early as 1826 to encourage the legalisation of their unions and the legitimation of their children.[73] Even twentieth-century historians (most notably Louis Chevalier) while avoiding the moral strictures of nineteenth-century commentators, have tended to follow the latter in representing concubinage as a key feature of working-class culture, a way of life chosen deliberately to flout bourgeois conventions.[74]

Some, indeed, go further. As we have already had occasion to notice, Edward Shorter and his followers have propounded the thesis that such working-class behaviour is part of the proletariat's historical mission to be the vanguard of a 'sexual revolution' which would eventually work its way upwards to the bourgeoisie. Hailing the arrival of sex before marriage, Patricia Branca declares illegitimacy statistics to be 'a clear indication of the new pleasure-seeking mentality'. [75] Many women, she suggests, 'bore their bastards gaily', though others, like the prostitutes in Rheims in the 1830s, appear guilty of sexual over-indulgence. [76] For the most affecting image of the happy, warm-hearted, sexually-fulfilled proletarian couple, however, we may turn to Michael Phayer who renders faithfully all the crudeness of thought, argument and expression so typical of Shorter and his disciples:

> We speak then, with justification of a sexual revolution. The proletarian family was socially revolutionary both as to its nature or ethos (affective bonds) and as to its effect (increased legitimate and illegitimate fertility). Faced with blanket disapproval on the part of farmers, they insisted on their life-style even though this led to an unprecedented jump in bastardy. In time proletarian families would learn to inhibit sexuality but for roughly the first half of the nineteenth century, they revelled in the freedom to love, marry and beget, or just to love and beget, that modernisation had brought them. [77]

Given the all-pervasive obsession with sex to be found in Western society in the late twentieth century, one should not be unduly surprised at attempts on the part of sensationalist historians to unearth a 'sexual revolution' in the recent past. That, however, is no reason why we should take the concept seriously or regard it as bearing any relation to the social realities of nineteenth-century France. The 'sexual revolution' is not a historical event but a fantasy sprung from the over-fertile imagination of its proponents. Why rising bastardy rates should be interpreted as a measure of sexual emancipation is by no means clear, when attitudes towards illegitimacy have varied considerably over time and place. In medieval Europe, for example, it would appear that greater indulgence was shown towards both bastards and their begetters than was the case in the period following the counter-Reformation. [78] Here, perhaps, is an opportunity for another Shorter or Phayer to investigate the proto-sexual revolution of the Middle Ages. As far as nineteenth-century France is concerned, it is certainly the case that the unmarried mother was not ostracised by the working-class community, but she herself would surely have been the first to be amazed to discover that she was the harbinger of a sexual revolution. Likewise the poor domestic servant, faced with dismissal as a consequence of pregnancy, and sometimes driven to the appalling expedient of infanticide, should hardly be regarded as a representative of the sexually emancipated proletariat. Pondering the lot of girls brought to trial for murdering their new-born babies (several cases documented in the *Gazette des Tribuneaux* are reported below) we might wish to reconsider the view that 'some women bore their bastards gaily'. As for the view that working-class girls who were forced onto the streets were merely over-reacting to their new-found sexual freedom, this quite plainly exemplifies crass insensitivity to the hideous poverty and exploitation which obliged these women to sell their bodies in order to keep them joined to their souls.

To reject the concept of a sexual revolution among the French working classes in the nineteenth century is not, however, to deny that the intangible and unquantifiable factors of romantic love and sexual attraction played a large part in the formation of the working-class household. Lawrence Stone's insulting remarks about the incapacity of the lower classes to experience the refined sentiment of 'affective individualism' are, if anything, even more of a travesty of historical truth than the thesis of a proletarian sexual revolution. No doubt, the female companion of the working man was formed in a different mould from that of the bourgeois housewife. As a young girl, she enjoyed considerable freedom of movement and sexual opportunities. Sexual misbehaviour was a matter not of extra-marital sexual relations but of the commercialisation of sex. Girls who became professional prostitutes were considered a scandal to their families and rarely allowed to return to the areas where they had been brought up. [79] In the working-class code of values, vice consisted of anti-social acts such as theft rather than making love. Thus, after a number of passing fancies, a girl would usually become attached to a young man whose intentions seemed serious, and, without bothering about the formalities of legal marriage, the couple would simply live together, perhaps after a simple family meal to consecrate the establishment of a new household. As a sympathetic student of working-class mores like Henry Leyret understood, these unions were most often cemented by strong bonds of affection between man and woman. Only if the man were a callous brute or a hardened alcoholic did he forfeit his companion's trust. If on occasion he came home drunk or got himself into a fight, she might become angry and give him a good scolding. Such an incident, however, would in no way imply a permanent breakdown in relations, for she would soon forgive and forget. A woman might complain of her man to the neighbours, but she would be the first to spring to his defence if anyone else tried to run him down. [80] Love, fortunately, neither was nor is a monopoly of the middle classes.

Furthermore, as a recent article in *Annales* has demonstrated, concubinage should not be regarded as an exclusive and distinctive feature of the working-class way of life. [81] To judge from a sample of cohabitation statistics for mid-nineteenth-century Paris, a significant proportion of female concubines (at least 40%) were of non-working-class origin. In addition, even if concubinage was more common among female textile workers than among any other group of women, marriage remained their ultimate aspiration. Concubinage was often only a temporary substitute. Significantly, some 80% of the cohabiting couples who attracted the attentions of the St François-Régis Society converted their unions into legal marriage. In many respects, the working classes were more genuinely committed to marriage than the bourgeoisie, since, able to earn their living at an earlier age and less concerned with the idea of marriage as a means of acquiring or transmitting property, they more readily entered into permanent relationships, whether matrimony or free union. Even disapproving bourgeois observers like Villermé and Jules Simon had to admit that, once settled, the working-class couple tended to stay together.[82] It would, of course, be naïve to romanticise these unions after the manner of late nineteenth-century propagandists: love and the promise of a new deal after the socialist revolution were not enough to eliminate the injustices of sex inequality in the everyday world of the working-class woman.[83] Divorce may have been virtually non-existent, but broken homes and separations were hardly unknown. Sometimes a man would abandon his common-law wife when she became pregnant: sometimes a woman would go off with another man. In general, however, the working-class household was held together by strong emotional as well as economic ties and the devotion of its members to one another was no whit inferior to that to be found in the 'modernised' middle-class family.

As misconceived as the accusation of immorality against working-class people of both sexes is the charge brought against the working-class housewife of being a failed household manager. True enough, her home was rarely the haven of privacy and security eulogised by bourgeois apologists for the cult of domesticity. A major reason for this was bad housing. René Michaud, a syndicalist militant, has given us a graphic picture of the wretched conditions under which he was brought up in the 13e *arrondissement* of Paris, revealing that if the hideous cellars and attics in which whole families were housed in Lille in the 1830s were now a thing of the past, lack of sanitation and overcrowding persisted into the twentieth century.[84] It must also be said that, in any case, quite apart from the poor quality of much of the housing in working-class areas, workers themselves were unwilling to spend a lot of money on accommodation. As the sociologist Maurice Halbwachs discovered, the main item in the budget of working-class families was food: the proportion of income devoted to housing was comparatively small, and not because workers were obliged to spend all their earnings on eating to stay alive, but rather because they preferred to have extra cash for expenditure on items such as clothes and leisure activities outside the home. [85] Drinking was the favourite male pastime, though in cotton towns it was not uncommon for women also to be seen in bars and cafés.

In spite of these deviations from the middle-class code of behaviour, it would be rash to conclude that the working-class woman in France lacked the prestige and influence of the bourgeois wife and mother. The working-class housewife was neither a passive nor submissive creature, crushed by the demands of advancing industrialisation. On the contrary, as Michelle Perrot has argued in a stimulating essay, women were in the forefront of working-class resistance to the new industrial order in the first three-quarters of the nineteenth century. [87] It was women, for example, who as organisers of the family's housing arrangements, took the initiative in struggles against high rents and profiteering landlords. As housewives, they did not confine their activities to the home itself, since many household duties – taking the children for a walk, shopping, doing the laundry – took them into the outside world. With men at work, Mme Perrot reminds us, the streets belonged to women. Meeting together in the market place or the *lavoir*, women exchanged gossip and grumbles, and perhaps above all gave one another support in times of need – when money was low, when a husband had run off with another woman, or when a daughter had an illegitimate child. In the working-class suburbs the women had a large role to play as defenders of community values: creating an appropriately festive atmosphere on feast days, assisting newly arrived provincials to adapt to the urban environment, and, not least, in their very language, maintaining a sense of the people's identity. Perhaps, as Mme Perrot suggests, these forms of popular resistance declined somewhat in importance after 1880, commensurate with the rise of an organised labour movement in which women played only a minimal part. Yet such a view may be too pessimistic when it is remembered that in the late nineteenth and early twentieth centuries working-class women continued to occupy a pivotal place in the working-class family. Though lacking both the resources and the time to adhere to the model of domesticity prescribed in the manuals of good housekeeping, the working-class woman knew how to stretch to the last *sou* the slender wages of her man. With warm admiration and deep gratitude, René Michaud has evoked the revered memory of his mother, left to fend for herself and three children after the suicide of her husband. [88] The capacity of women such as this to perform economic miracles and their willingness to sweat blood for the sake of their families expose patronising value judgements about the working-class woman's failure to modernise for what they are – travesties of the historical record.

Chapter III
WOMEN IN THE WIDER SPHERE: EDUCATION AND EMPLOYMENT

ACCORDING to the doctrine of separate spheres, the world beyond the home belonged to men. As we have seen in the previous chapter, domesticity did not necessarily reduce women to a kind of servitude but, on the contrary, more often gave them high prestige and not a little power. The fact remains, however, that from a feminist point of view attempts to deny women access to the male-dominated domains of politics, work and the higher reaches of the educational system add up to discrimination against women on the grounds of their sex. In any appraisal of women's status we must therefore weigh the pre-eminence which women enjoyed in the home against their marked inferiority in the wider sphere. The extent to which they were able to break down the barriers erected against them in the world outside the home may serve as an important measure of progress made in the direction of sex equality. Politics we leave to later chapters: for the moment we turn our attention to the milieux of education and employment.

Girls' education

From the earliest stirrings of the feminist movement, education was identified as a crucial element in the process of female emancipation. Following the lead given by the philosopher Condorcet, authors of pamphlets and *cahiers de doléance* at the outset of the French Revolution called for equal educational opportunities for women.[1] The feminists of the July Monarchy period likewise looked to education to bring about equality of the sexes. As Pauline Roland put it, an egalitarian relationship between husband and wife within marriage depended on 'l'éducation commune et égale des enfants des deux sexes'.[2] Under the Third Republic, just as the male political establishment had boundless faith in the power of education to forge the moral unity of the nation (not for nothing was the régime known as *la République des professeurs*) the feminists attached enormous importance to securing for women the right to participate in the educational system at all levels on the same terms as men.[3]

Such a connection between education and social advancement was a new idea in the nineteenth century. Under the *ancien régime*, it was unthinkable that a child – especially a female child – could attain a status higher in life than that of his or her parents as a result of success within the educational system. Eighteenth century church leaders and *philosophes* alike agreed that the purpose of educating the popular classes was to teach them to accept their proper (that is, inferior) place in society. Jean-Jacques Rousseau was not alone in thinking that to educate those who must gain their daily bread by manual toil beyond a certain point was not only unnecessary but dangerous. As the institution generally held to be best qualified to inculcate respect for God and the social hierarchy, the Church was entrusted with a virtual monopoly of female education. At the elementary level a girl from the popular classes (like her brother) was not expected to learn much more than a useful manual skill. The daughter of a notable, denied the classical education given to her brother to prepare him for a life of service to the state and of civilised leisure, passed her days at the convent school dabbling in fine arts and preparing for a life of domesticity.[4] It was only under the Third Republic that the clerical stranglehold over female education was finally broken, though as we shall shortly see, this has to be understood as a victory for anti-clericalism rather than for feminism.

The state was slow to accept that it had any obligation to make provision for female education.[5] When the Guizot law of 1833 stipulated that every commune must have its own primary school for boys, nothing was said about an elementary school for girls. Even after the Pellet law of 1836 decreed that girls too should be provided for, no element of compulsion was added to ensure that the law was applied. The Falloux law of 1850 contained a clause which required every commune with a population of more than 800 people to provide at least one girls' primary school. (The figure was reduced to 500 in 1867 by Victor Duruy, Minister of Public Instruction at the end of the Second Empire.) Duruy also tried to raise the status of the *institutrice* (woman primary teacher: but many posts continued to be occupied by incompetent teachers who took up jobs immediately upon leaving their convent schools. In 1870 there were only nineteen training schools (*écoles normales*) for women elementary teachers in the whole of France.

Matters were even worse at the secondary level.[6] Such institutions as existed provided only a very modest continuation of primary school studies which in no way corresponded to the programme available in the boys' *lycées*. Some girls went to the Legion of Honour schools which Napoleon had founded after the battle of Austerlitz 'for the free education of girls, sisters or nieces of members of the Legion of Honour'. All the great plans to expand these schools, however, had collapsed with the Empire: although reconstituted by a decree of 16 May 1816, they never became important centres for the dissemination of secondary education to girls. There were also boarding schools run by lay mistresses. But, for the most part, such education as could be had was provided in the *pensionnats* run by the female religious orders, whose dramatic expansion under the restoration and the July Monarchy was one of the principal traits of religious renewal in France in the first half of the nineteenth century. In 1850, the enactment of the Falloux Law gave a further boost to convent schools in that restrictions placed upon private education by the Napoleonic institution of the University were now removed. With teachers no longer required to obtain a certificate attesting their competence to teach, nuns were able to open girls' schools which were more interested in recruiting pupils than in attaining high academic standards. Even if republican historians of female education in nineteenth-century France can hardly be regarded as unbiased commentators, their strictures on the *pensionnats* appear basically sound, as may be seen from the fact that in the upper echelons of society parents increasingly tended to have their daughters instructed by male private tutors rather than consign them to the mediocre teaching of the nuns.

Improvement came about, however, not as a result of parental or feminist pressure but as a consequence of the Third Republic's overriding preoccupation with establishing a viable democracy and a morally and socially united nation. Under a democratic system of government, it was felt by the country's new masters, that teachers had the duty to propagate the republican faith among the masses, for education was identified as the key to progress and happiness. In the 1860s a massive campaign was launched by the Education League on behalf of free, secular and compulsory schooling. The founder of this movement, Jean Macé, was to be canonised as one of the lay saints of the Third Republic (despite the fact that the movement developed in directions different from his original intentions). The humiliating defeat of 1870 in the Franco-Prussian War was widely attributed to the superiority of the Prussian schoolmaster and served to reinforce the idea that the school system would ultimately determine the fate of the nation. To politicians such as Jules Ferry and Camille Sée, the Republic could be established on a secure and permanent basis only if the régime won the battle against the Church for the minds of men – and more especially of women.[7]

The first attempt on the part of the state to wrest control of girls' education from the hands of the clergy came, in fact, before 1870 with the appointment of Victor Duruy as Minister of Education towards the end of the Second Empire. At a time when Napoleon III faced mounting clerical criticism on account of his attitude to the Roman Question, Duruy made out the case for reorganising the secondary education of girls, stressing that in part at least, 'our present embarrassments stem from the fact that we have left this education in the hands of people who are neither of their time nor of their country'.[8] Accordingly, in 1867 Duruy set out to transform this situation by establishing secondary courses for girls to be given by male teachers from the Sorbonne and the *lycées*. The idea was that girls should follow these courses for three to four years, six or seven months a year, proceeding on the basis of examination results until eventually a diploma was obtained. But despite promising beginnings, the experiment ended in almost complete failure. By January 1870, the courses survived in only fourteen towns and by 1879, in only five, including Paris.[9]

In part, the Duruy experiment failed on account of clerical hostility, in particular because of the campaign conducted by Bishop Dupanloup, who objected not only to the idea of more advanced studies for girls than was conventionally available, but also to the fact that in provincial towns the courses were usually held in the town hall, that is, a public place where all kinds of men would be in the vicinity, and, still worse, 'evil-living women'.[10] In his *Second Letter* he accused Duruy of being motivated solely by a desire to detach women from the Church, and denounced him as one of the odious creatures (Darwinists) 'who saw man as a perfected orang-outang'.[11] Other members of the episcopate and clergy rallied round the Bishop of Orleans: for example in Besançon, Bordeaux, Perigueux and Agen clerical intimidation caused the withdrawal of pupils, though it is true that in other places such as Rennes and Troyes the local bishops lent their support to the scheme.[12] But it was not clerical hostility alone which wrecked the experiment. In most places – with the notable exception of Paris – the courses themselves were badly organised, in that each town was left to devise its own curriculum, which led to wide discrepancies both in the type and in the quality of courses offered.[13] In addition, they catered almost exclusively for girls from the highest social circles, and these turned out to be somewhat dilettante pupils, reluctant to do any homework or any real classwork and attending 'the way one goes to a public lecture or a show'.[14] Finally, it is worth noting that even if the courses had turned out to be more successful, their effects would hardly have been revolutionary. Duruy's ideas on the actual content of girls' education were not all that different from Dupanloup's. Like the Bishop, he believed in the ideology of separate spheres and regarded domestic duties as women's essential preoccupation.[15] Developing their minds was a way of turning them into more interesting companions for their husbands and increasing their authority in the family and in society.

Whatever the reasons for the failure of the Duruy experiment, it fell eventually to the legislators of the Third Republic to enact measures which amounted to a genuine new deal for female education. After the experience of the 'Moral Order' and monarchist threats to the security of the régime in the 1870s, Republican leaders were more convinced than ever of the need to establish a lay and national education system. Introducing his bill to set up state secondary schools for girls, Camille Sée made no attempt to conceal his anti-clerical objectives. So long as women's education ended in the primary school, he said, it would be impossible to overcome the old prejudices, superstitions and routine. In his view, priestly power over women was already so great that through them the Church enjoyed political mastery, for, although women could not vote themselves, they could influence the vote of their husbands, in keeping with the directives they received from their confessors.[16] The Sée law of 21 December 1880 which created *lycées* and colleges for girls was not inspired by feminism but rather by the anti-clericals' design to laicise the state and to consolidate the republican régime.

Reform of girls' primary education was a product of the same strategy. It will be recalled from Chapter I that Jules Ferry, the principal architect of this legislation, had in a famous speech pleaded the necessity of rescuing women from the Church in order to win them for science. The alternative, in his view, was to place a barrier between husband and wife within marriage.[17] His first concern, reflected in the law of 9 August 1879, was to ensure that teaching in girls' primary schools was carried on only by trained, qualified teachers, since every department now had to have at least one training school for women primary teachers. The teachers in the training schools had themselves to be of very high quality, graduates of the new Ecole Normale Supérieure established at Fontenay-aux-Roses. Another law of 16 June 1881 provided for free and secular education for all children, girls as well as boys. Compulsory attendance between the ages of six and thirteen was required by the law of 26 March 1882.

The massive expansion of educational opportunities which followed the enactment of the school laws was regarded by the Republicans as one of their greatest achievements. On the whole, historians have been right to endorse this claim, although we should bear in mind Theodore Zeldin's point that the consequences of the laws were not always those envisaged by their authors.[18] In the case of girls' primary education, one should also remember that the law requiring obligatory attendance proved difficult to enforce. One inspector noted in 1903 that 'almost everywhere' young girls left school at eleven or twelve, or even earlier. Absences were particularly high in the west (where more than 50% of the pupils were affected) and in the Bourbonnais, the Allier and Lorraine. Thus, among poorer families, the expectation that girls would continue to make some kind of contribution to the family budget frustrated the hopes of the legislators of the early 1880s.[19] As for the new secondary schools, it was in any case no part of the original plan to put girls on an equal educational footing with boys. The curriculum of the new colleges and *lycées* prepared girls not for the *baccalauréat*, the passport to higher education and the professions, but for a largely ornamental diploma of secondary studies. Camille Sée's intention was to reinforce the ideal of domesticity, not to destroy it. The aim of girls' secondary education as established by the law of 1880 was merely to broaden the cultural horizons of girls in order to make them less susceptible to 'superstition' and more capable of taking an intelligent interest in the intellectual preoccupations of their husbands. As Sée put it, if girls learned about science it was to make them aware of matters such as the influence of the atmosphere on health, the best types of food and clothing for children and how to treat ailments until a doctor could be fetched. Nothing was further from his mind than the creation of female lawyers, doctors or politicians.[20]

Nor did the Sée law become effective overnight. Much indifference, if not actual hostility, towards girls' secondary education had to be overcome, particularly in the provinces. The law, after all, had been passed not in response to public opinion but in order to bring the popular mentality into alignment with the enlightened views of the new élite. In 1885 the Rector of the Academy of Aix had to report that Digne was the only town in the department to have consented to the sacrifices involved in establishing secondary schooling for girls. He envisaged no improvement in the immediate future as the population was too sparse and too poor to allow courses to be established with any chance of success.[21] Clerical opposition was still creating difficulties in some places at the turn of the century, as at Le Mans in 1900, where the mayor told the municipal council that girls' education was almost completely under the control of the clergy, with the result that good republican families had of necessity to send their daughters to religious establishments.[22] Such schools as did exist often had to cope with immense material problems, not the least being the lack of a proper school building because municipalities would not contribute towards construction costs. Thus at Castres courses continued to take place in the building owned by a private individual who would not carry out necessary repairs,[23] while at Carpentras the only improvement was that the lavatories were no longer 'veritable homes of infection'.[24] At Calais, the building was also badly in need of repair and there was an acute lack of teaching materials, especially science equipment, while no books apart from the personal library of the headmistress were available for teaching literature.[25] The root of the trouble was that the central government was excessively tight with money grants: it wanted to establish secondary education for girls on the cheap. Every minute item of expenditure had to be accounted for to the Minister of Education, who personally checked every last detail. In the early days the élite at

Sèvres (the training school established to educate future teachers in the new *lycées* and colleges) was allowed to take a bath only once every three weeks, though in a moment of generosity the Minister consented to the installation of showers in 1888. An enquiry was ordered to see that there was no unnecessary usage of heating and lighting, as when the students were not in their rooms. A request for an increase in the school's hospital budget was turned down.[26] With such a cheese-paring outlook typical of most French governments of the period, they can hardly be said to have done everything in their power to promote secondary education for girls in the years before the First World War.

In the end, however, the secondary education of French girls was to develop in directions which the legislators of 1880 had not anticipated. Intended largely for the daughters of the upper middle classes, the schools came to recruit their pupils mainly among lower middle-class girls: almost one third were the daughters of teachers or civil servants while another third were the daughters of self-employed businessmen. Although in Paris the pupils tended to come from a higher social bracket (parents were frequently top civil servants or fairly wealthy bosses) in the provinces most girls – particularly in the colleges – came from the ranks of the petty bourgeoisie. Thus the girls often came from backgrounds where parents were less interested in the acquisition of the diploma than in obtaining a primary certificate which would qualify their daughters for some kind of employment. In this way many establishments came to provide what was in effect a higher primary education with a distinctly vocational bias.[27]

In certain schools another very different development also served to undermine the original dilettante ideal. This was the clandestine introduction of Latin classes, which allowed girls to prepare for the *baccalauréat* and therefore for university entrance. Here, private educational establishments took the initiative, with the Collège Sévigné, a private secular school founded in 1880, leading the way, and a number of Catholic schools following suit. It would be wrong to think that the Catholic initiative is to be attributed to a sudden conversion to feminism. Rather, it was prompted by the vigorous anti-clerical measures which were enacted in the aftermath of the Dreyfus Affair and which culminated in the law separating Church and State in 1905. By way of retaliation against these attacks and of refuting republican allegations about their inferior educational standards, Catholic headmistresses seem to have decided to upstage their rivals by making provision for the teaching of Latin in their schools.[28] Faced with such a challenge from the private sector, some heads of state establishments in Paris and other large towns saw no alternative but to allow their own pupils to study Latin and to sit the *bac*. In the Academy of Poitiers Latin teaching began in 1909, the courses being given by a male teacher from a boys' *lycée*. In 1910 five candidates were successful in the *baccalauréat* examinations. By 1913 there had been twenty-nine passes.[29] Though still small, these figures were a sign of the times: female secondary education was now set on a course towards identification with the male programme, much to the dismay of Camille Sée, who continued to argue the case for a distinctive syllabus for girls, even if the diploma were to be replaced by a special female *baccalauréat*.

The number of girls who succeeded in going on to higher education remained comparatively small. In 1880 only the Medical Faculty in Paris expressly allowed women students to take its courses: even so, there were only thirty-two females registered there in 1879. By 1914, this figure had risen to 578. In other faculties of the University of Paris the situation was somewhat confused. In 1864 some women protested at the exclusion of women from the Sorbonne, yet a handful of exceptional women did succeed in enrolling in Science and Arts. In 1867 Mlle Emma Chenu became the first woman to take a degree in mathematics in the Science Faculty, while Julie Daubié, the first woman to obtain the *baccalauréat* (in 1861), also became the first to graduate in Arts in 1871. Thus, in practice, if not in theory, women established their right to a university education from the 1860s, though it was only in 1890 that Julie Chauvin became the first woman to graduate in Law, and later in the same decade that institutions like the Ecole des Chartes and the Ecole des Beaux-Arts opened their doors to women students. By 1900 there were 624 native French girl students in the French higher educational system. As more and more girls took the *baccalauréat*, numbers reached 1148 in 1905 and 2547 in 1914. One should note, however, that in the French faculties the proportion of French women students exceeded that of foreigners for the first time only in 1912-13.[31] Moreover many girls, even those who had worked furiously to obtain a place, failed to complete their course, opting out as soon as they met a suitable husband.[32]

Bourgeois parents often showed no interest in the academic attainments of their daughters. As Louise Weiss recalls, her father was unimpressed by her scholarly success at school: far from encouraging her to go on to university, he wanted to send her to a college of domestic science.[33] Progress in the field of women's education over the period 1870-1914 was undoubtedly real, but it was also slow and undynamic.

The ambiguous status of women teachers confirms the impression of only a limited advance in the educational sphere. At the primary level, the *institutrice* was very often an isolated figure, misunderstood by a public who saw her as the agent of Ferry's anti-clerical revolution, even when she herself remained loyal to her religious upbringing and was

only vaguely aware of the 'laic ideal'.[34] This of course was most true in
areas where clerical influence was strongest. The reactionary newspaper *Autorité* took great delight in informing its readers that in the
commune of Le Montiel in Savoy, the two secular women teachers
could attract only one solitary pupil to their new school, since the local
parish priest had raised money to keep the old school, run by nuns, in
existence.[35] Material hardship was also common. Mlle N of
Selles-Saint-Denis in the Loir-et-Cher department complained bitterly
that her school was housed in the filthiest building in the commune and
that she herself had inadequate living space, having no kitchen – or
rather a kitchen which also served as a classroom. Consequently, she
had begun to take her meals out at the village hotel, but this in turn gave
rise to gossip and scandal, and she was obliged to eat at home again. A
strained relationship with her male colleague did not make life easier:
and even her one pleasure, going for solitary walks in the woods, set the
tongues wagging anew.[36]

Mlle N may have been an atypical case and she may even have been
given to exaggeration, but it seems abundantly clear nevertheless that
the private life of a village *institutrice* could be intolerably difficult.
Others, too, stressed that loneliness was the greatest problem which
they had to face, a problem exacerbated by the difficulty of finding a
suitable marriage partner. Many, particularly those of bourgeois
origin, driven into the career by a reversal of family fortunes, could not
bear the idea of living with a peasant or worker of lower culture. In any
case, in the early days of the Third Republic, a married *institutrice* gave
scandal, even when married to a fellow schoolteacher.[37] One young
mistress told the feminist newspaper *La Fronde* that a jealous inspector
had prevented her from marrying a colleague in a neighbouring canton
on the grounds that she would be 'compromised in the eyes of the
population'.[38] It is true that at the beginning of the twentieth century
official policy on this matter underwent a dramatic about-turn, so that
marriages between male and female primary teachers were actually
encouraged. But the *institutrice* still had plenty of other difficulties to
contend with. The question of dress could prove vexatious (with male
colleagues among the harshest critics) in that she was expected to dress
elegantly enough to be distinguishable from the peasant woman, but
yet not so fashionably as to attract too much admiration.[39] M Bédorez,
Director of Primary Education in the Seine, laid down that his *institutrices* could cycle only on Sundays and in the countryside: they were
forbidden to arrive at school on their bicycles on the grounds that if an
accident occurred in front of the pupils the teachers' authority over them
would be diminished.[40] Finally, to complement these moral sufferings,
the salary of a woman primary teacher was equal to that of a man only
at the bottom of the scale: in the higher grades they were paid less.[41]

If anything, the position of *femmes professeurs* in the new secondary school was even worse. They too fared badly by comparison with their male colleagues. They worked longer hours for lower salaries. If they had passed the *agrégation* they did not receive the annual bonus of 500 francs given to men. Absences for illness (and pregnancy was deemed to fall within this category) led to deductions from salary, though this was never the case with male teachers. Women *agrégées* were not allowed to present a thesis for the *doctorat d'état* and women did not have the right to vote in elections to the *conseil supérieur d'instruction publique*. For society at large, the woman secondary teacher was a dangerous creature, threatening the natural order of male supremacy, the kind of person who ought to be seen only rarely in public. Ideally, she should be 'moderate in her opinions, neutral in her dress, nil in her personality and ugly for preference'. Living under a constant régime of 'liberty under surveillance', many succumbed to nervous depression. As was pointed out in the *Revue Universitaire*, this took a particular toll on the health of unmarried women, who formed the majority of the profession: they failed to eat properly and suffered from the continual intellectual strain, exacerbated by solitude and the pressure from prejudiced public opinion.[42] Thus these women rarely saw themselves as agents of profound social change or as militants on behalf of the rights of women. Rather, they seem to have conceived their role as being that of secular missionaries whose essential task was to see to the moral education of their pupils. Here it is interesting to note the significant number of Protestant women who entered the profession, including the first Directress of Sèvres, Mme Favre.[43] Reflections on the fate of the *femme professeur* and of the *institutrice* should discourage any tendency to exaggerate the extent to which the Third Republic's educational reforms contributed to the emancipation of French women.

The employment of middle-class women

If a positive but tentative advance in the realm of education was one aspect of a general improvement in the standing of middle-class women in the world beyond the home, another was the availability of new opportunities for employment in the years from about 1880. In the first half of the nineteenth century the strength of the ideology of separate spheres had made it simply unthinkable that a bourgeois woman should even contemplate the prospect of taking a job, except possibly as a schoolteacher. But partly as a result of the reforms in education, partly because of a general expansion in industry and commerce from the time of the Second Empire, women of the middle classes began to enter the labour market in significant numbers in the late nineteenth century. Technical advances, such as the invention of the telephone and the typewriter, taken alongside the ever-growing complexity of the industrial economy and the widening spheres of government interest, all combined to bring women into every kind of 'tertiary' employment – as clerks, shorthand typists, secretaries, cashiers, post-office workers, telephonists, shop assistants in the luxury stores such as the *Louvre, Bon Marché* and *Printemps*. In these, and in banks, credit houses, government departments, railway companies and so on, women came to represent an increasingly large proportion of the total number of employees.[44]

The Post Office (PTT) provides a good example of this process of 'the feminisation of office-work'.[45] The postal services had employed women under the *ancien régime* but they had been deprived of their positions in the course of the French Revolution. The few provincial postmistresses who retained their jobs were subjected to repeated attacks in the nineteenth century, as in the insulting series of articles published in *La France Administrative* between 1841 and 1846. It was only in 1877 that women were once again employed in Paris, initially at the *Central Télégraphique*, then in the Postal Savings Banks opened in 1881, and finally in the telephone company after it had become a state monopoly. The *Journal des Postes, Télégraphes et Téléphones* kept up the barrage of criticisms of women employees in the 1890s, but their numbers continued to grow until they reached 21,457 in 1906 (22% of the labour force).[46] The general trend can perhaps best be illustrated by some statistics. In 1866 only 238,000 women were employed in commercial professions (25.5% of all such employees); by 1896 they numbered 1,602,000, a proportion of 35.6%; while by 1911 the percentage had risen to 40.6%.[47] To put the expansion another way, 170 women in every 1000 working women worked in commerce in 1906, whereas in 1866 there had been only eighty-two.[48]

But as in the sphere of female education, it would be a mistake to exaggerate the extent of the progress made in the sphere of women's employment before 1914. Access to the liberal professions did mark a turning point, but once again the full effects were to be felt only in the future. Only about 7% of working women were engaged in a liberal profession, and of these the vast majority were independent schoolteachers rather than lawyers or doctors. In the legal profession, open to women only from 1900, the proportion was tiny – 0.29%. In the medical profession as a whole, women provided 49% of the numbers, but this inflated figure reflects the almost exclusively feminine professions of midwife (100%) and nurse (96%) as well as the women who made up 68% of hospital personnel. Those who were actually doctors numbered only 573 in 1906 – 3% of the profession.[49] Moreover, in both the law and medicine, women were advised by careers guides that their best chances of success were to specialise exclusively in cases involving women or children.[50] Women did supply a higher proportion of French dentists (8%) even if their numbers were lower than the doctors (280). The 659 women pharmacists added up to only 3% of the profession. A mere 2.6% of French chemists and engineers were women.[51] It was still impossible for a woman to become a senior civil servant as a law of 31 August 1908 permitted only males to take the appropriate examinations.[52]

In general, the commercial and administrative jobs held by women were those involving little initiative and no authority. In government departments, women were employed mainly as shorthand typists, and the usual motive was to keep down salaries.[53] Until at least the turn of the century, many of the new office jobs were restricted to female relatives of male employees. In the railway companies, for instance, preference was given to the wives, daughters and sisters of men already on their staff, though some others did get taken on.[54] In one of the main Parisian banks, the *Comptoir National d'Escompte de Paris*, women employees were recruited exclusively from relatives of their male staff, while the examinations set for candidates to the *Crédit Lyonnais* and the Bank of France counted for little beside recommendations and influence. Not surprisingly, there were many more applicants for office jobs than there were places available. The Bank of France had 5000 applicants, but could offer jobs only to 20–25 candidates; the *Crédit Lyonnais* had 7000–8000 competitors for 80–100 places; while the *Société Générale* could accommodate only 64 out of 1000 applicants. The Post Office had 250 posts and 5000 aspirants.[55]

Underlying this situation was the lack of establishments to provide girls with an adequate technical training for a career in commerce or industry.[56] The earliest attempts to meet this deficiency were made by Elisa Lemonnier, who founded the Society for the Professional Education of Women and established the first of her vocational schools in 1862. After her death Mme Julie Toussaint carried on her work, but the state remained slow to follow their example. Eventually, on the initiative of MM Gréard and Buisson at the Ministry of Education, a law of 11 December 1880 created a number of manual apprenticeship schools, which was followed by further legislation establishing practical schools of commerce and industry. But despite the encouragement which all of these schools received from various governments before 1914, the type of training they provided was intended only to prepare girls for the lower reaches of business life – as typists, secretaries, drawing mistresses and so on. Managerial positions remained almost exclusively in the hands of men.

Thus, in the field of employment, it is necessary to note that although considerable evolution did take place, the changes were hesitant and far from dramatic. The ambiguity of the situation is well illustrated by certain authors of careers guides written to help girls take advantage of the new opportunities. Mme Georges Regnal, while insisting on the obligation of every mother to prepare her daughter for a working life, observed nevertheless that society was still reluctant to allow women to live by the fruits of their own labour, since customarily they were paid only 'pin money'.[57] Mlle Razous still clung to the old view that only girls from families which had suffered a reverse of fortunes should have to go out to work, though she could see that women married to men with incomes insufficient to let them live in the style to which they had been accustomed might also have to find a job to supplement the family income. Under normal circumstances, the proper place for a woman remained the home:

> 'The best, the healthiest, the most noble of situations is that of the woman as wife and mother, conscious of her duties towards her husband and children.'[58]

The old traditions died hard.

The plight of the ouvrière

As we saw in Chapter II, the very commitment of working-class women to the welfare of their families often obliged them to violate the ideal of domesticity by taking up paid employment either inside or outside the home. As daughters and as wives they were expected to contribute to the family's income as circumstances required. The conditions under which working women carried on their labour, however, hardly seem to support the view that participation in the labour force opened the door to female emancipation. Class and sexual exploitation was the most common result of the *ouvrière*'s involvement in the world of work in the years before the First World War, as will be evident from a survey of the situation of women workers in industry (we shall look in particular at textiles and the clothing industry), in domestic work and in domestic service.

FACTORY WORKERS IN TEXTILES

For the working women of the textiles industry, long hours, low wages and bad conditions remained the rule for most of the nineteenth century. Jeanne Bouvier, the daughter of a cooper who also owned a small farm in a village of the Isère, has related the harrowing story of how she became an *ouvrière* at the age of eleven in 1876.[59] Starting work at 5 am and finishing at 8 pm, with rest breaks of two hours for meals, she was paid 50 centimes for her thirteen hours' labour a day. To supplement this meagre pittance, she spent her evenings at crotchet work, sometimes working through the entire night so that the house might have bread:

> I recall that one time among others I went almost two days without eating. In the evening, on coming home from the factory, I got down to work. My mother spent

the night with me to give me a shake when in spite of myself I fell asleep. She said: 'Don't go to sleep, you know that you mustn't sleep. Tomorrow we won't have any bread.' I made superhuman efforts to stay awake. It was very cold. The snow hammered against the windows. Despite all these tortures, I kept working until 4.30 am, the time at which I got ready to return to the factory.[60]

Before 1900, no effective legislation existed to mitigate such horrific exploitation. A law of 19 May 1874 banned children under the age of twelve from any type of factory or manufacturing work and limited the maximum number of hours as twelve for those over this age. Girls under twenty-one were not to be allowed to do nightshifts, while women and children under the age of twelve were to be excluded from work underground. This law, however, was totally ineffective for lack of any adequate machinery of control to enforce it.[61] Likewise, the law of 2 November 1892, intended to ban night work for women, to give them an eleven-hour day and provide them with a weekly day of rest, was never properly implemented.[62] A decree of 26 July 1893 acted totally against the original intentions of the law by permitting work until 11 pm, which overturned the provisions on the working day, and by making exemptions from the provisions on night work and weekly rest in a large number of specified cases. In textile factories, another way round the law was the adoption of shift work in teams (the *système des relais*) which often kept women workers on the premises for longer than eleven hours a day in cases where they lived too far away from home to go back at their break.[63] The relay system was not effectively suppressed until the application of the law of 30 March 1900, which was intended to bring a woman's working day down to 10½ hours after two years, and finally to ten hours by 1904. It seems, however, that the average day in weaving in the years before 1914 continued to be ten hours, and even eleven in the cotton mills of the Nord and the silk factories of the Rhône.[64] Another decree of 27 December 1911 improved on that of 1892 as regards night work for women by conforming to the stipulations agreed by the International Convention of Berne in 1906. Obligatory weekly rest became more widespread after the law of 13 July 1906, whose terms applied not just to industrial workers, both male and female, but also to employees in commerce.[65]

By the 1890s the conditions under which women carried on their labours were no longer quite as fearful as at the time of Villermé's investigations, when girls in textiles factories doing work of beating by hand often contracted 'cotton pneumonia', and when girl silk workers died young from tuberculosis. But dangers were still much in evidence. Women weavers at work on Jacquart looms had to be wary of the toxic poisons given off by the little counter-weights of lead when they rubbed together.[66] In linen mills the heavy, hot, humid atmosphere was a constant threat to the workers' health, while in the silk factories

defective machines for conducting steam away meant that girls had to
work enveloped in clouds which prevented them from seeing their
neighbours and which soaked their light garments, so that the slightest
drop in temperature could bring on chills capable of developing quickly
into pneumonia. [67] Also, quite often the silk workers stayed overnight
at their factories, going home only at weekends. Factory inspectors
discovered that their sleeping arrangements could be atrocious. One
inspector reported that the dormitory was an attic where air and light
never penetrated; in other places, no wash basins were to be found, and
beds consisted of piles of straw over which were strewn filthy sheets
and blankets. A further report of 1901 noted a few changes for the
better, but deplored the fact that girls generally still slept two to a bed. [68]

Legislation did something to improve these conditions before 1914.
A law of 1894 brought some action on the problem of the temperature
in textiles factories while better provision was made for conducting the
dust from the carding rooms. [69] The law of 9 April 1898, penalising
employers who were responsible for industrial accidents occasioned by
their machinery, led to a tightening up of security in factories by
measures such as fencing off machines and providing female employees
with protective clothing. [70] In 1913 the Minister of Labour was able to
say in reply to a parliamentary question that the factory inspectorate
was vigilant in enforcing the regulation that women should not clean
out power looms in textiles mills. [71]

But one area where legislation had no effect whatsoever was the
all-important one of wages. Here no significant improvements can be
observed in the period 1880–1914. Kaethe Schirmacher, author of an
exhaustive statistical survey on the situation of the *ouvrière* at the turn of
the century, calculated that the maximum wage of a woman employed
in industry did not reach even 50% of the maximum obtained by a male
worker. [72] There were a few exceptions to the general rule: for instance,
the matchmakers, whose wages rose by 76% in the years between 1890
and 1904, and the tobacco makers, whose pay went up 21% between
1894 and 1904. Women typographical workers, too, earned well above
the average wage for women, but their 5–6 francs a day still left them
well below the 7–8 francs earned by their male workmates. [73]
Nevertheless, it remains true that in the early 1890s the average pay
taken home by a woman in a large to middling firm in the Department
of the Seine was 3 francs to a man's 6fr.15, with the corresponding
figures in the provinces being 2fr. 10 and 3fr. 90. [74] From the statistics
released by the Ministry of Labour in 1914, no significant diminution in
this gap can be discerned in the years just before the Great War.

WOMEN WORKERS IN THE CLOTHING INDUSTRY
In the world of the clothing industry, the situation of the woman

worker was equally grim. The Parisian dressmakers, for example, may
have had a reputation for coquetry and good humour, and doubtless
cherished their leisure hours when they could devour romantic novels
or spend Sunday with their boy friends on outings to Suresnes,
Meudon or Robinson. [75] Their relish for life, however, flourished in
spite of rather than because of the conditions in which they worked
before 1914. If excessively long hours of frantic toil were the rule at the
height of the season, long hours of unemployment followed when
business slackened off. Before a big society occasion – a ball, a Grand
Prix, a funeral – girls put in astonishing overtime hours, known as
veillées, as they desperately tried to finish the garments in time. A
vigilant labour inspector reported that when Czar Alexander III died in
1894, all the great Russian ladies placed orders with Parisian fashion
houses, who then required their dressmakers to slave day and night to
meet the deadline. [76] Jeanne Bouvier has recalled how she frequently put
in long *veillées* till 2 am, in most cases without stopping for dinner and
sustained only by a roll and a bar of chocolate taken at 4 pm. Absolute
silence was imposed to make life even less bearable. At 2 am, she faced a
walk of some three-quarters of an hour before she reached her lodgings
– a daunting prospect on an empty stomach in freezing winter. On
reaching home, more often than not, she was not up to preparing a
meal: it is hardly surprising that after such a season she needed hospital
care. On one occasion, she worked a shift from 8 am to 5 am the
following morning. [77]

The legislation of 1892 and 1900 led to no serious dimunution in the
practice of *veillées*; before a Grand Prix race of 1900, a case of thirty
hours of continuous labour was unearthed by the inspectorate. [78]
Industrialists resorted to every kind of subterfuge to get round the
provisions of the law. At the end of the legal ten-hour day, they
sometimes gave work to their employees to finish off at home and bring
back completed first thing in the morning. Another device was to send
girls home when the inspector appeared, with instructions to come
back after his departure. Legal technicalities were also effectively
exploited: for instance, an inspector had a legal right to enter a factory
after 9 pm only if he had good grounds for thinking that he would
discover a breach of the law. (The position was that he could enter night
or day as long as work was in progress.) But even when the inspector
had sufficient evidence to gain right of access to the premises, he might
come up against an employer who sent his *ouvrières* to work on the
higher floors in his bourgeois apartment: there the inspector would be
unable to search further without violating the domestic rights of the
employer. Such a situation came to light in 1906 in the horrible case of a
young girl who died of suffocation in the wardrobe of a prominent
couturier; after the departure of the inspector, he had forgotten to let

her out and she was discovered only thirty-six hours later. In any case, sanctions were not severe enough to act as an effective deterrent (Article 26 of the law of 1892 provided for a fine of between 5 and 15 francs). For all these reasons, enforcement of the law was very difficult: any improvements that did result after 1900 can be credited to the dedication of the factory inspectorate.[79]

Veillées were not eliminated until the decree of 17 February 1910, restricting female labour between the hours of 9 and 11 pm to the fabrication of articles required for funerals by women and children, and the law of 22 December 1911, supplemented by a decree of 27 December 1911 which had the effect of fixing the minimum duration of night rest for women at eleven hours, with 10 pm as the extreme limit of the working day.[80] Of course some bosses continued to break the rules. A woman inspector, Mme Maître, discovered overwork at the Maison Alexandre in Paris. Arriving at 7.40 am, she found that work had already begun, though she had previously been told that starting time was 9 am. No notice was displayed giving the hours of the working day, nor was any register kept.[81] By 1914, however, *veillées* had become exceptional, perhaps the best result of protective legislation on behalf of women in the pre-war period. Yet it should still be remembered that in season these *ouvrières* worked a twelve-hour day, returning home only about 9.30–10.00 pm; and since most of them had to travel back to working-class suburbs like Clichy, Batignolles and Levallois, they were often too exhausted to eat, and consequently failed to look after their health properly.[82]

At no time did the state consider intervention to try to raise the derisorily low wages paid to women workers in the clothing industry. Between 1893 and 1900, wages remained fairly stable: no significant difference resulted from the (theoretical) reduction in the working day, since dressmakers were paid by the day rather than by the hour. Towards 1908 there were some slight improvements, followed by small increases after 1910. But these pay rises served only to keep pace with rises in the cost of living, which went up by 5% between 1900 and 1914. In small and middling houses, workers were only marginally better off by 1914. Apprentices who in 1893 lived *au pair* with their employers and received no wage at all were paid 50 centimes a day in 1914; small hands who got between 1–1fr.50 in 1893 received between 1fr.78–2fr.25; while first hands got at least 4 francs instead of 3 francs. In the bigger houses improvements were even less marked – insignificant in the case of apprentices and second hands and perhaps attaining about 0.50 francs in the case of first hands who could count on earning 5–6fr.50 a day in 1914.[83]

These pitifully low wages were exacerbated by the irregular and seasonal nature of employment in the clothing industry. A dressmaker had to reckon with the grim fact that she would be unemployed for long stretches during the year: top hands could count on earning a full wage on only 260-300 days, while a second would be lucky to have full employment on 200-15 days. [84] Thus even in the few cases where daily wages were relatively high, annual salaries still remained low. A girl who in 1895 could earn 4fr.75 a day, but had to survive 160 days of dead-season, told Charles Benoist that she would rather be paid only 3fr.50 a day if she could be guaranteed 300 days' full employment in the year. [85] At the time of Benoist's enquiry, girls in the clothing industry were not being paid a living wage, as he showed by drawing up a list of specimen annual budgets. To give only one example, there was the case of a small hand in ready-made clothes who earned 1fr.25 a day, and had an annual income of 375 francs, which was divided up as follows:

Yearly rent	100
1 dress at 5 francs	5
1 fichu at 2 francs	2
2 pairs of stockings at 0.65 a pair	1.30
2 pairs of shoes at 4 francs a pair	8
1 jacket at 1fr.25	1.25
2 handkerchiefs at 0.40 each	0.80
Lighting (a year)	4
Total	125.68 francs

This left 250 francs a year for food, in other words 0.65 francs a day, which she spent thus:

Morning: milk	0.05
bread	0.20
Lunch: black pudding	0.10
chips	0.05
cheese	0.10
Evening: sausage	0.10
chips	0.05
Total	0.65 francs [86]

Other studies of yearly budgets show that there were still many women in a comparable situation in 1913, earning barely subsistence wages. With an abundance of skilled labour available on the market, the laws of supply and demand worked very much to the advantage of the employer. The author of a report in the *Bulletin* of the Ministry of Labour concluded that even in 1914 'the level of the daily wage barely provides for the indispensable means of subsistence: it does not even permit independence, nor the least saving, or leisure or pastime which promotes intellectual or physical development'.[87] For girls living at home, this 'pin money' was acceptable as a contribution to the family income; but for women living alone and trying to earn their own living, the material difficulties presented by these pitiful wages could usually be overcome only by cohabitation with a man, prostitution or, in the most desperate cases, suicide. Among Jeanne Bouvier's neighbours on the seventh floor of an apartment building were some who were even poorer than she was. The most wretched was a young seamstress who worked for a big fashion house on the rue de la Paix: despite the high quality of her work, she could afford only 0.15 francs a day for food (bread and milk). Unable to pay her rent, she had to move to another place nearby where she survived miserably until, overcome by the strains and pressures involved in merely staying alive, she jumped out of a seventh floor window.[88]

SHOP ASSISTANTS

Having looked at the plight of women workers in the clothing industry, we now turn briefly to the situation of a related category of *ouvrières*, the shop assistants of the luxury stores (the *demoiselles de magasin*). Many of these came from working-class suburbs such as Pantin, Saint-Denis and La Chapelle, from where they commuted into the centre of Paris. Although enjoying a relative superiority in status over their brothers who worked in the industrial factories of the *banlieue*, these girls, too, suffered from extensive exploitation, since they were poorly paid and constantly made to feel inferior by the hierarchical structure of power in the store.[89] The rapid development of the *grands magasins* such as *Printemps*, *Bon Marché* and the *Galeries Lafayette* took place under the Second Empire and their internal functioning has been graphically depicted by Zola in his *Au Bonheur des Dames*. Liable to instant dismissal, denied the right to answer complaints by a customer, the shop assistants worked on average a thirteen-hour day, having to arrive before opening time at 8 am and not being able to go home after closing time at 8 pm until all goods had been rearranged. Apprentices were kept busy all day long with the most menial tasks – sweeping up and running errands. Other girls had to sell the shop's wares on the street pavement, where they could freeze in winter and stew in summer. But perhaps the most distressing aspect of their situation was the isolation and ferocious rivalry which existed among them as a result of the *guelte* system of payment (a bonus system based on the quantity of sales). Assistants regarded one another as competitors and few made friends with their colleagues. The customers, too, were rivals, for, as Zola saw, the sales girls depended on them for their livelihood. While they envied their wealthy and well-dressed customers, they themselves were the object of the bitter resentments of their petty bourgeois clients, who took pleasure in ordering them around in the most humiliating fashion before making purchases worth a few pence. In front of the counters, observed Zola, it was a case of woman eating woman.[90]

Because the laws regulating the hours of women's work in industry did not cover commerce, there is no doubt that shop girls were overworked. With the exception of food stores, in general the bigger the shop the worse were the conditions: girls were continually overworked in a confined and unhealthy atmosphere. According to Dr Paul Berthod, tuberculosis was a not uncommon consequence.[91] Some were lodged by the shop in a *mansarde*, a small, cramped, extremely uncomfortable attic with no washing facilities and where they were forbidden to have visitors. Placed under the strict surveillance of a *concièrge*, they had to return to their miserable dwellings by 11 pm, which left them only a few hours in which to meet a lover or just relax on their own. The smiling, elegant *demoiselle* of the daytime belied the lonely, miserable girl of the *mansarde*.

DOMESTIC WORKERS

As has already been pointed out, a very large proportion of the female labour force in manufacturing industry in France (above all in the clothing industry) was made up of women (frequently married) who worked neither in a factory nor a small workshop, but at home. Of all working women, these were, generally speaking, the most hideously exploited. As analysis of 510 such *ouvrières* in an inquiry carried out for the Musée Social in 1908 found that, out of 217 who gave their wage by the hour, 109, that is 60%, got less than three sous, and 186, or 83%, got less than 5 sous.[92] Some unfortunates, the victims of the 'truck' system, might see hardly any money wages at all, but receive only some token in kind.[93] No limitation (beyond the strength of the worker) existed on the duration of the working day: the official enquiry into the state of domestic work in needlework in Paris found that 43% of the women workers laboured between ten and twelve hours a day, while 13% did more than twelve hours.[94] Even children were cruelly exploited: as one contemporary observer pointed out, it was complete nonsense to argue that small industry and domestic industry preserved the family better, for reality showed 'the little girl of ten kept from going to school and made to do housework and look after the smaller children, while the mother sews at her machine'.[95] Few of these women could afford to eat properly or to live in decent lodgings: 'those who have 95 centimes or 1 franc a day for food constitute the aristocracy. Others don't have more than 50 or 75 centimes'.[96]

The various enquiries initiated by the Labour Office confirm this picture of surpassing misery. Occasionally, an extremely skilful woman capable of prodigiously hard work could make more than enough to survive on. Such was Mlle B, aged thirty and a former dressmaker who claimed to have earned 1200 francs in 1904 by putting in sixteen hours daily for ten months and managing some irregular work in the other two. She declared that she had got used to long hours of work with her *veillées* and did not mind them much now that she was able to remain at home.[97] But in sharp contrast, and much more typical of the average Parisian domestic worker in sewing, was Mme I, at twenty-eight the widow of a policeman with no family to help her out. Although able to sew, she lacked the skill of a professional and earned only ten centimes an hour, working an eleven hour day. Out of an income of about 30 francs a month, she had to pay 12 francs towards the cost of her machine which left her with only about 1 franc a day for food, whereas she reckoned that she needed to spend at least 1fr.50 if she were to maintain a proper diet. Usually her meals consisted of milk and sugar in the morning, cutlet or beefsteak at 30 centimes and a vegetable for lunch, with three pounds of bread to last her two days. She took no evening meal. The rest of her resources went on washing, heating and lighting, though fortunately she had her rent paid by the widow's pension she received. For the previous fifteen months she had been able to get by only because of her savings: she had no idea how she could cope once these ran out.[98] For a single woman with children the situation was even more desperate. One woman, aged twenty-six, and abandoned by her husband at the birth of their second child, was able to earn only about 600 francs in 1904. She now lived with her two children and her mother in a filthy hotel room near the Panthéon and told the interviewer that no one had eaten since the previous day. Her female employer exploited her situation to pay her less than other women workers, humiliating her because of her irregular marital situation. When she tried to get help from another woman, she found herself even more cruelly exploited, receiving only 2fr.50 for a week's work in which she worked three days and three nights: that is, she was paid less than 5 centimes an hour.[99] A single woman was likely to survive only if she had someone else in her family to help her out. Mme H, a forty-three year old widow living in Plaisance who said she made only 2fr.25 a day (though the inquirer thought she possibly made more) was able to live quite comfortably because two of her three remaining children were gainfully employed, so that the annual resources of the household totalled 1779fr.50.[100]

Overall, the Paris survey of domestic seamstresses discovered that a sizable proportion (17%) were over sixty years of age. Out of 540 interviewed, some eighty were suffering from ill-health and probably a lot more refused to reveal the real state of their health. Around 25% seem to have experienced a deterioration in their eyesight. 50% were married, while 33% were either widowed or, very rarely, divorced. 16% were single women, of whom ten out of eighty-three said they had children. The majority (60%) earned less than 400 francs a year, 24% got between 400-600 francs, while 15% made more than 600 francs. Accommodation was usually poor: 135 lived in a single room and twenty-four of these were occupied by households with three or more persons. The average rent was between 150-300 francs a year. 68% of the residences could be considered satisfactory from the point of view of hygiene, but 32% were extremely bad.[101]

The horrors uncovered by the Parisian enquiry were matched in almost every respect by the findings of provincial surveys. In the Cher, domestic seamstresses averaged a maximum of 0.10 francs an hour (59%); a mere handful (1%) earned more than 0.21 francs.[102] In the Loir-et-Cher 52% of the women workers earned a maximum of 200 francs a year.[103] Fairly representative would be Mme C (department of the Indre), aged thirty-five, married with four children. Her husband earned about 100 francs a month working in a chemical laboratory. For the previous sixteen years, she had made all kinds of articles for an entrepreneur specialising in military equipment – shirts, flannel belts, jackets, etc. – working fourteen hours a day and receiving a little help from her mother, who also helped the children with some of the housework. Her daily wage usually came out to be about 0.80 francs net.[104] Once again, the hardest lot was that of the single woman fending for herself: a widowed shirtmaker from Rouen said that only a very good worker could hope to make 1fr.25 a day, and only then by doing with a minimal amount of sleep. She herself had made 127 shirts in a week, sleeping only two hours a night, but for this her net gain had been a mere ten francs. She was one of the many who had to buy thread from her *Maison* at an inflated price or else be refused work. The interviewer summed up:

> this worker, who is forty-seven, looks as if she is sixty. Her food is made up of little more than little balls of minced pork, salted herrings and the cheapest of vegetables. She says that she gets no help from anyone and that life for her is an unalleviated burden.[105]

The same pattern is to be found in other domestic industries, though in the case of artificial flowers it would be true to say that wages were generally somewhat higher. Essentially a Parisian trade, the artificial flower industry was designed to complement the products of the great fashion houses and a skilled specialist could do very well. Mme N, who specialised in natural flowers, and had learnt the art at fourteen, was able to make a gross income of 631fr.25 working a six hour day in

1907-8. Her husband, a mechanic with a bus company, earned a good wage and her daughter brought in 90 francs a month. The family lived comfortably in bourgeois style in a flat in the Clignancourt area and the wife felt that she would be able to stop working altogether in a year or so. Another of these better off women workers was Mme V, whose income in 1907-8 amounted to 1088fr.50 for an average eleven hour day. Her husband, an electrician, earned 1127 francs a year and they lived comfortably with their two children in the Combat *quartier*. But by no means all of the women working in the artificial flower industry were as fortunate. Mme S, a widow of thirty with five young children, one of whom had recently died and of whom two others were seriously ill, was unable to continue working for a large store because she had to live in Ménilmontant, on the outskirts of the city, where they all lived in one big room. Herself tubercular, her work was often interrupted by illness; the physical effort involved in her work of making artificial chrysanthemums periodically caused her to vomit blood. Another poor woman was Mlle C, aged forty-eight, who suffered from a liver complaint and lived in a squalid furnished room. For meals she took only a sou's worth of horsemeat with a sou's worth of bread. Working irregularly, she probably made about 456 francs the previous year. Likewise thirty-one year old Mme G, whose pale, ravaged face bore the marks of excessive effort and a life of deprivation, struggled to earn enough to bring up her family by making violets 10-12 hours a day, without ever receiving more than 1 franc for her labours. Her husband, a casual labourer, was of no great help since he was often out of work.

In general, for Paris and its suburbs, 81% of the women engaged in making artificial flowers at home had worked at some previous stage in a workshop, and had therefore obtained some kind of training and skills. 52% were married, 22% were widowed or divorced and 21% were single. Most worked at home for family reasons and were prepared to put in long hours – more than 40% did between 11-18 hours a day. Wages varied considerably. Top skilled workers, making natural flowers and roses, could expect at least 3 francs a day, and the very best working for a famous fashion house might make up to 50 francs a week. But those making small flowers and fruits would be likely to average only about 2fr.50.[106]

As in the case of industrial factory workers and women working in the clothing industry, the domestic worker was not expected to earn enough money to allow her to lead an independent existence. This at least was the conclusion reached by Louis Bonnevay after an extensive study of wages and budgets of domestic workers in the Lyons area in 1896.[107] All sections of opinion, from the Catholic social reformer Albert de Mun on the Right through to the Socialists on the Left, were agreed that it was a matter of deliberate policy on the part of employers not to pay women a living wage. As the socialist Briquet put it:

A woman's wage is only a pittance [*un salaire d'appoint*]: it is fixed in accordance with a calculation which holds as axiomatic that a woman 'must have recourse to someone who helps her'. Normally, this someone is her husband, from which flows women's subjection in marriage: but he is not always the husband, wherein lies the profound immorality of the capitalist régime which not only pushes women into prostitution because of the deplorable conditions of work it imposes on them, but, even worse, speculates on the ability which women workers have to find an addition to their wages in the trafficking of love in order to pay for their labour at a derisory rate.[108]

Finally, it should be remembered that domestic work by no means accounts for all the economic activity of women in the least industrialised sectors of the economy. Women (again they were often married women) were to be found doing all sorts of odd jobs, most of which cannot be mentioned at any length here. These would include bread-carriers, fruit-sellers, fish-sellers, toy-sellers, news-vendors and so on. There were also girls who worked in small shops, selling bread, cheese, jam, and all sorts of other specialities such as herbs (herbalists were also said to be frequent practitioners of back-street abortions).[109] No survey of female employment would be complete without at least a reference to that most characteristic of women workers, the laundry-woman. In the mid-nineteenth century a soaping-woman would work a laborious fourteen-hour day for 2fr.50 and an ironing-woman, more skilled and having served a longer apprenticeship, would still get only 2fr.75 for a twelve-hour shift.[110] According to Octave Uzanne, a close and sympathetic observer of working women, most laundry-women were clean, pretty and even coquettish – though their language tended to be vulgar in the extreme. The washerwoman, however, was in a different category. Arriving by the Seine at 6 am to start work, she was rarely able to leave before 7 pm. Exposed to the wind in winter and sweltered by the heat in summer, they easily became bronchial or rheumatic: and 75% suffered from hernia as a result of carrying their heavy loads of washing. The only highlight in their back-breaking day was around 3.30 pm when their *patronne* traditionally brought over coffee or a glass of wine. They were also well known for their strong language and willingness to exchange insults as they fought each other for the best washing places.[111] For the washerwomen life was every bit as hard as it was for the vast majority of women who worked in domestic industries.

DOMESTIC SERVANTS

For the prosperous middle classes, at least one domestic servant in the household was a necessary status symbol. In 1906, there were 206,000 servants in Paris, some 11% of the population.[112] Before the French

Revolution the profession had numbered as many men as women, but in the course of the nineteenth century the male proportion fell drastically. In 1851 in Paris there were still thirty-one men for every sixty-nine women: by 1872 men constituted only 29% and in 1901 only 17% of the total servant population.[113] Though heavily concentrated in Paris most domestics were provincial in origin (in 1831, 60% of the servants who died in Paris had been born elsewhere).[114] Theresa McBride has argued that domestic service should be seen as an important avenue by which women from a rural background came to join the modern, urban way of life; but the fact remains that many domestics entered service in the hope that eventually they would be able to save enough money to allow themselves to retire or establish themselves back in their native region.[115]

Domestics were far from forming a homogeneous body: on the contrary the structure of the profession was extremely hierarchical. At the top of the female hierarchy came the chambermaid, generally aged between seventeen and twenty-five. Her tasks included dressing her mistress, some darning and occasionally some ironing. According to Octave Uzanne, she was given to snooping and searching in drawers and was an avid reader of other people's letters. One of her main aims was to squeeze as many old dresses and hats out of Madame as she could. Generally ugly, she was an opinionated prude who would go to Mass on Sundays and make her Easter Duties. In family quarrels she invariably took the side of the mistress against the master of the house. Earning between 40-75 francs a month, she was generally in a position to go back to her local village at about thirty-five, where she would marry and perhaps open a small store. Her great rival for pre-eminence was the cook: big, fat and moon-faced and excessively proud of her culinary talents. Should one of her dishes prove unsuccessful, she would fly into a rage, venting her spleen usually on the hapless dishwasher. It was common knowledge that a cook would appropriate some of the household's food for herself and her husband, though she was quite indignant and resentful if Madame came shopping with her. Her earnings worked out at about 50-75 francs a month.[116] The rivalry between cooks and chambermaids also carried over into their social life. At a big dance organised by domestic servants at the Salle Wagram in 1898 it was remarked that the younger, more coquettish chambermaids clearly enjoyed dancing the waltz or the quadrille while the heavier, more gauche-looking cooks looked on enviously.[117]

The children's maid might be a foreigner (English or German). Aged 20-25, often pretty, her chief ambition was to wring more old clothes out of Madame than the chambermaid. Frequently, she was bored by the children, paying attention to them only when out on a walk or in the park in order to attract men's attention. In her free time she read romantic fiction, fantasised about the possibilities of marvellous adventures, and haunted the *brasseries* of the Latin Quarter, where, unlike most domestics, she habitually squandered her 35-50 francs a month.

The maid-of-all-work was likely to be a sturdy country girl of limited intelligence who had to be ready to do any kind of job. Rising early and going to bed late, her day was spent in trying to avoid scoldings or breakages, which would be deducted from her wages. Her fresh looks often compensated for her lack of beauty and made her attractive to the male servants and even to Monsieur, all of whom hoped to get her to bed in her hovel in the attic. Fundamentally a good honest girl, she received between 20-40 francs a month and tended to marry a peasant farmer back in the country, where she would sweat blood to make the farm pay – 'a beast of work and a beast of pleasure', in Uzanne's view. Finally, at the bottom of the hierarchy, there was the poor cleaning woman, who would leave her village with her children and husband (typically a factory worker or coachman, or maybe a porter at the *Bon Marché*) to come to look after a bachelor. Rarely did she end her days back in her native parts, dying worn out in Paris after a life of hardship, having suffered beatings from her husband and undergone frequent pregnancies, yet remaining to the end honest, tender and devoted – all for 20 sous a day. She was 'the real woman of the people'.[118]

Despite all these gradations in the ranks of domestic service, it is important to emphasise what servants had in common rather than what might appear to keep them apart. One feature they shared was the necessity of working long and hard: usually their day began at 7 am and did not finish before 10 pm or even 11 pm, with only one hour off to attend to personal matters – hence their habitual lack of cleanliness. Only a few got one afternoon a week free – certainly general maids never did – while others counted themselves lucky to be off every Sunday, or perhaps once a fortnight. A holiday was possible only at times when the family was away. This lack of any time to oneself explains why servants were continually dodging and trying to steal time in desperate attempts to have some freedom and privacy.[119] Jeanne Bouvier in her varied career as a working woman was for a time a domestic servant and she supplies ample evidence of the incessant demands placed upon a young maid by an exacting mistress. Obliged to look after two spoiled and insolent children – though their mother would not hear a word against them – she had in addition to do all the shopping and the housework, which included the particularly heavy task of the laundry. When the family entertained lots of friends before the holiday of 14 July, this washing load was made almost intolerable as she struggled down stairs with two large buckets of water heavier than her own weight. The last straw came when the old clothes line broke and she was both insulted and punished by her mistress.[120]

It was this kind of reaction which produced in the servant class as a whole another common trait: a bitter class hatred of their masters and mistresses, intensified by an ever-increasing awareness of themselves as a distinct social group, almost a caste. Most of the literature on servants has of course been written by the master class and therefore represents only its point of view. Nevertheless, it is interesting and instructive to note the virtual unanimity on several points: the lack of any kind of sentimental bond of loyalty which they supposed had existed in a feudal relationship between masters and their *anciens serviteurs* and, on top of this, exclusive emphasis by domestics on the cash nexus, as well as a certain truculence and barely concealed resentment against their betters. As early as 1837 Marius Mittre wrote: 'Everyone complains about domestic servants! If you train them yourself they leave you, it is said, as soon as they can find a place elsewhere with higher pay.'[121] Mme Romieu also lamented the readiness with which Parisian servants quit their positions and concluded that the most powerful force at work in relations between masters and servants was mutual hatred.[122] Other commentators said much the same thing, one even bemoaning the abolition of the *livret*, in which he saw the 'only real security for the masters'.[123]

From such remarks, it seems reasonable to deduce that bourgeois masters and mistresses felt themselves to be confronted by a discontented servant class, and sound reasons for their discontent are not hard to find. Even if the legendary devoted *ancien serviteur* was largely a myth – Ernest Legouvé described the chambermaids in the plays of Molière and elsewhere as 'the confidantes of young girls, the messengers of amorous correspondence, the born enemies of husbands and fathers'[124] – it was true none the less that servants had once been more fully integrated into family life. A major development in the nineteenth century, mainly associated with the large-scale building of blocks of luxury flats under the Second Empire, was the separation of the maid from the rest of the family by having her live in a tiny room at the top of the apartment (*la chambre de bonne*): this could only make masters and mistresses more indifferent to the fate of their servants and in turn encourage them to feel more independent and even less loyal.[125] In these garrets it was not always possible to find somewhere to stand up straight. The windows were often too small to admit sufficient light or air, making for excessive heat in the summer, while it was perishingly cold in the winter. The only furniture would consist of a small iron bed, a washbasin, a table, a chair and a waterpot. Outside would be a filthy toilet. A domestic servant lacked not only the time but also the means of keeping herself clean. At a congress on tuberculosis held in Geneva in 1906, one delegate claimed that the designer of these rooms, the engineer Mansart, had done more than any other man to promote the spread of this disease.[126]

To compound these material sufferings, domestics were continually demoralised by their superiors' assertion of rank. Jeanne Bouvier has a very revealing story of how she lost another domestic job by getting on a bus before the two children whom she was paid to look after, and then sitting down on the only seat available. Madame, who saw the whole incident, was outraged at such an example of *lèse-majesté*: 'I was told I was ill-bred and bad mannered – I could only have served with louts who did not know how to behave'.[127] Of course, critics were able to point out that many servants wanted only to emulate their betters: Frantin Fournier was scandalised by their desire to eat the same food as their masters and their aping the manners and dress of their mistresses.[128] But what he fails to realise is that a servant girl like Mirabeau's Celestine was not necessarily taken in by all Madame's finery and grand, civilised airs, for she could see through the outer trappings to the stains on her petticoats, and had witnessed the sagging breasts which she scrutinised before the mirror, as well as the hypocrisy and corruption that often underlay her conventional piety.[129] Living in such proximity to their mistresses domestic servants saw all the weaknesses of individuals and knew all about family quarrels and family secrets: it was hard for them not to mingle contempt with their envy and resentment. Sometimes a maid would be humiliated by a summons to the master's table where, condescendingly, she would be offered a few titbits from the lavish meal and be expected to go away more grateful than ever to her benign employers. Under normal circumstances, she would be made to feel her inferiority by taking the special meal prepared by the cook for the servants. Only in the simplest homes was there the possibility that the servant would eat the same food as her master and mistress.[130]

Domestics were acutely conscious of their lowly status. Although their wages rose continually throughout the nineteenth century, they were still aware of their lack of prestige in the eyes of the public. Evidence of a desire to improve their standing can be seen in their insistence on being called *gens de maison* rather than *domestiques*, and in their attempts to form trade unions and mutual aid societies. It was men who were mainly responsible for these initiatives, but there are indications that their efforts were appreciated by women domestic servants also.[131] One reform demanded by the Catholic Union *Le Ménage* particularly affected women – namely the suppression of the placement bureaux. These often fictitious employment agencies were responsible for hiring many innocent peasant girls to non-existent jobs in the towns, others were simply fronts for brothels. A law was passed in 1904, establishing free placing, with remuneration for the agents to come entirely from the employers. But, as with a previous decree of 25 March 1852, the law was not rigorously enforced and abuses continued. *Placeurs* were still able to obtain large sums from prospective employees as a result of wide advertising campaigns in the provinces. One legal improvement from which domestics did benefit, however, was the law of 3 July 1890 which obliged a master to give his servant a certificate at the end of the term of service, stating only factual information about the date of entry to employment, the date of departure, and the nature of the work done: no derogatory comments were allowed. [132]

Bourgeois writers were agreed on one other universal feature of domestic servants: their 'immorality'. That servants indulged in extra-marital sex is hardly surprising, given their state of enforced celibacy and the promiscuous conditions of life on the fifth or seventh floors, where all would gather in someone's room after the long day's work to chatter incessantly until midnight, and where the male servants could make contact with equally frustrated maids. To judge by Celestine's experiences, a chambermaid was also regarded as fair game by the master and his sons, though pregnancy brought instant dismissal. [133] Even if, as Cusenier suggests, serving girls acquired considerable familiarity with contraceptive techniques, large numbers of them did become pregnant. [134] Hence it was entirely predictable that domestic servants would provide a disproportionately high number of the prostitutes, unmarried mothers and perpetrators of infanticide in France.

Seventh floor promiscuity or dismissal consequent on pregnancy often led girls into the life of the streets. In general, they swelled the ranks of unofficial, clandestine prostitution. Dr Commenge found that out of 6842 known non-registered prostitutes arrested in Paris between 1878-87, 2681 (31.18%) were domestic servants (his main concern in advertising the fact was, as we have seen, to warn bourgeois householders of the possibility of infection in their midst). [135] Likewise, if a baby were found abandoned, there was a good chance that it would belong to a domestic. One discovered in the Church of St Louis d'Antin in 1914 turned out to be the child of Marie Changala, a chambermaid from the Basque country. [136] Equally, they figured among the victims of back-street abortionists, like poor Ernestine Zaramarcaz, who died with her baby at the hands of a herbalist in 1885. [137]

Their predominance in known cases of infanticide can be documented from a random survey of the *Gazette des Tribuneaux*. A classic case was that of Marie Savage, aged twenty-two, a domestic servant of a milliner on the rue St Honoré. Such information as was available showed her to be from a good family background. Her crime was committed solely on impulse and under stress, and a sympathetic jury acquitted her.[138] Those with a previous history of misconduct, however, were unlikely to escape so lightly. Solange Mignet, twenty-four, employed as a cook in an apartment on the Boulevard St Michel, and also from a good family, already had a child which was being brought up by her parents. When arrested on the Boulevard St Michel, she was trying to conceal the corpse of a new-born child to which she had given birth the night before in a furnished hotel in the nearby rue St Jacques. She was given six years' hard labour.[139] The same sentence, plus a fine of 50 francs, was passed on Clara Quevreux, who had previously had four children.[140] Of course, not all the servants who committed infanticide in Paris actually became pregnant there; some came to avoid the opprobium of their local village, like the nineteen year old Alsatian girl, Marie Baré, pregnant by a Prussian officer: she too got six years' hard labour.[141] By 1914 the number of infanticide cases seems to have been diminishing but in those reported by the *Gazette des Tribuneaux* the pattern remained very much the same. In one case in 1913 where the accused, for once, was not a domestic servant, the newspaper commented that such an event was 'happily . . . rare enough to merit being pointed out'.[142] But in August of the same year there was a particularly grotesque example on the classic model. Victorine-Marie-Louise Relland, a maid in the service of a hairdressing family of the Boulevard Haussmann, gave birth to a child and immediately killed it by stuffing a handkerchief down its throat; she then cut it up into pieces with a knife in the hope of being able to flush the remains down the toilet. She was yet another girl who had good references to her credit: her sentence was three years imprisonment with reprieve.[143] As a last example there was Adèle Duval, who at Créteil in 1914 delivered herself of a child in the toilet, strangled it, banged its head against the wall and then buried it in a dung heap. She got two years.[144]

Ultimately the fate of such girls does not inspire confidence in the theory that domestic service was one of the routes to the 'modernisation' of French women. Rather, their sad histories illustrate only too well how in the so-called *belle époque* the inequalities of class were exacerbated by those of sex.

Chapter IV
THE STRUGGLE FOR SEX EQUALITY: FEMINISM IN FRANCE 1870-1914

IT is one of the little recorded facts of the Third Republic's history that the inequalities of sex became a matter for widespread public discussion in the years before 1914. This development owed much to the emergence of an articulate feminist lobby, a body, unlike its counterparts in Britain and America, largely neglected by serious historians. The task of this chapter will therefore be threefold. First, to explain how a movement for women's rights came into being in the late nineteenth and early twentieth centuries; secondly, to analyse its distinctive character; and thirdly to assess the degree to which it was able to influence the status of women in French society.

The history of feminism in France

Feminism was not a new phenomenon when it began to grow under the Third Republic, having first appeared in France in the course of the Great Revolution. It cannot, however, be said that feminism was a prominent feature in the demands of the men of 1789.[1] At the theoretical level, its only champion of stature was the philospher Condorcet, who even before the Revolution argued that in any enlightened society there could be no place for discrimination against women any more than there could be toleration of black slavery or the civil disabilities imposed upon Protestants.[2] In his *Essay on the Admission of Women to Civic Rights* (1790), Condorcet maintained further that the logic of the Declaration of the Rights of Man was that these sacred principles should be extended to include the rights of women to civil and political equality.[3] A number of pamphlets and *cahiers* written as a response to the summoning of the Estates General echoed the ideas of Condorcet. The authenticity of many of them cannot be guaranteed, but among the genuine were the *Petition des Femmes du Thiers Etat au Roi* (1 January 1789) and the *Cahier des doléances et réclamations des femmes*, written by a Norman woman, Mme B....B. Both reiterated Condorcet's call for the amelioration of women's education. Other petitions written at the end of 1789 and the beginning of 1790 with a view to influencing the Constitutional Assembly in its work of national reconstruction stressed additional areas where reform was necessary if women were also to profit by the Revolution. For instance, the *Motions addresées à l'Assemblée Nationale en faveur du sexe* concentrated on the employment of women, while the *Vues législatives sur les femmes* by Mlle Jodin strongly advocated divorce. [4]

The most celebrated statement of the early feminists was the *Déclaration des droits de la femme et de la citoyenne* drawn up by Olympe de Gouges in September 1791. [5] Modelled on the Declaration of the Rights of Man, it demanded complete political equality of the sexes, arguing that since women had the right to mount the scaffold, they ought equally to have the right to mount the tribune. It further advocated the abolition of marriage, which would be replaced by a new kind of contract between men and women. The boldness of Olympe's demands did not endear her to many male revolutionaries, and in any case her brief political career was terminated when she was executed for her defence of the King and her attacks on Robespierre. Her revolt was essentially personal and rhetorical: she did nothing to make feminism into an organised force.

A more successful feminist propagandist during the Revolution was the Dutch woman Etta Palm d'Aelders, who, fascinated by the events in France, came to Paris and joined the *Cercle Social*, a club founded in 1790 by the abbé Fauchet, one of the few male revolutionaries to champion women's rights. Having acquired a reputation as a speechmaker at the *Cercle*, Mme d'Aelders brought out a pamphlet, the *Appel aux françaises sur la régénération des moeurs et nécessité de l'influence des femmes dans un gouvernement libre*, which was marked by its insistence on the need for women to organise themselves into an effective feminist lobby. Her idea was that women should form societies in each department, which would tackle problems such as wet-nursing, public education for women and social services generally.

A number of women achieved a certain notoriety as female revolutionaries. Pauline Léon and Claire 'Rose' Lacombe of the Society of Revolutionary Republican Women were first and foremost active supporters of the Jacobins and then associates of the *Enragés*. (Leclerc was to marry Pauline Léon, having probably earlier been the lover of Claire Lacombe.) Though the Society did provide an example of women engaged in independent political action, their prime concern was never with the rights of women but rather with the zealous promotion of the aims of the more extreme male revolutionaries. They wanted all nobles removed from the army, thorough repression of all internal enemies, action against food hoarders and speculators (a demand which involved them in street brawls with the market women, the *dames des Halles*) and the strict enforcement of the law of the Maximum. The most advanced claim they could make on women's behalf was the right – or rather the duty – of women to sport the revolutionary cockade. The strongly anti-feminist leaders of the

Convention were more embarrassed than pleased by the revolutionary ardour of the Republican women, and suppressed their Society along with other women's political clubs. [6] Quite apart from the fact that the activities of the women revolutionaries tended to highlight shortcomings in government policy, the Jacobins – and indeed the *sans-culottes* themselves – had highly patriarchal views on women's proper role. Fabre d'Eglantine was applauded for his speech to the Convention of 8 brumaire, Year II, when he observed that in the women's clubs there were no mothers or daughters who cared about the younger children in the family, only liberated adventuresses. [7] The Revolution, said one *sans-culotte*, had been made by men and for men. [8]

The French Revolution, therefore, did very little to promote women's rights. On the contrary it left a legacy of antipathy towards feminism and reinforced the ideology of the woman by the hearth. A second and more significant wave of feminism arose with the rise of utopian socialist movements in the period before the outbreak of the 1948 Revolution. In the Saint-Simonian vision of a new world order based on a religion of love, the figure of woman was deemed to have an essential role in the search for peace and harmony. The human race was to be regenerated on the basis of complete sex equality which would itself be derived from the union of man and woman in the 'social couple' as the fundamental unit in society; the highest form of this union was to be the *'couple-prêtre'*, the union of priest and priestess who disdained earthly and sensual pleasures. The original Saint-Simonian doctrines, however, were developed in new and bizarre directions by the master's disciple Enfantin. Rejecting the exclusive monogamy of the Christian tradition, he became the prophet of 'the rehabilitation of the flesh'. He also believed in the existence of a female Messiah who would be his associate in this work of redemption, and led an expedition to the Middle East to search for her. [9] Other Saint-Simonians, such as Pierre Leroux, refused to follow Enfantin's lead and the movement split. [10] Nevertheless, all continued to believe that in their new society the status of women would be dramatically improved, especially within marriage. Claire Demar, author of an *Appeal to the People on the Emancipation of Women*, proclaimed that real freedom and greatness could only be achieved when the female half of the human race was set free from the exploitation which weighed on their sex. [11]

The utopian socialist theories of Charles Fourier (1772-1837) also contributed to the development of advanced libertarian feminist ideas. [12] In his *Theory of the Four Movements* (1841) he insisted that social progress was to be measured in terms of the degree of liberty accorded to women in a given society. In his ideal community, the *phalanstère*, the family was to be abolished and women's right to free love established. Victor Considérant, Fourier's principal disciple, later eliminated some of these ideas on sex but he remained a firm advocate of women's rights (as a deputy in the National Assembly of the Second Republic he was to argue the case for the enfranchisement of women).[13]

Stimulated by these utopian socialist ideals, a new generation of feminists made its appearance in France in the early years of the July Monarchy. The Saint-Simonians brought out a feminist newspaper which, after going through a number of changes of title, was finally called *La Tribune des Femmes*. Founded by Désirée Veret and Reine Guindorf, both of whom were seamstresses, its staff consisted almost entirely of working-class women. After the two co-founders left to embrace Fourierism, it was subsequently edited by Suzanne Voilquin, an embroiderer who had become a midwife, and then by Jeanne Victoire, who may have been Jeanne Deroin.[14] For the first time in the feminist press we can see a manifestation of class consciousness, a linking of the struggle for women's rights with that of the cause of the proletariat. This theme was further developed by Flora Tristan (1803-44), the grandmother of the post-impressionist artist Gauguin, and perhaps the most famous of the early utopian feminists. Born in Paris the daughter of a Peruvian noble and a young French *émigrée*, at the age of fifteen she began to work in the studio of the painter lithographer André Chazal, whom she married and by whom she had three children. Having left her husband on account of his brutality, she eventually came to England where she was appalled by the wretchedness of the working classes. Converted to Saint-Simonianism, she came to see herself as their female Messiah and in her book *L'Union Ouvrière* explicitly formulated the theory that the emancipation of women was bound up with the general question of the emancipation of the working class.[15]

Less well remembered by historians but more effective among contemporaries were three feminists: Eugénie Niboyet, Jeanne Deroin and Pauline Roland. They all came under the spell of Saint-Simonianism for at least a time and were to espouse the cause of revolution in 1848.[16] Eugénie Niboyet was born in 1800 into a Protestant family which believed in the Englightenment and the Napoleonic legend. In the early years of the July Monarchy she became actively involved in charitable and literary activities, espousing the cause of prison reform and translating Dickens into French. After her conversion to Saint-Simonianism, she founded a newspaper, *Le Conseiller des Femmes*, in which she preached a humanitarian socialism. She brought out a number of other newspapers, including the pacifist *La Paix des Deux Mondes*, before founding in 1848 *La Voix des Femmes*, which was to be the principal feminist organ of the 1848 Revolution. Herself a moderate, Eugénie Niboyet was disappointed at the establishment of a Republic and confined her feminism to promoting better education and better employment opportunities for women.[17]

One of her principal collaborators in 1848 was Jeanne Deroin (1805-94), an uneducated seamstress who had learnt to read by attending evening classes. She, too, had founded a number of newspapers after coming under the influence of Saint-Simonian and other utopian socialist ideas. Her main concern was with the condition of working-class women and, true to the spirit of 1848, she saw the solution to their problems in the organisation of the labour force in associations. Her hope was that a number of individual working-class associations would eventually form a general Union of Associations.[18] The same theme was adopted by a number of other ex-Saint-Simonian women, notably by Pauline Roland (1805-52), the daughter of a postmaster from Falaise who was introduced to Saint-Simonian ideas by her tutor. Having become a schoolteacher, she decided at the age of twenty-eight that the time had come for her to put Enfantin's doctrine of the rehabilitation of the flesh into practice, and deliberately chose to become un unmarried mother. After living and working in the community of Pierre Leroux at Boussac, she returned to Paris in December 1848 and with Jeanne Deroin founded the *Association des Instituteurs et Institutrices Féministes Socialistes*.[19] Other important advocates of female associations were Désirée Gay, a seamstress who had experience of the English Owenite communities, and Suzanne Voilquin.[20] The presence of these working-class women alongside the bourgeois feminists makes 1848 a significant date in the history of French feminism.

To the authorities, especially after the June Days, the feminists of 1848 appeared as dangerous radicals. Not only as old Saint-Simonians and Fourierists were they tainted by their connection with libertarian sexual theories, but, perhaps more importantly, in their preoccupation with the plight of working-class women, they leaned towards vaguely socialistic solutions. Jeanne Deroin and Pauline Roland were both arrested and sentenced to six months' imprisonment in 1849. Satirists like Daumier depicted the feminists of 1848 as man-haters and enemies of the family because they campaigned for the reintroduction of divorce[21] – although in fact most of them believed in marriage founded on romantic love, with divorce available only as a last resort to extricate unfortunate women from an intolerable position.[22] Despite their essential moderation, they acquired an unjustified reputation for being social and sexual misfits.

With the establishment of the Second Empire, this second phase of feminism in France was definitively closed. Feminism ceased to exist as a movement and appeared only in the guise of individual literary polemics. Stung by the attitude shown to women in the writings of men such as Michelet, Emile de Girardin and above all Proudhon, author of the infamous statement that women could only opt to be either housewives or whores, a number of women from very different backgrounds took up their pens to launch a counter-offensive. Jenny d'Héricourt wrote *La femme affranchie* in 1860. Juliette Lamber (the future Madame Adam, wife of the prominent Republican politician Robert Adam and celebrated society hostess) brought out her *Idées antiproudhoniennes sur l'amour, les femmes et le mariage* in 1861, while Andrée Léo (the pseudonym of novelist Léonie Bréa, widow of the forty-eighter journalist and Saint-Simonian Grégoire Champseix) produced *Les Femmes et les moeurs*.[23] A particularly virulent, not to say slightly deranged, polemicist was Olympe Audouard, who in 1866 decided to declare war on men (apparently because she was refused permission to turn her literary journal *Le Papillon* into a political organ).[24] Likewise Louise Michel, soon to be famed as the 'Red Virgin' of the Commune, entered the feminist lists to reply to 'Junius', an anti-feminist journalist on the staff of the *Figaro*.[25] Another future *communarde*, Paule Mink, the daughter of an émigré Polish army officer, was also a feminist activist of this period.[26]

What gave coherence and a measure of solidarity to the nascent feminist movement at this time, however, was not just a preoccupation with women's rights but, more importantly, a close connection with the cause of republicanism.[27] Out of this alliance, a new wave of feminism emerged in France, destined this time to have a less ephemeral existence than its predecessors. The credit for launching this modern movement goes largely to two people, Maria Deraismes and Léon Richer.[28] Maria Deraismes, perhaps the most distinguished of the early feminists of the Second Empire, discovered her feminist vocation in 1866 when stung into replying to a vicious article by Barbey d'Aurevilly on *Bluestockings*. Born into a freethinking and Republican family of the *grande bourgeoisie*, she was an exceptionally well-educated and cultured woman. She attacked Barbey in a series of lectures at the Grand Orient, the Freemasons hall, and, having joined forces with several other literary feminists, she established the *Société de la Revendication du Droit des Femmes*, which can be seen as the first important feminist society of the modern period. Léon Richer was a former notary's clerk turned journalist, and a militant Republican and Freemason. It was at his suggestion that Maria Deraismes gave her lecture series at the Grand Orient in 1866 and in 1869 he brought out *Le Droit des Femmes*, the longest lived of French feminist newspapers. Out of the collaboration of Richer and Deraismes, the modern feminist movement was born.

First of all, through their joint efforts, was founded an *Association pour le Droit des Femmes* in 1871. Renamed the *Société pour l'Amélioration du Sort des Femmes* in 1874, the organisation encountered problems

under the extremely conservative 'Moral Order' régime of Marshal
MacMahon and was dissolved in 1875. Nevertheless, the Richer-
Deraismes partnership continued to put down the foundations on
which the future of the French feminist movement would be built. In
1878, to coincide with the international exhibition in Paris, they staged
the first international congress on women's rights, which brought
together women from eleven countries and sixteen feminist organisations.[29] Their Society for the Amelioration of Women's Lot was
re-established and in 1882 Richer founded his own *Ligue Française pour
le Droit des Femmes*, an organisation which exists to this day.[30]
Organised feminism in France was now a reality.

This is not to say that all those women who entered the feminist
movement were content to follow the lead of Deraismes and Richer.
One of their earliest associates, Hubertine Auclert,[31] the daughter of a
landowner and a rebel against her pious convent education, founded a
society called *Le Droit des Femmes* in 1876 but broke with Deraismes and
Richer when they would not allow the issue of the female suffrage to be
put on the agenda of the international congress of 1878. In 1881 she
started her own newspaper, *La Citoyenne*, to campaign for votes for
women, for, as she put it, political rights were 'the master key' which
would open the door to all other rights. In 1883 she changed the title of
her group to *Le Suffrage des Femmes*. Altogether, she adopted an
approach to feminism which was closer to that of an English suffragette
than to the tepid gradualism of Deraismes and Richer. Through her
newspaper, she collected signatures for petitions to parliament (one
presented in 1881 by the socialist deputy Clovis Hughes contained 1000
names). Despite female ineligibility, she also entered her name as a
candidate in municipal elections. Her most spectacular tactic was to
correlate the payment of taxes with the right to vote, arguing that 'in a
country where women don't have any rights, neither can women have
any obligations'.[32] In the eyes of the police, she was written off as
'suffering from madness or hysterics which made her think of men as
equals'.[33]

The more moderate Deraismes-Richer wing, however, remained the
more influential and the more typical of the movement as a whole. In
1889 they organised a second international congress of women's
rights,[34] while in the 1890s their ranks were reinforced by new groups
such as the *Union Universelle des Femmes* and the *Avant-Courrière*. The
former was founded by Marya Chéliga-Loevy,[35] a Pole by birth, and
had as president Mme Clémence Royer, renowned for her translation
of Darwin. The *Avant-Courrière* was the creation of Mme Jeanne
Schmall,[36] an Englishwoman, who intended that the Society should be
disbanded once its two objectives – the right of women to be civil
witnesses, and the right of married women to dispose freely of their

own salaries – had been achieved. (These goals were in fact attained in 1897 and 1908 respectively.) The *Groupe Français d'Etudes Féministes*, founded by Jeanne Oddo-Deflou,[37] likewise concentrated on legal reform. But the more advanced spirits were by no means inactive. Mme Vincent,[38] the daughter of a Republican and utopian socialist father, was, like Hubertine Auclert, an ardent apostle of women's suffrage, and the founder of a society, *Egalité*, whose aim was to promote the recovery of rights allegedly lost by women since the Middle Ages. Mme Maria Martin,[39] another Englishwoman, was for a time Hubertine Auclert's closest collaborator on the *Citoyenne*, but after a quarrel she broke away to found her own newspaper, *Le Journal des Femmes* which advocated much the same programme as the *Citoyenne*.

Some degree of unity was injected into this burgeoning movement by Mme Eugénie Potonié-Pierre,[40] a Saint-Simonian and pacifist whose group the *Solidarité des Femmes* had hopes of bringing together feminism and the working-class movement. Having canvassed the idea of a French Federation of Feminist Societies, she organised a congress in 1892 out of which emerged a Central Committee whose principal task was to draw up a list of grievances which would be presented to parliament. But what put feminism on the map as never before was the launching in 1897 of the newspaper *La Fronde*, not merely the first ever feminist daily but one printed and administered as well as written and edited by women. The paper was the creation of Marguerite Durand,[41] an ex-actress at the Comédie Française and former journalist on the *Figaro* who had been converted to feminism at a congress organised by Eugénie Potonié-Pierre in 1896.[42] Thanks to the contributions of the talented team assembled under Durand's direction, *La Fronde* won for feminism a new prestige and authority and came to be regarded as the feminine equivalent of *Le Temps*.[43]

The final stages in the development of organised feminism in France before the First World War can be quickly traced. In addition to the continual appearance of new groups like the *Fédération Féministe Universitaire*[44] and the *Union Fraternelle des Femmes*,[45] two major federations were founded to co-ordinate the activities of most societies which belonged to the mainstream of French feminism. The first was the CNFF, the National Council of French Women, established in 1900 and presided by Mme Sarah Monod, daughter of the famous Protestant pastor. By 1914 the National Council had about 100,000 members belonging to 123 different societies.[46] The other federation was the UFSP, the French Union for Women's Suffrage (and the French section of the International Woman Suffrage Alliance) which was founded in 1909 to concentrate on winning the vote. By 1914 it had sixty-five groups and 12,000 members.[47] These two organisations soon established themselves as the principal representatives of feminism in

France, receiving official approval from politicians and government ministers who frequently attended their congresses.[48]

The character of French feminism

The history of feminism in France has been sketched at some length in order to make clear the distinction to be drawn between the organised movement of the Third Republic and the earlier waves associated with the Revolutions of 1789 and 1848. Indeed, the character of the later movement may perhaps best be understood as a conscious reaction to what had gone before. As has already been suggested, modern French feminism owed its existence, in the first instance, to its close association with the rising fortunes of republicanism. Now, just as the Third Republic's new breed of moderate politicians wished to obliterate the connotations of republicanism with the violence and disorder of the Commune, the June Days and the Terror, so too the feminists were equally anxious to dispel memories of previous links between feminism and political and sexual radicalism. Intent on living down the past, republicans and feminists alike sought above all to establish their respectability. Given the links between the two movements in the early days, it is hardly surprising that from the outset mainstream feminism in France opted for a course of prudence and moderation which might better be described as timidity.

Maria Deraismes and Léon Richer were not simply (or even primarily) feminists: first and foremost they were militant Republicans, anti-clericals and Freemasons (Deraismes became the first woman Freemason in France). Richer initially hoped to model his LFDF on the lines of Jean Macé's Education League, which had conducted a highly successful campaign for free, secular and obligatory education.[49] Most significantly, 50% of the membership of the LFDF was accounted for by men (including twenty-one professional politicians) and it was the men who took charge of the League's day-to-day operations. Richer and Deraismes were both convinced that women's rights could only be achieved through cooperation with male legislators. But because, in their view, the Republic was still threatened by right-wing clerical enemies, the male feminists had to join hands with anti-feminist Republican colleagues for the safety of the régime. At the same time, they considered that to grant women the vote prematurely in France could endanger the democratic system. As Richer wrote in 1888:

> I believe that at the present time it would be dangerous – in France – to give women the political ballot. They are in great majority reactionaries and clericals. If they voted today, the Republic would not last six months.[50]

Thus the link between feminism, anti-clericalism and Freemasonry was not necessarily one which worked to the benefit of feminism. On the contrary, the Pecq Lodge, which had initiated Maria Deraismes in 1882 after she had been rejected by the Grand Symbolic Scottish Lodge in 1881, regretted its decision and refused to admit any additional woman members. This remained the situation until Deraismes decided that, rather than force a lodge to secede from the federation over the question of woman members, it would be better to constitute a new mixed lodge. Her Grand Symbolic Scottish Mixed Lodge was duly admitted in 1893. Many of the most prominent figures in the feminist high command, particularly those who were members of the LFDF, lost no time in becoming Freemasons.[51] In Paris the mixed Stuart Mill Lodge was founded specially to promote the emancipation of women.[52] In general, however, Freemasonry continued to have reservations about women members and it was the militantly anti-clerical senators of the Radical Socialist Party who were to be the most intransigent opponents of women's suffrage in the inter-war period.

The post-Deraismes-Richer generation, less exercised perhaps by the question of the régime's survival, were none the less concerned to demonstrate their fidelity to the Republic and their capacity to act as good and loyal *citoyennes*. Some indeed had very close links with the male Republican establishment. Mme Brunschvicg, secretary, then president of the UFSF, was the wife of the philosopher Léon Brunschvicg and one of the first woman members of the Radical Party. Mme Siegfried, the second president of the CNFF, was the wife of the industrialist and deputy Jules Siegfried. Mme Avril de Sainte-Croix, the next president of the National Council, was the first woman to be appointed to an extra-parliamentary commission (that on morals in 1901). In general, the French feminists considered that the best way to advance their cause was to make friends with leading politicians – hence their immense satisfaction at the presence of deputies, senators and academicians at their congresses. By obtaining official recognition from the government for the International Congress on the Condition and Rights of Women in 1900, and by including prominent political figures on the honorary committee of the congress of 1908, and by having the congress of 1913 opened by Klotz, the Minister of the Interior, they felt that they were making important progress. They could begin to imagine that the 'Republican synthesis' – to borrow the phrase of Stanley Hoffmann – was being extended to include women as well as men who were loyal to the régime.

To emphasise their civic virtue, the feminists of the mainstream took pains to ensure that their cause could not be identified with the standard of reaction. To be sure, the Church, despite the dire suspicions of the anti-clericals, had little sympathy with the demands of the feminists, remaining faithful, as we have seen, to the misogynous tradition of St Paul and the Early Fathers. Church leaders, however, did not ignore the feminist challenge but organised instead their own so-called Catholic feminist movement under the direction of Mlle Maugeret.[53] Her monthly newspaper, *Le Féminisme Chrétien*, appeared in 1896, and in 1900 she founded the *Fédération Jeanne d'Arc*, which affiliated all existing Catholic societies. In 1904 the new organisation held the first Joan of Arc Congress at the Catholic Institute in Paris, presided by Mgr Péchenard, with many other members of the hierarchy in attendance. Speakers included priests such as Father de Sertillanges, who put the case for improving girls' education, a favourite theme of the Christian feminists.[54]

Some organised groups of Catholic women did take an interest in politics – but not to advocate women's emancipation. Rather, like the League of French Women and the Patriotic Association for Women's Duties, they saw their main function as being to combat Freemasonry and to lend their support to right-wing and nationalist political organisations. Other female political societies such as the Union of Christian Women of the Loire, the League of Women from Rheims, and the League of Women from Lorraine, concentrated their efforts on the diffusion of right-wing propaganda among male electors.[55] The existence of these groups was an embarrassment to the French feminist leaders, who contended that the emancipation of women would not rock the Republican boat. Indeed, one of their favourite themes was the special contribution which women would bring to public life once they were enfranchised.[56]

If the mainstream feminists took care to distinguish themselves from the organisations of right-wing women and Christian feminism, they likewise refused to associate themselves with the politics of the Left. Solidarity with the bourgeois Republic kept feminism isolated from the socialist movement, despite socialism's theoretical commitment to the cause of women's emancipation.[57] Following the example of the moderate Republican politicians themselves, the leaders of French feminism repudiated the radical and libertarian tendencies of earlier waves of feminism. The recent episode of the Paris Commune of 1871 served only to reinforce their conservatism. Although, as in previous French revolutions, feminism itself was very much a minority theme in the Commune, many women from the most disadvantaged sections of the female proletariat – notably sweated workers in the clothing industry and a contingent of washerwomen – marched behind the banner of the Commune, demanding an end to male-dominated and clerical standards of morality as well as the right to employment and a living wage. The army of *pétroleuses* who are supposed to have set fire to Paris as the Commune drowned in its own blood belong to the realm of myth. But women such as Louise Michel, Paule Mink, Nathalie Lemel and Elizabeth Dimitrieff, a friend of Marx who organised the Union of Women, the female section of the First International, were among the most dedicated supporters of the Commune, participating in debates in the political clubs, tending the sick and wounded, and, in the last resort, fighting with their male comrades on the barricades.[58] Here was a tradition which the mainstream feminists, in their bid for respectability and acceptance, had little desire to commemorate.

A handful of women did subsequently attempt to bring socialism and feminism together. Léonie Rouzade, an embroiderer and daughter of a watchmaker, founded the *Union des Femmes* in 1880 in the hope of uniting the cause of women's rights with that of the proletariat, as in the dreams of Flora Tristan. It was her agitation within the ranks of the Broussist socialist group which led to their adoption of women's emancipation as part of their programme.[59] After Rouzade and the reformist socialists parted company, a second feminist socialist group was formed in 1899 by Elizabeth Renaud, a private schoolteacher, and Louise Saumoneau, a seamstress from Poitiers, with the help of two other women workers from the clothing industry, Estelle Mordelet and Florestine Malseigne. At the Congress of 1900 on the Condition and Rights of Women the socialist women clashed openly with the bourgeois feminists, who denied the inevitability of class conflict and preached class reconciliation.[60] Thereafter, Louise Saumoneau became so virulent in her denunciation of bourgeois feminism that she virtually denied the existence of a sex problem distinct from that of the class struggle. When a new group of women socialists was formed in 1913 (the *Groupe des Femmes Socialistes de la Seine*) the issue of sexual oppression did not feature in its programme, and the group served as the official feminine section of the French Socialist Party.[61]

Thus feminism and socialism ultimately went their separate ways, although individual feminists might retain links with various kinds of socialism. In any case, for the sorts of reason already suggested in Chapter I, male socialists had very little enthusiasm for women's rights or the organisation of women. The *Groupe Féministe Socialiste* and the *Groupe des Femmes Socialistes de la Seine* were tiny, sectarian bodies. Women made up at most 3% of socialist party membership, and even then two-thirds of these women were the wives of male party members.[62] Madeleine Pelletier, a militant on the advanced Hervéiste wing, noted sourly that the equality of the sexes proclaimed by the socialists remained highly theoretical:

> In practice, only the woman who comes along with her husband, her father or her brother is welcomed without objections, but against the admission of a woman coming on her own impediments are always found.[63]

Refusing to engage in radical politics and accepting the values of the Third Republic except in so far as these discriminated against the rights of women, especially of married women, the French feminists concentrated on developing a brand of 'social feminism' relevant to their conception of the needs of French society.[64] Social feminism was not peculiar to France but, more than in the United States or in Britain, it was the unifying force within the movement. The distinctive orientation and emphasis of French feminism derive not just from its association with republicanism but also from its connections with philanthropy – very often with Protestant philanthropy. The first president of the CNFF, Sarah Monod, was the daughter of Pastor Monod and had begun a long career in charitable works in 1870, when she started the first feminine ambulance section in France. Her successor, Mme Siegfried, was likewise the daughter of a Protestant clergyman and also had a brother in the ministry. Both she and her husband were actively involved in a wide range of charities. Another Protestant, Mme de Witt-Schlumberger, the grand-daughter of Guizot, was president of the UFSF after a longstanding involvement in the work of rehabilitating prostitutes. Though an active suffragist, Mme de Witt-Schlumberger never regarded the vote as an object in itself. Rather, it was only a means of promoting a general improvement in women's social and moral condition which could also be fostered by charitable methods. On the International Council of Women she was a vehement advocate of the abolition of regulated prostitution, and she also presided the International Commission for a Single Standard of Morality and against the White Slave Trade. After prostitution, the vice which she attacked most resolutely was alcoholism (she suggested that one should never drink oneself, nor even offer alcohol to one's guests). She was honorary president of the Union of French Women against Alcohol and also a member of the National League against Alcoholism. Later, during the First World War, she was to organise a number of charities on behalf of soldiers and the families of refugees from the invaded regions. Herself the mother of six children, she worked zealously on behalf of the natality lobby, exhorting French women to replace the losses in the population inflicted by the war.

Not all of the philanthropic feminists came from a Protestant background.[65] Mme Isabelle Bogelot, who, as an orphan had been raised in the household of Maria Deraismes and later became an honorary president of the CNFF, was an ardent opponent of regulated prostitution and president of the *Oeuvre des Libérées de Saint-Lazare*, a charity founded by the Catholic Pauline de Grandpré to help prostitutes find employment when they were freed from the notorious women's prison.[66] Mme Brunschvicg (secretary, then president of the UFSF) was the daughter of a rich Jewish industrialist. Her involvement in the feminist movement was primarily political but she also found time to direct several charities. It was as a delegate of one of the charitable organisations which she herself founded that she joined the CNFF, where she developed strong links between its activities and those of the UFSF. In the case of another non-Protestant, Mme Avril de Sainte-Croix (secretary-general then president of the CNFF) once again it was the fight against the state regulation of prostitution and the attack on the double standard of morality which led her into the cause of feminism.

If feminism in France never came to place the same emphasis on winning the vote as, say, the English suffragettes did, the explanation lies mainly in the domination of the movement by these women from the world of philanthropy. For them, feminism was only a logical ultimate step, a better means of tackling a problem like prostitution. The franchise assumed importance in their eyes only in that, once women were allowed to vote and to elect their own representatives, they could legislate all the great social scourges out of existence.[67] Under their leadership, mainstream feminism was given both moderate and diverse goals. The point cannot be over-emphasised that the CNFF was a feminine as well as a feminist society: the suffrage section was merely one among many.[68] French feminists spread their efforts over many areas – legal reform, employment, education, protective legislation for working women, public health and, above all, moral reform. Certainly, by 1902 there was unanimous agreement on the necessity of obtaining the vote, as the indispensable means of promoting their social and moral action.[69] But at no time did they develop the massive concentration on this one issue in the manner of the British or American movements. Indeed, if mainstream feminism can be said to have had any one overriding goal, it was to obtain a single standard of morality by abolishing the regulated system of prostitution and by making men conform to the standards of sexual respectability demanded of girls and women.[70] Feminism in France was very largely a 'purity crusade'.[71]

The limitations of French feminism

From the standpoint of the contemporary woman movement, the most obvious failure of the early twentieth century French feminists was their inability to develop a new consciousness of themselves as women. Confining their aspirations to institutional reform and shackled to conventional ideas about femininity and the family, they often failed to identify, let alone to solve, the sexual and social problems to which contemporary feminists now address themselves.[72]

It would, of course, be anachronistic to judge the early feminist movement by the standards of the late twentieth century: all the more so in that the values of the women's liberationists are far from being

universally accepted in our own time. Nevertheless, around the turn of
the century, certain French feminists did attempt a radical re-thinking
of the place of women in society. If the mainstream feminists did not
call for a profound re-examination of women's role, it was not because
they were unfamiliar with the arguments of the advanced integral
feminists but rather because they disagreed profoundly with their
analysis. It was the desire for change, rather than ignorance of the
possibilities of change, that was lacking.

The isolation of the radical wing can be seen most completely in the
case of Madeleine Pelletier, the most outstanding of the integral
feminists despite her eccentric practice of always dressing like a man.[73]
Anne 'Madeleine' Pelletier was born on 18 May 1874, the daughter of a
small shopkeeper in Paris. After a desperately unhappy childhood and a
great deal of struggle, she succeeded in becoming a doctor, specialising
in the treatment of mental illness. Having joined the Freemasons, she
continually denounced their refractory attitude towards women.[74] A
revolutionary socialist and pacifist she eventually became a militant in
the violently anti-militarist faction of Gustave Hervé. After the Russian
Revolution, she was for a time to sympathise with communism, until a
trip to the Soviet Union shattered her illusions, after which she reverted
to the milieux frequented by anarchists and libertarians.[75] Having taken
over as director of the group *La Solidarité des Femmes*, founded by
Eugénie Potonié-Pierre, she then started her own radical feminist
newspaper *La Suffragiste*. For her, as for Hubertine Auclert, full
political equality with men was the most important right which women
should demand. As long as women were not on the electoral roll, she
argued, they would obtain nothing in a régime of universal suffrage,
since only voters mattered to the politicians. The argument that this
would pave the way to clericalism and reaction she dismissed as absurd,
ridiculing the paradox by which the advocates of free thought were
prepared to deprive half of humanity of its rights on the pretext that its
thought differed from theirs.[76] An admirer of the English suffragettes,[77] she herself stood as an electoral candidate on a number of
occasions. Backed by the socialists, she polled 340 votes in the
hopelessly conservative 8e *arrondissement* in Paris in the legislative
elections of 1910. (In the course of the campaign she also resorted to the
suffragette tactic of smashing windows.)[78]

In so far as she looked for a social and moral revolution to be carried
out at the ballot box, Pelletier differed from the mainstream feminists
more as regards tactics than as regards fundamental goals.[79] Where they
irrevocably parted company was over their radically different
conceptions of women's proper role in society. Unlike the bourgeois
feminists who claimed to be reinforcing the family, Pelletier wanted to
see its destruction: only this, she maintained, would set women free to

choose their own destiny (and in the process emancipate men and children also). [80] The only valid reason for marriage was to provide for the socialisation of children: alternative arrangements could be made for this task. Sexual activity was only 'a physiological function, neither more noble nor more shameful than any other'. Women should be left to choose their partners with the same freedom as men already selected their mistresses. The social cell of the future should be not the family but the individual, for the individual was not made for society but society for the happiness of the individual. Sex was for pleasure and could be profitably enjoyed from the age of about sixteen. Girls should be taught how to avoid pregnancies and the concept of illegitimacy should be abolished to prevent any stigma being attached to children born out of wedlock or to their mothers. There was no inherent reason why mothers should have to feed their own children, who were better brought up collectively in any case. [81] Women who desired an abortion should be able to have one. Only women should decide whether or not to have children and there was no necessary law to say that they should, since they might be better able to serve society without them. [82]

Pelletier had nothing but scorn for those feminists who made a virtue of their femininity while demanding sex equality. In her view, those who flaunted their bare arms and nude breasts, their powdered faces and their elaborate hairstyles were in no position to claim equal treatment, hence her own habit of wearing masculine clothes. Feminism, she maintained, had to renounce any kind of special favours or privileges for women; if this meant equality of duties such as the obligation to perform military service, then this should be accepted as just. [83] If women wanted to be emancipated they had to renounce their servile habits and rid themselves of their traditionally 'feminine' attributes. [84]

At least some of the questions posed by Pelletier were taken up by other integral feminists. Nelly Roussel, the wife of the sculptor Henri Godet, concerned herself principally with the issue of contraception. She argued that the most important right for women was the freedom to control their own bodies and constantly spelled out the horrors of excessively large families and over-population. [85] The widow Gabrielle Petit, like Pelletier an extreme anti-militarist and advanced socialist, also actively supported the birth control movement both in her newspaper *La Femme Affranchie* and in lectures she gave to anarchist and libertarian circles. [86] On the political front, a number of women apart from Pelletier followed the example of Hubertine Auclert in running for election, none more successfully than Elizabeth Renaud who got 2869 votes (more than 25%) in the Isère thanks to strong local feminist support. [87] Various women's groups reacted against the excessive caution of the CNFF and the UFSF (who were prepared to settle initially for the right to vote in municipal elections) and demanded the immediate implementation of full universal suffrage. The old warrior Hubertine Auclert launched a new society called the *Ligue Nationale pour le Suffrage des Femmes* which advocated taking to the streets to agitate on behalf of their cause. [88] Marguerite Durand, now associated with an organisation called the *Ligue Nationale pour le Vote des Femmes*, was one of the principal organisers of a rally held on 5 July 1914 to honour the memory of Condorcet and to demonstrate in favour of women's suffrage. In her speech at the demonstration she chided feminists for having been too mild in their demands. [89] Even some of the mainstream feminists came to recognise that perhaps their prudence had been excessive. Maria Vérone, secretary-general then president of the LFDF and a prominent barrister, was a member of the committee which planned the Condorcet rally, while Pauline Rebour of the UFSF was one of the speakers. [90]

The old guard of the official feminist movement, however, refused to bow before the pressure of the radicals. Jane Misme, editor of the newspaper *La Française*, which can be regarded as the main organ of the majority movement, took issue with the radicals' claims to full suffrage rights and/or sexual liberation, arguing that such demands could only put in jeopardy the more modest but more plausible ambition of first securing the municipal franchise. It was all very well for the English to have suffragettes, she asserted, but France required only *suffragistes*. [91] Street demonstrations were in her view harmful to the movement's prestige. French women, she insisted, were much more discreet and reserved than the women of England or America and should never appear on the streets for the sole purpose of being seen. In any case, since France was a nation which respected intelligence, the feminist cause could be carried by words and arguments rather than by protests and demonstrations. The feminist congress was the best place to impress the validity of their arguments on the public. [92]

Ultimately, the extreme conservatism of the French feminists has to be related to the profoundly conservative nature of French society. Despite the frequent political scandals and crises, French society remained remarkably stable in the nineteenth century, with 17.5 million people, 46% of the total population, still making their living from agriculture in 1891. [93] The Left may have continued to glorify the revolutionary tradition but the very existence of this tradition also acted as a powerful brake on change, since it could be invoked by the Radical politicians who came to dominate the governments of the Third Republic to justify their failure to promote any far-reaching political or social reforms. Within this larger context, it is hardly surprising that the mainstream feminists rejected both the ideas and methods of Madeleine Pelletier, and concentrated their efforts on establishing their social respectability and their sexual orthodoxy. Far from wishing to be rebels against society, the leading French feminists stressed their regard for convention and therefore their capacity to be good citizens of the bourgeois Republic. Colourful and unorthodox figures such as Marguerite Durand and Maria Vérone[94] were conspicuously few in the movement. In particular, on the issue of marriage and the family (seen as the touchstone of their respectability), mainstream feminists were loud in their defence of both institutions to protect themselves against the charge that feminism recruited only single women to its ranks.[95] Certainly the majority of the leaders were either married or widowed, and most had children. According to Jane Misme, at the society of the *Française*, out of 121 members, only twenty-seven were single and only one of these by deliberate choice.[96]

The fact that the movement did contain a genuine lunatic fringe served only to consolidate the natural tendency towards conservatism, since the cranks provided fair game for the anti-feminist lobby. Perhaps the most vitriolic of the extremists was Mme Remember, the pseudonym of Mme Beverley-Dupont, who became a professional man-hater after an unhappy marriage.[97] Like Christabel Pankhurst, she propagated the idea that the overwhelming majority of men were syphilitic.[98] She also proposed that women should at all times carry guns for protection against the omnipresent threat of assault by the predatory male.[99] Still more extreme – indeed rejected in the end even by Remember – was Mlle Arria-Ly, who advocated universal virginity for all women in order to exterminate the odious species of men.[100] Madeleine Pelletier's feminism may have been of a different stamp, but the fact that she allowed women such as Remember to contribute rabid anti-male pieces to the *Suffragiste* was in itself enough to place her beyond the bounds of respectable feminism, quite apart from her revolutionary views on the family.[101] Pelletier herself admitted in her diary that she attracted much unwanted attention on account of her masculine attire.

However sensible the gradualism of the mainstream feminists might have seemed at the time, its decisive shortcoming was that it produced no far-reaching transformation of women's status in French society. It could claim to be instrumental in the realisation of a number of legal reforms. The *Avant-Courrière*'s campaign to obtain the right for women to be civil witnesses and the right of married women to dispose freely of their own salaries prompted legislation on these issues in 1897 and 1908 respectively. Feminist pressure, too, contributed to the enactment of the law of 27 March 1907, by which women were allowed to vote in elections to the *Conseil de Prud'hommes* (a kind of arbitration tribunal). Equally, the law of 1912 which introduced paternity suits had long been sought by the principal feminist organisations, even if it did not satisfy all their aspirations. Despite all their efforts, however, the feminists could not induce the male legislature to enact their most fundamental legal demand: full civic equality for married women under the law. Unlike Josephine Butler's campaign against the Contagious Diseases Acts in England, the French attack on the double standard of morality was not crowned with success. Apart from sensational newspaper articles alleging high-handed and arbitrary brutality on the part of the Vice Squad, the most that the abolitionists (spear headed by feminists such as Avril de Sainte-Croix, and men sympathetic to feminism like the liberal economist Yves Guyot) were able to achieve was the setting-up of an Extra-Parliamentary Commission on Morals.[102]

Success proved equally elusive in the matter of the municipal suffrage for women. A bill to bring about this reform was introduced by the deputy Dussaussoy in 1906 and was the subject of an impressive and favourable report by Ferdinand Buisson in 1909, yet the Chamber of Deputies had not got round to enacting a law by 1914 when the war provided an opportunity to postpone all further discussion of the project.[103]

On the credit side, the feminists could claim to have made some impression on public opinion. Politicians of all parties made sympathetic noises about the justice and inevitability of women's participation in the political process. The President of the Republic himself, receiving a deputation from the CNFF, told them that it was high time that women who shared the duties of men, should also share the same rights.[104] Even some clerics showed a willingness to move with the times; for example, the abbé Naudet wrote a book advocating the progressive emancipation of women.[105] Not all Catholic feminists remained blinkered reactionaries. Lucie Félix-Faure-Goyau (daughter of the President of the Republic) defended the traditional role of women as wives and mothers but could see no reason why this precluded participation in civic life or professional activity.[106] But perhaps most indicative of the long road along which feminism had travelled by 1914 was the result of a ballot conducted by the Parisian daily newspaper *Le Journal*, which had become an ardent convert to the now fashionable cause of women's suffrage. Timing its survey to coincide with the general elections of 1914, it issued a ballot sheet on which all women who supported female suffrage were invited to register their opinion: they could vote either by depositing the sheet in special booths erected on election day itself, or by mailing the ballot to the newspaper's offices (these postal votes were to be accompanied by a stamped addressed envelope to ensure authenticity). The response was enormous: by 3 May 1914 *Le Journal* claimed to have received 505,912 expressions of a desire to vote.[107]

On the other hand, it has to be admitted that though feminism had made indubitable progress, it still had to reckon with much hostile criticism. The *Assiette au Beurre*, drawing on a long satirical tradition stretching back at least to Daumier, continued to represent feminists as deviants from their sex, an ambiguous species more male than female.[108] Many of the books written to familiarise the public with the stages in the growth of the new phenomenon were the work of militant anti-feminists. The obvious example is Turgeon's two volume *Le féminisme français*, which was the fullest consideration of French feminism published before 1914 and which took a contrary line to most of the feminists' main demands.[109] A female commentator, Anna Lampérière, also set herself the task of refuting the errors of the feminist campaign, basing her argument on the old theory that women were equal but different and accusing the feminists of mixing up masculine and feminine roles.[110] Even writers who claimed to be basically sympathetic to feminism might retain a nostalgia for traditionalism. Thus Emile Faguet, who wrote a reply to Turgeon, denouncing it (rightly) as boring, contradictory, wrong-headed and repetitive, himself expressed a desire to see women reconciled to their time-honoured role, prepared to show their husbands not servile obedience but a certain 'docility' or 'deference'.[111]

More consequential than these literary polemics was the failure of feminism to make converts in the world of the working class. For most of this pre-war period, leaders of organised labour simply ignored feminism – it was not something which impinged on their existence to any noticeable degree. In so far as they were aware of the feminist movement, they tended to associate it exclusively with suffragism, which, as anti-parliamentarians, they naturally rejected.[112] One of the few dissenters from this general line was Marie Guillot of the Schoolteachers Federation, who consistently argued that the cause of feminism went hand in hand with the organisation of working women.[113] This, however, was not a popular view even among the ranks of militant schoolteachers. P Guérin suggested that there was no need to organise a society in which women would have equal rights since they would not know what to do with their new found freedom.[114] Marie Vidal depicted the National Council of French Women as a bourgeois organisation fraught with dangers for the female proletariat. Its interest in class reconciliation was a plot to woo the working class away from the ideal of social revolution and its concentration on the suffrage was an attempt to make working women think that they were exploited by men rather than by capital.[115] As F Berret contended, political rights were illusory. The real problem confronting women of the working class was the large size of their families and bourgeois feminists had done nothing to alleviate this situation.[116] On the contrary, as C Gété noted, the CNFF was a vigorous supporter of the natality crusade.[117]

From about 1907, the attitude of syndicalist leaders towards feminism shifted from a general indifference to a more virulent hostility, as Pierre Monatte and others came to realise how feminists could have a disruptive impact on the working-class movement. Evidence of this existed from at least the turn of the century and the affair of *La Fronde*, the feminist daily newspaper founded by Marguerite Durand. In keeping with her all-women policy for the production of the newspaper, Durand had organised a female printers' union which the *Fédération du Livre* did not recognise. In 1901 during a strike of printers at Nancy, Marguerite Durand agreed to send twelve of her woman workers to take the place of the men on strike. It is clear from her correspondence that she was willing to repeat this service for the same employer and in the eyes of the printers' federation she and her union represented blackleg labour.[118] In 1907 Durand again antagonised syndicalist militants by organising a Labour Office Congress in an attempt to put pressure on the Ministry of Public Works to fulfil its promise to establish a special department dealing with the problems of female labour. Her interference was deeply resented by a number of *syndicats* (for example those of Montluçon, Valence and Bordeaux) who castigated female unions as 'yellow'. At the Congress itself (all the expenses for which were paid by Durand) a militant delegate, called Mme Roques, was constantly ruled out of order from the Chair and finally expelled after she had described the gathering as lackeys of capital.[119] But it was the Couriau Affair in 1913 which finally made syndicalists take note of the feminist movement, since the Feminist Federation of the South-East was among the couple's earliest champions and their case generated support throughout the feminist movement.[120] These stirrings were not appreciated by male militants. Pierre Monatte wrote that working-class women did not need any help from women of the bourgeoisie, however sincere their motivation.[121] For syndicalists feminism was no longer a force to be dismissed but to be opposed.

PART TWO

THE FIRST WORLD WAR
AND THE SOCIAL CONDITION OF
WOMEN IN FRANCE

In Part Two of this book we address ourselves to the important question of whether or not the First World War represented a decisive stage in the process of female emancipation in France. As was mentioned in the General Introduction, most historians to date, following the line taken by contemporary commentators, have judged that French women, through their participation in the war effort, reaped a rich return in both material and moral benefits. First of all, it is argued, the war broke down the barriers which still separated women from the wider sphere in the period before 1914, the crucial breakthrough being made in the hitherto predominantly male domain of work. Women – above all middle class women – are alleged to have conquered not merely the right to work but also, thanks to their new-found economic independence, a new and recognisably higher status in both the family and society. Working-class women, for whom wage labour was hardly a novel experience, are deemed to have benefited from wider job opportunities and increased earning power, along with the discovery of a new sense of their own importance in the industrial labour force evident in a tendency towards greater militancy. Secondly, the war is assumed to have led to a revolution in social mores. The appearance of a new woman, epitomised by the heroine of Victor Margueritte's novel *La Garçonne*, is cited as evidence of the collapse of the moral values which were instilled into young bourgeois girls of the pre-war period. Changes in fashion, greater freedom of movement and enhanced opportunities for making contact with men all seemed to testify to the emancipation of the bourgeois woman.

In the following chapters, our primary concern will be to contest the validity of the thesis that the First World War should be seen as a turning point in the history of the feminine condition in France. Chapters VI and VII discuss whether the tangible, material rewards of participation in the war effort were as great as either contemporaries or later historians would have us believe. In the case of middle-class women, by examining their post-war situation in employment, in education and in the family, we shall be in a position to judge whether the ideal of domesticity was seriously undermined. As regards women of the French working classes, having analysed the harsh realities of their war work, we shall want to dispute the claim that participation in the labour force during the war was any more of a liberating experience than it had been in the pre-war period. With regard to the war's alleged ideological impact, we consider first the social mores of the post-war period, focusing attention on the durability of the double standard of morality. Secondly, we examine the fate of the French feminist movement, particularly with respect to the outcome of the suffrage campaign. Both chapters will provide little evidence for the view that the war brought about 'the destruction of all the old arguments about women's proper place in the community'. Before turning to these matters, however, we pause to consider how French women endeavoured to cope with the cruel and tragic consequences of war in their everyday lives.

Chapter V
WOMEN AT WAR

The experience of war in everyday life

FOR the inhabitants of the invaded regions of northern and eastern France, the experience of war was particularly harsh.[1] Many families were ruined and saw their members scattered throughout the country; those who remained behind were subjected to all the trials and humiliations of military occupation: requisitions, forced labour, morale-sapping propaganda, even arbitrary shootings. Women as well as men were forced to work for their German masters. Around Easter 1916, girls and young women from the larger towns were systematically deported to the countryside and obliged to do heavy work in the fields of the Ardennes and the Aisne. Lille provided most of these victims (some 16,000 were dispatched in April 1916) while others came from Roubaix and Tourcoing.[2] The local villagers received them sullenly, having been told by the Germans that these were no respectable women but fallen 'femmes à Boche', an impression rendered the more credible by the inclusion of a handful of real and regularly patronised prostitutes. Few of these unfortunate women of the northern industrial towns can have given much thought to the war as an agent of social change.

Even if the war came as less of a total disaster in Paris and other large urban centres which remained free from invasion, it still brought in its wake widespread anguish and suffering. This is not apparent from the contemporary (heavily censored) press and innumerable publications, all of which tried to create the impression of French womanhood solidly united behind the civil and military authorities, caught up in a tidal wave of patriotic enthusiasm, and ready to make any sacrifice in order to sustain the struggle against the German aggressor. Playwright Maurice Donnay, for example, extolled the transformation of the frivolous, pleasure-seeking Parisienne of the *belle epoque* into a devoted, dutiful servant of the community: 'Disorder, independence, selfishness, blindness, all that becomes order, discipline, altruism and lucidity.'[3] Another writer, Lucien Descaves, marked out women for the special role of haranguing *embusqués*, those who shirked their patriotic duty, and claimed to see in the knitting activities of women who sent off parcels of socks, scarves, gloves, etc. to the soldiers at the Front 'a little of the aggressive ardour of 1793'.[4] Such propaganda should be regarded with much suspicion especially in the light of reports compiled by various sections of the *Sûreté Générale*, where the evidence suggests that attitudes were a good deal more complicated. For most women, the war represented a scourge, inflicing on them the pain of separation from the men in their families and precipitating many of them into a rude world where for the first time it was necessary to earn their own living by their own toil and sweat. For a bourgeois woman like Marguerite Lesage, the wife of a factory owner in the Compiègne region taken prisoner at an early stage in the war, this could be a daunting prospect, as she confided to her diary:

> I know nothing about business, I am afraid, I've never had to display much energy, life having been very kind to me, so it's a question of going beyond what I've been, of what I've given up to now.[5]

And yet there were other women for whom the war came as a release, providing uncustomary outlets for diversion. Disenchanted wives had ample scope to seek amorous adventures in the absence of their husbands; young girls, previously allowed out only accompanied by a chaperone, found themselves able to arrange romantic rendez-vous with soldiers home on leave; and naturally business boomed for the *cocottes* of the boulevards and fashionable cafés. Reactions to the war among the women of France were not only a lot more varied than the patriotic propaganda would allow, but also usually involved much more mundane considerations than the greater honour and glory of the fatherland.

The most crucial practical problem that confronted the average French woman between 1914 and 1918 was how to cope with rising prices, particularly rising food prices. The prefects and the special superintendents who conducted the 'permanent inquiry' on the state of public opinion were in no doubt about this and gave it the largest place in their reports. For instance, the report of December 1915, drawn up by the Prefect of Police, described the situation in the 10e *arrondissement* of Paris:

> As for the high cost of living in the 10e *arrondissement* almost like everywhere else, it remains the greatest preoccupation of the housewives. The recent price rise of potatoes in particular is causing anxiety among them: the absence of frozen meat is unanimously deplored, likewise the scarcity of milk.[6]

For the housewife, especially in a working-class area like the 20e *arrondissement*, the over-riding question was when her 'economic difficulties' would come to an end, and it was a constant source of complaint that government action against speculators remained ineffectual.[7] It is true that the food supply in France never reached the proportions of scarcity attained in Britain. Mary Vincent, a real old English 'sweetie' who had lived in Paris for forty years, recalled 'that there was no real shortage of food in Paris during the war', since she was able to buy 'delicious butter, eggs, vegetables and also small joints of meat, two or three times a week'.[8] Nowhere had rationing to be employed on the English scale though restrictions were imposed on the sale of sugar, bread and meat from 1917. On 1 February 1917 tea-rooms and restaurants were placed under strict surveillance. At the beginning of 1918 coupons were introduced for the purchase of bread, sugar and some other items.[9] But though France may have been relatively better off than most belligerent countries from the point of view of food supply, the hardship necessitated by food shortages and high prices was real enough. Throughout the duration of the war, the market-place remained one of the most sensitive areas for testing the state of public opinion and there the overwhelming obsession of housewives was the ever-increasing rise in the cost of living. At Vincennes in December 1917, they complained about the poor quality of red sausages, and expressed alarm at rumours of an impending rise in the price of potatoes; others made a catalogue of their grievances, recalling how they had been obliged the previous year to queue for coal and deploring the present necessity to do so for petrol, oil and tobacco. They wanted an end to the war which alone could terminate all these *ennuis*.[10] To countless French women, housewives with families to feed, it must have seemed that the real battle was less against German imperialism than against the endless rise in prices.

Of scarcely less importance to them was the absence of their husbands, sons and brothers. These were not given blindly or willingly as the patriotic propagandists made out. Undoubtedly, especially during the earlier stages of the war, there were women who adopted a position of intransigent belligerence. Returning home on leave, Michel Corday was disgusted to find women abusing and ostracising 'any man who is not dropping to pieces with age for not being at the Front'.[11] One prostitute, seeing her pimp off to join his unit, is supposed to have exclaimed, 'Go and rape lots and lots of them!'[12] More usually, however, the loss of the men was sorely felt at home, and as hostilities began to appear interminable, led to mounting protests. Especially after the failure of the April–June offensive in 1917, widespread support for an early peace developed among the civilian population in general and among the women in particular. Reports to the War Office show that this was true all over France, both in Paris and in the provinces. For instance in Clermont-Ferrand it was noted:

> In general the women don't comfort the soldiers. They have a tendency to welcome and to exaggerate alarmist rumours.[13]

While at Toulouse:

> The civilian population deplores the long duration of the war, but it accepts it as a necessity and doesn't let itself become discouraged, except perhaps in the feminine element (wives and mothers).[14]

Many women clearly felt that there were limits to the sacrifices which they could reasonably be asked to make. One who had already lost two sons aroused much sympathy outside the town hall of the 15e *arrondissement* where she was lamenting the imminent departure of her third boy. Some cursed the war along with her, and a cry was heard in denunciation of the government for not considering such a special case.[15] By 1918 disatisfaction was being expressed in some places of popular entertainment. In the rue de la Convention, a one-act vaudeville show called *Le Retour du Poilu* received loud applause from the audience for its anti-war sentiments, especially when one of its artists sang 'that she didn't care a hoot for stripes and decorations which her tommy could have, and prefers that he should bring back his skin'.[16]

At the very least, it was commonly felt, women should be able to see their husbands a lot more frequently than the military authorities allowed. Discontent always arose when stories got about that some men had obtained leave before others who had spent more time away at the Front.[17] Even after they had been placated by the return of their men, wives might soon turn to complaining about the censorship of mail sent home from the trenches.[18] Another stock grievance was the presence in a *quartier* of able-bodied youths who gave the impression of escaping military service through nepotism; up at the Gare du Nord some wives whose husbands had been mobilised staged a protest at the excessive number of young male railway clerks employed by the Orleans Railway Company.[19] Likewise, there was a good deal of resentment against foreigners, like the Russians and Poles in the 19e *arrondissement* who were of age to bear arms and who frequently conversed among themselves in German.[20] The kind of question which preyed on the minds of loyal French wives was concerned with whether or not their husbands were being well-fed, well-clothed and generally well looked after, and why they should be prevented from sending back underclothes to be cleaned and mended.[21] In other words, they cared about all the minute details relating to their men's material welfare rather than the contribution they were supposed to be making to the ultimate victory of the Allies.

For their own part, women had to live in a state of permanent anxiety, forever fearing the arrival of some dreadful news and wondering for how long they could maintain their courage, as

Margaret Lesage has testified in her diary.[22] And yet, even though the war did appear as an unreal and endless nightmare, disenchantment at no time swelled to the proportions of massive revulsion, expressed in anti-war demonstrations. War aims were an abstraction, reality a daily struggle to survive in the absence of fathers, husbands and sons, a time of mental anguish and material difficulties. But despite the tormenting thoughts about the fate of their men, despite all the problems of finding food for their families, and despite all their trials and sufferings, the women of France remained loyal to their country and accepted everything with dignity and resignation. Margaret Lesage, weary of the war and sick to see her husband again, could still feel that all had to be borne for the sake of the fatherland.[23] If police reports can be believed, this view was representative: for the author of the *rapports Dausset* concluded his survey of feminine morale during the war by writing:

> You have all seen at the doors of food shops the disciplined and almost smiling queue of housewives waiting their turn with their milk cans and shopping bags under the complaisant eye of the veteran who acts as policeman. No, their faces in no way betray discouragement, but reflect a quiet confidence which demands acceptance without murmur of the necessary restrictions and sufferings.[24]

In short, the average French woman accepted the First World War as a cruel and evil necessity. She was prepared to make immense sacrifices, but she did so with her eyes open. She did not attempt to delude herself that here was a crusade to be supported with a kind of mystical patriotic fervour. Without wanting the French government to purchase peace at any price, she was well aware that the war brought misery and privation.

On the other hand there was a sizable minority of women who did not mind the indefinite prolongation of the war at all, either because it left them totally unaffected or because it provided them with unaccustomed opportunities for enjoyment.[25] Such were the women who frequented the bright bars and smart cafés of the *grands boulevards*, hoping to be picked up by a soldier home on leave, or better, an English or American serviceman passing through Paris with money to throw around. Gabriel Perreux relates several stories of disillusioned officers who discovered that in a place like Maxim's no one cared about the war.[26] Contemporary newspapers denounced the few who could indulge in scandalous, profligate living while others were dying wretchedly in the trenches, and while a thorough investigation of these charges revealed that most of the accusations had no foundation in fact, it did admit the existence of certain 'establishments which left much to be desired'. The bars, apparently, were the most serious dens of iniquity:

The bars have suffered little from the state of war. You find there the pre-war clientèle of *demi-mondaines* and dubious looking individuals.

Among these establishments, those of Montmartre are the most frequented, notably the Brasserie Cyrano, 82 Boulevard de Clichy, the Café de la Place Blanche, the Brasserie La Nouvelle Athènes, 9 place Pigalle. These are the haunts of prostitutes who come from the Pigalle and Place Blanche area: the Brasserie Cyrano is also patronised by pederasts, drug-takers, pimps, etc... All these people talk and laugh there noisily, the women smoke and call out loudly to each other, the conduct of this establishment leaves much to be desired. [27]

Restaurants were usually animated, full of soldiers, especially officers, 'coming to spend the forced savings of several months at the Front in the company of chance female acquaintances'.

Prostitution, naturally, was rife. At first the professionals had feared that they would be deprived of their livelihood and perhaps be recruited into the Red Cross, so they took to the countryside or went into hiding. [28] But discovering that their services were more indispensable than ever, they soon re-emerged in even greater force, establishing themselves at convenient spots behind the front line with the more or less open cooperation of the military authorities. Real money was to be made there – sometimes as much as 400 francs a day – though the gruelling eighteen-hour shifts meant that a regular rest in Paris was necessary at least once a month. Robert Graves tells how recourse to the brothels of Amiens, Abbéville, Le Havre, Rouen and all the other large towns behind the lines took place on a massive scale. Three out of ten young officers under his command contracted venereal disease after a visit to the 'Blue Lamp' in Rouen. [29]

Business also picked up again in Paris from 1915 onwards. The number of clients grew as soldiers returned home on leave or to convalesce and more and more allied troops passed through the city. Increased demand was met by new recruits to the profession – 'prostitutes for the duration of the war' – who might be short of money, lonely in the absence of their husbands, or just patriotic. From 1916, new houses were opened up to try to keep pace with the inordinate sexual needs of men who lived under the constant shadow of death. In the area near the Etoile the girls were particularly hard-worked:

The few moments of rest that they could find they consecrated to the study of English, and classes were organised. No doubt their pronunciation wasn't perfect: but they could make themselves understood without much difficulty and even the Portuguese managed to understand the English with a Montmartre accent of their young companions. [30]

The authorities objected only when men attempted to see their wives and sweethearts rather than prostitutes – as the feminist press repeatedly protested. [31] Michael Corday describes the elaborate ruses adopted by some wives to visit their husbands: some even got hold of cards from the police to say that they were official prostitutes. A poor woman who succeeded in reaching the Front by this device, and wanted to stay a little longer, was told to go away because the section in question had now been satisfied.[32] Similarly, Léon Riotor arranged for a Parisienne to be taken clandestinely to her husband hidden among sacks of oats.[32] As the war wore on, prostitution became increasingly flagrant and widespread, much to the horror of a puritanical police officer who would have liked to round them all up and set them to work in the war factories. In his view the increase in debauchery was to be explained by the prolonged absence of married soldiers, the presence of large contingents of troops far away from their homes, and 'the quasi-masculine morals of women factory workers'.[34] But what made a bad situation irretrievable was the arrival of American troops in France:

> Since the American soldiers have been here, you see them going off with prostitutes. These take good care to spend all their money for them and to infect them with venereal diseases. So these unfortunate men will end up with a fine opinion of the French people in general.[35]

The sleazy rue de Malte was the scene of some particularly sordid encounters between young French girls and drunken English soldiers.[36] In the rue de Sèze, however, it turned out that the 'little girls' promised to prospective clients by the prostitutes of a brothel in the rue des Mathurins were 'women aged thirty to thirty-five more or less capable for the job'.[37]

On the other hand at least some people believed that these ephemeral encounters had their part to play in serving the Allied cause. Ettie Rout, an English woman who spent the last two years of the war helping New Zealander and Australian troops to have a good time in the Paris brothels without catching disease, distributed protectives to soldiers and prostitutes alike, all in the name of patriotism. Among her instructions in the use of a particular ointment was the following reminder:

> REMEMBER that if you have a disease, not only are you doing yourself serious harm by delaying treatment, but you are helping the enemy by rendering our men unfit to fight.

The French government evidently thought highly of Miss Rout's contribution to the war effort: it awarded her 'the premier decoration for women, the Reconnaissance Française'.[38]

Some statistical evidence can be produced to support this general picture of a soaring rise in the amount of prostitution. F Masson has observed that among the refugees to arrive in Marseilles in November 1914 were 200 public prostitutes evacuated from the Toul region, a figure more than the total to be found in the ten *maisons* boasted by the city.[39] But what really swelled the numbers was the personnel of innumerable furnished hotels and furnished rooms, where prostitution was practised clandestinely. Whereas the Vice Squad had only some 700–800 women registered on their files, the unregistered total was reckoned to be higher than 7000. Passing troops, especially those billeted in camps around Marseilles, provided a more than reliable clientèle, though the attraction may often have been mutual, since the women seem to have displayed an 'unhealthy curiosity' in such foreigners as the British, Hindus, North Africans, Senegalese and Annanites. Another index is the dramatic increase in cases of venereal diseases in the army. Gabriel Perreux cites figures which show a rise of almost 4000 in a matter of four months.[40]

Prostitution, however, was only one particular instance of the heightened sexual activity generated by the war. There seems to be little doubt that many wives found the strain of living alone intolerable, while others took the opportunity to practise an infidelity that perhaps predated the war in their hearts. Anatole France claimed that a major reason for the prolongation of hostilities was that wives were enjoying themselves so much in the absence of their husbands.[41] Adultery was a recurring theme in the diary of Michel Corday. In May 1915 he wrote: 'Signs of retrogression: women are leading fast lives from one end of the social scale to another. "Must have a man about the house" is the popular phrase.'[42] According to Léon Riotor, the problem of the absence of men was so acute that General Mangin had to prevent troops from entering Laon, otherwise general debauchery might have taken place since the remaining civilian population of 6000 included some '4000 women thirsting for love'.[43] He also claimed that cohabitation with the invader had become extremely common and no longer gave rise to social ostracism.[44] (This was by no means the case everywhere: in other parts of the invaded regions, women who became the mistresses of German soldiers were generally reviled. In the reactionary press, it was even suggested that their illegitimate offspring should be put to death.)[45] Finally, Raymond Radiguet's classic novel, *Le Diable au Corps*, (like the film *Hiroshima, Mon Amour*) reminds us that a time and place associated with public disaster might represent a happy phase in the lives of individuals. For both the young married wife whose husband is away at the Front and the adolescent who becomes her lover, the war permits an expansion of their personalities towards a greater maturity and a deeper sensibility than they would have experienced under normal peacetime conditions.[46] In a way that the historian cannot hope to emulate, the artist can depict the immensely complex response of women to the demands placed by the war on their fundamental needs and loyalties. Probably the most profound insight into women's emotional life at this time is to be found in the novel of Maxence van der Meersch, *Invasion 14*. [47]

Supporting the war effort

To suggest how ordinary, everyday life could be made up of a strange mixture of the tragic and the banal is not to diminish the magnitude of the contribution which women did make to the war effort. French women may not have served under the flag, as Serbian women did, but as 'substitutes' in agriculture, industry and the public services, as the organisers of a bewildering number of charities, as 'godmothers' who sent out letters and parcels to their 'godsons' at the Front, in a multitude of ways they contributed enormously to the ultimate victory of French arms. In their quiet courage and unfailing tenacity most French women were – and had to be – heroines during those terrible years.

But France also had its share of heroines of a more traditional kind, women who displayed outstanding bravery or daring. Just as England had its Edith Cavell, so France produced Louise de Bettignies. [48] Born in 1880 into an aristocratic family with its roots in the Hainault, from October 1914, in collaboration with the French intelligence service, she organised a vast information network at Lille, where twice a week reports would arrive from Folkestone which she would often distribute herself. In August 1915 she set up bases for a second organisation at Valenciennes, herself becoming the chief of the Secret Service for Northern France, with almost 200 agents under her direction. Throughout this time her house was a constant refuge for English soldiers and aviators. In October 1915 she was betrayed by one of her collaborators and arrested by the German police. Incarcerated at the prison of Saint-Gilles, she escaped the firing-squad only because of the outrage provoked by the shooting of Edith Cavell. Given instead a long prison sentence, she resisted all attempts to make her work on munitions for use against the Allies, which earned her solitary confinement in an unspeakable cell measuring 2 x 1.5 metres, with neither straw nor blankets. In a glacial winter she contracted the blood poisoning which eventually killed her.

The risks run by Louise de Bettignies and the fortitude with which she bore her sufferings represent heroism on the highest plane. But there were other women too who were fit to join her company. Louise Thullier, a close collaborator of Louise de Bettignies, was also condemned to death after her arrest and would have passed before the firing squad but for the outbreak of the German Revolution in 1918. [49] Another to have the death sentence commuted was the Countess Jeanne de Belleville, this time thanks to personal interventions by the Pope and the King of Spain.[50] Most celebrated of all, perhaps, is the almost legendary Marthe Richard, who as a spy succeeded in becoming the mistress of Baron von Krohn, chief of German Naval Intelligence, and obtained invaluable information for the French authorities.[51] The examples of extraordinary heroism displayed by French women are legion; here we can only single out certain categories for special mention.

None can occupy a higher place on the roll-call of honour than the military nurses who carried out their duties at enormous risk to their own safety. Such for instance was Mme Charlotte Maître, cited as a:

> nurse of the élite, courageous and devoted beyond praise: since the beginning of hostilities has given the most valuable services to surgery and medicine. Posted as a volunteer at the front line, has borne the dangers and the fatigue of the life of the Front in the underground shelters, has shown in the face of repeated bombardment an exemplary courage and decision. Wounded by shell bursts while carrying out her duty, refused to allow herself to be evacuated. Has contracted two serious infections in the course of her service while caring for men with contagious diseases. Has already been cited twice by the order of the day.[52]

Another figure to stir the imagination was the village schoolteacher left not only to carry on with her teaching but also to take charge of the municipality in the absence of the mayor, and even on occasion to negotiate with the enemy invader.[53] Likewise the postoffice clerkess who remained at her post was another popular heroine. One woman kept services going singlehanded, despite having to make bicycle journeys under artillery fire.[54] Another continued to telephone news from Etain during the bombardment of the town until she communicated her last message: 'a bomb has just fallen into the postoffice'.[55]

Indisputably the most striking folk figure was the nurse. Lauded with extravagant tributes in the press, and celebrated in a flood of novels, she was singled out for admiration by almost all contemporaries who wrote accounts of women's involvement in the war effort. As nurses, women were held to be infinitely superior to men, possessing greater moral qualities of devotion, obedience, discretion, calm and order.[56] A sympathetic nurse could not only care for her patient, but also console his grief and sustain his courage to return to the fray.[57] A favourite theme with popular novelists was how the mutual attachments between patient and nurse could blossom into romance. As usual, Marcel Prévost was quick to produce an example of the *genre*, in his *Mon Cher Tommy*, in which the aristocratic heroine who has converted the family *château* into a hospital eventually falls in love with a likable English aviator entrusted to her care.

Some contemporary observers noted that among the recruits to the booming nursing profession there was a certain number who seemed to be motivated principally by a desire to be seen doing the smart thing. These girls took care to make sure that their appearance was different from that of the common nurses and saw their role as being to flirt and chat with the wounded rather than to employ themselves in regular chores.[58] Nevertheless, even the coquette was much appreciated by the wounded.[59] Ultimately, what mattered was the colossal scale on which service was mobilised. At Marseilles, 17 auxiliary hospitals and annexes were created, whose 3714 beds received 80,000 soldiers and provided for 3,800,000 days of hospitalisation. To these can be added some twenty-one private benevolent hospitals established by industrialists, doctors, religious, and the like, who supplied another 1450 beds.[60] In Bordeaux the *Service de Santé* had only 880 beds at its disposal in 1914: by the end of the war the total had risen to 8042, thanks to the creation of sixteen new auxiliary hospitals.[61] As a whole the response of the women of France to the desperate need for nurses can only be described as magnificent.

Perhaps the greatest need felt by the soldier at the Front was for some reassurance that his sacrifices and sufferings were not being forgotten by the people at home. The arrival of a sympathetic letter could work wonders on sagging morale. In ministering to this desperate longing for appreciation by acting as 'godmothers' the women of France performed another valuable service to their country. A scheme was started whereby women and girls would adopt a 'godson' to whom they would write and send presents, having obtained his name from the columns of newspapers such as *La Croix* and the *Echo de Paris*, in which Maurice Barrès was one of the scheme's most enthusiastic supporters.[62] There can be no doubt about the uplifting effect of this correspondence among their recipients. One soldier wrote back to his 'godmother':

> You can't believe the joy I experienced on receiving your letter showing me that someone thinks of me and is interested in what happens to me.
>
> I considered myself to have no family, having had no news of my dear ones at Lille for 639 days, but I see with satisfaction that I'm mistaken for I have found in you a kind soul.
>
> You have made me weep for joy and sorrow in thinking of my wife and two little children who themselves will be equally happy to learn that there are still generous and compassionate hearts in France.[63]

The organisation of charity was another area where women worked wonders. Innumerable charities were founded on behalf of soldiers and their families, some on private initiative, others on the initiative of feminine or feminist societies. To give a complete catalogue is impossible, but at least the main spheres of action can be indicated. The soldier himself was given priority: charities with self-explanatory names like The Soldier's Home, The Soldier's Shelter, The Soldier's Warm Clothes, The Soldier's Packet and so on began to mushroom everywhere. Canteens were organised at stations and on trains carrying soldiers to and from the Front. At Marseilles, a charity called Godmothers for the Soldiers of the Invaded Regions tried to ensure that men who had lost contact with their families after the invasion could receive news and encouragement from home. It is noteworthy that many of these charitable initiatives were sponsored by aristocratic women who, even if they had little respect for the Third Republic as a political régime, welcomed the opportunity to serve France. Perhaps the most active was the duchesse d'Uzès, who in her time had conspired against the régime (she had heavily subsidised the Boulangist campaign of the 1880s), though other aristocratic ladies such as the marquise de Noailles, the duchesse de Clermont-Tonnerre, the comtesse de Béarn and the baronne d'Eichthal featured prominently in the organisation of good works.[64]

The principal feminist groups, too, played their part. As the war dragged on, Jane Misme advocated exemplary self-abnegation by forming a League for Restrictions.[65] The CNFF established a Central Office of Feminine Activity under Avril de Sainte-Croix to assist unemployed women to find work.[66] It also had an Information Office for Dispersed Families in the charge of Mmes Pichon-Landry and Siegfried which attempted to develop links between the members of scattered families.[67] Mme Brunschvicg of the UFSF helped some 25,000 families from the north and east to find new homes.[68] Altogether, the official feminists were quite stridently patriotic. Propaganda on behalf of the right to vote was dropped in favour of exhortations to serve the *patrie*.[69] A peace initiative launched by Dutch feminists in 1915 received short shrift from the most powerful of women's organisations in France. Refusing an invitation to attend an international feminist congress at the Hague, the CNFF and the UFSF drew up a joint manifesto 'To the Women of Neutral Countries and Allied Countries' in which they said that it was impossible for French feminists to meet women from enemy countries when these had not disavowed the actions of their governments or protested at the violation of Belgian neutrality and the crimes of their armed forces. French women believed that France was fighting a just, defensive war and it was impossible to talk of peace while French soil remained occupied. The struggle had to be seen right through to the day of ultimate victory.[70]

Opposing the war effort

Compared to the enormous amount of patriotic activity, opposition to the war effort among French women was almost negligible. Even the Group of Socialist Women, who might have been expected to take the

lead in anti-militarist campaign, followed the official socialist party line
and supported the 'Sacred Union'. The Executive Commission refused
to send a delegate to the International Conference of Socialist Women
held at Berne between 26-28 March 1915 and organised by the leading
light among German socialist women, Clara Zetkin. Like the later and
more celebrated gathering of international socialists at Zimmerwald,
the Berne conference passed a resolution declaring war on war and
calling for mass action to bring about an early end to hostilities. Among
the twenty-eight women present at Berne, there was only one French
woman, the indefatigable Louise Saumoneau, who attended as a private
individual and not, as she tried to claim, as the representative of the
French Group of Socialist Women.[71]

As we have seen, Louise Saumoneau had a record of militant action
stretching back some fifteen years, having been one of the founder
members of the Socialist Feminist Group in 1899. As if to atone for the
sell-out of her socialist colleagues, virtually single-handed she
conducted a furious propaganda campaign against the war. Her view
was that socialists, having failed to prevent the outbreak of war, should
exert every effort to bring it to a close. In January 1915 she published the
Appeal of Clara Zetkin to all Socialist Women in all Countries obtained
from 'a female Russian comrade', presumably one of the couple of
Russian students who helped her constitute the Administrative
Commission of the Socialist Federation of the Seine once her anti-war
stance had been repudiated by the majority of the GDFS. On her return
from Berne, she distributed the manifesto *Women of the Proletariat –
Where are Your Husbands? Where are Your Sons?*, as well as churning out
pamphlets of her own such as *The World is Spitting Blood*. Between June
1914 and February 1915 she even continued to produce her own
brochure *La Femme Socialiste* in longhand. For these activities she was
arrested and jailed for six weeks in October 1915.[72]

A somewhat more substantial organisation than Louise Saumoneau's
Administrative Commission was the CIFPP (Comité International des
Femmes pour la Paix Permanente). This grew out of the feminist
congress at the Hague which the French leaders had refused to attend.
Presided by the Dutch feminist Dr Jacobs, the CIFPP aimed to spread its
pacifist ideas in every belligerent country. Its chief agent in France was
Mme Duchêne, president of the CNFF's labour section and one of the
very few mainstream feminists to have any truck with pacifism. The
secretary-general of the French branch of the CIFPP was Jeanne
Halbwachs, wife of the philosophy teacher Michel Alexandre and a
pupil and friend of the philosopher Alain. Supporters were not numerous – by March 1916 they had only 118 sympathisers in the whole of
France – but the Committee's links with pacifists in Switzerland, who
included Romain Rolland, gave the authorities cause for concern.[73]

Dissatisfaction with the war was more widespread in the School-teachers Union, which numbered almost as many women as men. Women primary teachers were much in evidence in the development of the Federation's pacifist campaign. Marie Mayoux, who taught in the Charente, was responsible for organising a meeting of some twenty militant teachers at Tours in June 1915, which ended by issuing a pacifist declaration. Chosen to represent the Teachers' Federation at the international pacifist congress at Kienthal, she was refused permission by the authorities to travel to Savoy, where another pacifist primary teacher, Lucie Colliard, was to get her across the frontier. Marie Mayoux, her husband François, with whom she published a pamphlet *Les instituteurs syndicalistes et la guerre*, and Lucie Colliard were among the first victims of Clemenceau's repressive measures at the end of 1917.[74] Another to suffer at this time was Hélène Brion, a thirty-six year old teacher at the nursery school at Pantin. Her advanced political and feminist views made her the object of vile abuse in the reactionary press, where she was accused of Malthusianism, defeatism, anti-militarism, anarchism and incompetence at her job, as well as a preference for masculine clothes. The examining magistrate even decided to have her mentally examined. At her trial a number of prominent radical feminists like Séverine, Marguerite Durand and Nelly Roussel stood by her, as did a number of socialist and syndicalist militants.[75]

Altogether, it cannot be said that women took part in anti-war activities on any significant scale. The Zimmerwaldien movement, the most revolutionary challenge to the war, was supported, inevitably, by Louise Saumoneau, who became a leading figure in the CRRI (the Committee for the Resumption of International Relations). Two other working-class militants, Stéphanie Bouvard and Louise Couteaudier, joined the cause.[76] There were also several women journalists who tried to mobilise opposition to the war, notably Marcelle Capy, the author of a pamphlet entitled *Une voix de femme dans la mêlée* which contained a preface by Romain Rolland and a contributor to both *La Vague*, the pacifist newspaper of the deputy Pierre Brizon, and to *La Voix des Femmes*, a radical feminist newspaper started in 1917. Marianne Rauze, ex-editor of *L'Equité*, the organ of the socialist women's group, became extremely active in the minority socialist movement after the death of her husband in 1916 and also wrote frequently for the socialist newspaper *Le Populaire*. In the end, however, the dissident voices seem to have been drowned by the shrill shrieking choruses of the patriotic choir.

Nevertheless, perhaps the most important conclusion that can be drawn from this rapid survey of women's position on the French home front during the First World War is that *both* the 'patriotic' and the 'pacifist' camps were in a distinct minority in the country as a whole. Only propagandists on either side campaigned for or against the war, even if there were more of the former than of the latter. To the vast majority, the war was a *fact*, a part of daily existence, something with which people came to terms in a multitude of different ways, including indifference. To be sure, the moral and material effort of French womanhood did reach spectacular proportions, and we have still to look at the magnitude of the female contribution in taking over men's jobs in the war factories. But in a way this communal achievement was almost accidental and incidental. Some women cursed the war because it brought grief, misery, hardship or inconvenience and not because of doctrinaire pacifist convictions. Likewise, other women worked hard, pulled together, tried to help out, acted generously, showed pity, kindness and decency because these were the obvious human responses in a crisis where survival depended on solidarity – again not out of an ideological commitment to nationalism. Between 1914 and 1918, as at any other time, what happened in the private lives of women was likely to mean more than the great public events like military victories or defeats. Just as the supposed achievements of the French Revolution often remained remote for large numbers of ordinary people in the 1790s, so too the 'glory of French arms', the 'National Honour', 'Duty to the *patrie*' and the rest could equally mean very little or nothing to countless French women during the war, when set beside the banal, tedious, painful or joyful experiences which, in different degrees, made up the course of their everyday lives. [77]

Chapter VI
THE SOCIAL IMPACT OF WAR: MIDDLE-CLASS WOMEN

DURING the course of the war and the period immediately following the cessation of hostilities, public opinion was prepared for a dramatic transformation of the role of women in French society. Female emancipation, it was thought, was on the point of becoming a social reality – 'emancipation' in contemporary usage being understood to mean essentially the expansion of women's activities beyond the domestic sphere, and, above all, into the field of employment. The middle-class woman's invasion of the world of work was expected to set her free from the shackles of domesticity while at the same time (one might think paradoxically) increasing her prestige as wife and mother within the family. The greatest enthusiasm for these changes was to be found among right-wing patriotic propagandists. Expressing their viewpoint with mercifully less bombast than was customary, Louis Narquet wrote that the war had brought the question of women's role into relief: by their contribution to the war effort they had more than adequately demonstrated their capacity for work in the world outside the home. In his opinion, since France faced a desperate labour shortage in the post-war period, the obvious answer was to expand the employment of women, rather than have recourse to large-scale immigration, which could bring many undesirables into the country. Narquet conceded that women's work was relevant to the burning question of maternity and depopulation, but argued that the crucial factors behind the declining birth rate were bourgeois ambitions for their sons, poor hygiene, alcoholism and bad housing. Altogether, Narquet found that the war had raised women's consciousness and placed them in 'a totally modified situation, completely turned to their advantage'.[1] In complete agreement with Narquet, the Director of the Conservatoire Nationale des Arts-et-Métiers stated that the war had broken down all the barriers erected against women's entry into careers from which they had previously been excluded.[2] As another nationalist spokesman declared, woman would no longer be 'a creature of luxury'.[3]

Naturally, feminists also hailed the bourgeois woman's discovery of work. Marguerite Clément saw it as a positive good that, as a consequence of the war, women should go out to work. Henceforth, she insisted, it was the duty of parents and teachers to prepare girls for a career.[4] Jane Misme expressed similar views in the pages of *La Française* and elsewhere. Although allowing that initially some women would doubtless be happy to return to the hearth, sooner or later she saw them becoming 'seized with nostalgia for the effort'. The transformation in women's attitude to work was, she maintained, something permanent, with the result that one of the principal causes of women's inferior status had been eradicated.[5] Champions of the domestic ideology, of course, were much less enthusiastic about the possibility of a new role for women in the post-war labour force. M Lambert, for instance, foresaw a 'crisis of the hearth', as women opted for work rather than maternity, neglected their children and their household duties, and, with their inflated wage-packets, indulged all their innate propensities to extravagance.[6] The point remains, however, that across a wide spectrum of contemporary opinion, the war was held to have shattered the ideal of the non-working woman. Such has also been the view of historians: 'a revolutionary chapter in the story of women's emancipation', in the words of John Williams.[7] The interpretation put forward here will be very different. Our argument is that contemporaries greatly exaggerated the extent of women's progress in the wider sphere while failing to appreciate the significant ways in which the impact of the First World War reinforced rather than weakened the cult of domesticity.

Employment

There were, to be sure, encouraging signs of progress. In the first place, statistics show that women made very real advances in the tertiary sector of the economy. In 1906, some 779,000 women were employed in commercial jobs and 293,000 in the liberal professions and public services. In 1921 these figures were respectively 1,008,000 and 491,000.[8] Moreover, in the immediate post-war years career guides for women mentioned jobs from which they had previously been excluded.[9] In response to the belief that women had a natural gift for commerce and ought therefore to be allowed to exercise these talents at the top level of management, a number of schools were set up to equip them with the necessary training in higher commercial education.[10] Mlle Louise Sanua was responsible for the creation of the Ecole de Haut Enseignement Commercial, a private establishment which was in due course recognised by the state and placed under the patronage of the Paris Chamber of Commerce.[11] The latter institution also founded an Ecole Commerciale de Jeunes Filles, while the Ecole Technique Supérieure de Physique et de Chimie and the Ecole des Travaux Publics also allowed women to follow their courses.[12] The initiative here was taken by the Ecole Supérieure de Commerce of Montpellier which asked the Ministry of Commerce for permission to accept women students.[12] There were also new openings in hotel management, such as the Ecole Hôtelière Féminine, founded by Valentine Thomson, and a similar establishment at Bescançon.[14]

At the lower level of technical competence, girls could learn the elements of industrial design in establishments such as the Ecole d'Enseignement Technique Féminin, opened by Mlle Hatzfeld, and the Ecole Rachel, founded by M Léonard Rosenthal.[15] In the provinces a number of schools provided a preparation for careers in both industry and commerce.[16] In the industrial sections, girls might learn the trade of dressmaker, corset-maker, sewing-maid, embroiderer, milliner or laundry woman, while the commercial classes prepared girls to be cashiers, shop assistants, typists and employees in the higher posts of banking and commerce. The success of this commercial education meant that parents could now hope to see their daughters employed in posts other than typing and primary teaching.[17]

In the post-war years some women found their way to responsible positions in industry and commerce. By 1929 Mlle Sanua's school had turned out 500 graduates. A survey revealed that among those who graduated in 1917 and 1918 were a future chief accountant, earning 27,800 francs a year; a manageress of a family pension earning an income of 24,000 francs; an accountant earning 21,600 francs; and various secretaries who earned between 15,000 and 18,000 francs. Graduates of 1919-21 went on to do even better, and one became a chief accountant with an income of 32,000 francs a year.[18] Among technical occupations, that of engineer was one where a woman might do particularly well. According to Lagorce's *Careers Guide*, old prejudices against employing women had been swept away, and instead they were now keenly sought by employers. Even if they did not yet direct workers on the site or workshop, they would be present in planning rooms, drawing-offices and technical services. Chemical and electrical engineering seemed to be the branches in which women could best hope to succeed; indeed in the latter case women engineers might find themselves in charge of workshops where most of the labour was feminine, as in the fabrication of electric lamps. On average, about five or six girls graduated from the Ecole Centrale each year; all had good prospects, since there were many more jobs than candidates available.[19]

Yet, despite all the signs of progress, it would be a mistake to think that all the middle-class women of France were escaping from their *foyers* into the brave new world of work. For the most part, the women who made up the cohorts of female employees in 'white-collar' jobs were not married. In 1906, the proportion of married women employed in commerce relative to the number of married women in the population was only 4.8%: by 1936, this had risen only to 6.4%. In the liberal professions and public services the comparable statistics are 0.8% and 1.9% for 1906 and 1936 respectively.[20] The female invasion of the tertiary sector, such as it was, was an affair of young, unmarried girls. In the family consumer economy of post-war France, the daughters of the bourgeoisie were permitted to work, but wives were still expected to devote their time and energies to rearing their children and organising their households.

Consequently, women were rarely able to break through into the top levels of management in industry, commerce, or administration. Time and again, the authors of careers guides for girls warned them not to set their sights too high. In banking, for instance, they were told to expect middling positions at most: only a few exceptional girls could hope to become supervisors or sub-principals. There was an extreme reluctance to give women 'indispensable' jobs when there was the possibility that they might suddenly leave, either to marry or to have a baby.[21] Women's progress in the tertiary sector therefore took place in subordinate positions, largely as secretaries or typists. Even at this level, to be successful a girl had to specialise, for in a tight economic situation it was anticipated that the simple shorthand typist would be the first to be sacrificed.[22] Another serious barrier to further advancement remained the lack of opportunities in higher technical education. By no means all of the establishments in this sphere took the view that women should be led away from their 'natural' vocation as a result of the First World War. In Paris the Ecole des Hautes Etudes Commerciales and the Ecole Pratique de Commerce et d'Industrie refused to admit women students, as did similar schools in Lyons and Marseilles.[23] It was only in 1966 that a government circular opened all commercial and technical schools to girls: until then most establishments remained separated by sex, with the result that women were excluded from numerous jobs because they could not receive the necessary specialised training.[24]

Likewise, women continued to be discriminated against in most administrative jobs. The transport companies, as before 1914, preferred to employ the wives, widows and daughters of male employees.[25] In the Civil Service, the need to replace men, during and after the war, led to the progressive opening up of most competitive examinations to women candidates after 1920.[26] But each department still had the right to decide for itself whom it should employ. Thus if women came increasingly to be employed in the Post Office, Bridges-and-Roads, Customs and in many prefectures and sub-prefectures, there remained state offices such as the magistrature and the Conseil d'Etat which refused to employ women at all.[27] The Ministry of War, under Pétain, reversed its policy of taking on women in the 1930s. Despite protests from women civil servants, this decision was upheld by the Conseil d'Etat on the basis of a law of 29 December 1882, which was itself abolished only in 1959.[28] Overall, the war certainly did help to expand the number of female civil servants, who amounted to more than 200,000 in 1921 as compared to 100,000 in 1906. But, overwhelmingly, the grades they occupied were inferior ones; only two women in the entire inter-war period succeeded in becoming *chef du bureau*.[29]

The new opportunities for girls in secondary and higher education were slow to produce any notable 'feminisation' of the liberal professions. The Bar, for instance, remained substantially a male preserve. Even Lagorce, who was keen to encourage girls to seek top jobs, had to admit that in the legal profession, despite the success of individuals, women were generally confronted by the weight of traditional prejudices. In 1929 only about one hundred women were enrolled at the Paris Bar, and several of these did not practise. In the provinces the woman barrister was an exceptional figure – almost an anomaly. There were three at Lyons, one at Le Havre, two at Caen and none in Marseilles. Lagorce remained optimistic about the possibilities of overcoming the barriers of prejudice in the near future, and drew consolation from the fact that those who did succeed in the profession could do very well indeed.[30] Certainly the heroic period when women had to struggle to be accepted at the Bar was long since over. Yet M Joseph Barthélemy, dean of the Law Faculty in Paris, considered that most of the girls who enrolled in law courses had no intention of pursuing law as a career. Law had come to be accepted as part of general culture, and was studied by them as amateurs engaging in a kind of intellectual sport. Only about one third might eventually be called to the Bar, although some of the other female law graduates would be able to find employment in ministries and prefectures.[31] All authors of careers guides stressed that success at the Bar required material resources and good connections as well as talent.[32]

Medicine was another career where success was not guaranteed by the possession of a paper qualification. Again it was necessary to have connections in order to be able to build up a clientèle, and this was difficult in big cities where there were already many male competitors. In the provinces, on the other hand, women doctors were still regarded with suspicion.[33] One careers guide written in 1921 did not even think it worthwhile to include information for would-be women doctors, since it was a most exceptional situation and one which was already well-known to the very comfortably-off families who alone could contemplate such a career for their daughters.[34] During the war many women doctors did replace mobilised male doctors in hospitals and private clinics, but it is not true to say that the war did a great deal to make medicine more acceptable as a career for girls. The Health Service was prepared to take on only a few women during the war and these were assigned to a subordinate role. Although there were some exceptions, many qualified women could not find employment as military doctors and, in order to have the opportunity of exercising their skills, had to resort to the subterfuge of joining the Service as nurses.[35] The post-war period may have revealed that women certainly had the capacity to undertake medical studies successfully, but their future in the profession was far from bright. The top positions in the medical hierarchy remained virtually closed to them and they were well advised to specialise in gynaecology and the ailments of women and children.[36]

Dentistry offered more possibilities to women; success came on more or less the same terms as for men.[37] But pharmacy, although considered a good career for girls, still placed handicaps in the way of their success. No candidate could take the final examinations without completing a period of practical training with a qualified pharmacist, and most often these openly favoured male trainees at the expense of girls.[38] One woman who did succeed claimed that she had done so against the odds, since there were three candidates for every post. Another drawback was the length and cost of studies.[39] Nursing was rated an excellent career for a girl on the grounds that not only was it an under-staffed profession but also an ideal preparation for marriage.[40] But the irregular hours of work made it virtually incompatible with family life and therefore an unsuitable career for a married woman. Apparently very few nurses married doctors; they also seem to have formed the main clients of marriage bureaux among women over the age of thirty-five. A Public Assistance supervisor declared that it was always a safe bet to address a nurse as 'mademoiselle': nine times out of ten one would be right.[41]

Social work offered many opportunities to women. As visiting nurses they might seem like the agents of a social revolution in that the pre-war generation would never have entertained the idea of young girls being allowed to go around on their own to visit people suffering from tuberculosis or venereal disease.[42] The factory superintendents, born of the war, survived into peace-time as intermediaries between workers and employers and the promoters of welfare in the factories. As 'social residents', bourgeois women might go to live in a working-class district to set up welfare and social centres.[43] Certainly the post-war period saw women enter social service professions in increasingly large numbers, but this only confirms the impression that the best opportunities for women lay in 'feminine' careers where their special 'feminine' qualities could receive maximum scope for development.

Teaching no longer required quite the heroism that was demanded of both primary and secondary school teachers in the early years of the twentieth century. Perhaps most importantly they could now expect to receive a decent salary which allowed them to live 'very honourably.'[44] But many of the drawbacks had not been entirely eliminated. Graduates of the training schools who were sent out to become village primary teachers still had to reckon with the loneliness stemming from the absence of either family or suitable intellectual companions, as well as the need to keep their distance from village society lest they be accused of favouritism. They soon learned of spitefulness and backbiting talk, no matter how irreproachable their lives, since they were placed in the almost impossible position of being an example to both their children and the community. Dignity without compromise was an ideal that was hard to attain to the satisfaction of all. The products of Fontenay aux Roses and Sèvres also had to face up to the trials of provincial life. Having committed themselves to secondary teaching for at least ten years of their lives, very often they had to live in less than comfortable circumstances – hotels were not uncommon as their place of residence. Posts in large towns were very difficult to come by and marriage might complicate life if one's husband did not work in the same town. In practice it was hard to change jobs even though the law provided that as far as possible husbands and wives employed by the state should be able to find work in the same locality.[45] Thus, after the war as before it, and especially in the more conservative parts of the country like the west, the woman secondary school teacher remained subject to the constraints imposed by small town mores: some headmistresses considered it improper for one of their staff to go out after 7 pm, even to post a letter.[46] For this reason very few women teachers joined the ranks of the feminists: as Jane Misme noted, in France, unlike most other countries where women teachers supplied much of the drive behind feminist movements, they had to practise a greater discretion and self-effacement in order to be the first examples of the intellectual and economic emancipation of women.[47]

Altogether, the First World War certainly played a part in bringing women into the tertiary sector of the economy but one which was subsidiary to a more general transformation already well under way before 1914.[48] The technological and demographic changes which created a more complex economy and generated greater material prosperity would seem to be more at the root of the increased participation than the upheaval of war. This would certainly conform with the experience of Western Europe and America after the Second World War and also bears out Jean Daric's thesis that women more readily than men abandon the primary and secondary sectors in favour of the tertiary, as may be seen from their greater predominance in towns, and especially those parts of towns where material prosperity is highest.[49] Ultimately, the First World War appears to have been much less of a watershed in the evolution of middle-class women's employment than either contemporaries or later commentators believed.

Education

As has been seen, the crucial battles in opening up secondary education to girls were won in the years before the war. But it still remained to permit them full equality with boys, notably in the matter of the leaving certificate, the *baccalauréat*, which outside of the Collège Sévigné and certain Catholic schools, could only be taken after a virtually clandestine preparation. The war gave this issue a new prominence, since it led to the mobilisation of many male secondary teachers and to their replacement by women, which helped to persuade at least some male educators that the case for equality was now irresistible. Professor Gustave Allais of Rennes University, for example, argued that there was now every reason why women should take the same examinations as men, and therefore have the right to study Latin in their own schools.[50] But when reform eventually came in 1924, it was the product not so much of the impact of war but of a long campaign to bring male and female secondary education into alignment which dated back to the pre-war period.

Once an extra-parliamentary commission had been set up by Viviani to examine the question further, considerable pressure was brought to bear on it by the reformist lobby. The *Revue Universitaire* and other pedagogic journals registered the rise in opinion favouring change. One of the most tireless campaigners was Mme J Crouzet-ben-Aben, whose advocacy of the absolute equality of educational programmes over some nine years was based on her own personal experience in struggling to master Latin and Greek with the help of a male tutor.[51] Yet despite the strength of the demand for reform, the Commission's recommendation was to keep the diploma and at the same time establish a new diploma to be taken over two years, which would be a kind of female equivalent of the *baccalauréat* – in theory enjoying the same status.[52] These conclusions produced an outcry throughout the educational world. The Arts Faculty at Rennes accused the Commission of acting upon the mistaken assumption that all girls were destined exclusively to be wives and mothers whereas many were destined for careers.[53] The *Société des Agrégées* (founded in 1920) denounced the recommendations for ignoring existing realities: unification was already partially a fact, if only in the most unsatisfactory way, and the diploma a meaningless decoration, without real value or prestige.[54]

A turning point was reached in 1922 when the powerful reformist lobby succeeded in enlisting the support of the Minister of Education, Léon Bérard. Though Bérard himself was not greatly interested in the question of female education as such, he was very concerned to restore classics to its former position of primacy throughout the secondary sector (a position which had been undermined by a reform of the *baccalauréat* in 1902). In the matter of girls' education, however, he was willing to take his cue from his secretary, Paul Crouzet, husband of Mme Jane Crouzet-ben-Aben.[55] In a speech in 1922, Bérard admitted that secondary education for girls no longer corresponded to the reality of things. Girls could no longer be content with the diploma: henceforth the problem was how to obtain a complete identity of programmes right through to and including the *agrégation*.[56] Having already given special permission to women candidates to take the male *agrégations* in grammar and philosophy, he authorised girls to attend classes in mathematics and philosophy at boys' schools in regions where it was impossible to set up a full class in a girl's school.[57] Intransigence still persisted in the ranks of some male – and even of some female – teachers. The Mixed Association of Secondary Teachers of Toulon strongly condemned equality (in the absence of four female representatives) on the grounds (among others) that male higher education was beyond the intellectual and physical capacities of women.[58] A woman teacher at Sèvres, Mlle M Guénot, also favoured a distinct feminine education which would develop and utilise 'all the feminine resources'.[59] But these traditionalist protests were raised to no avail: on 25 March 1924 the Bérard law was passed (by decree) to introduce complete equality into the curricula of secondary schools.

By this reform the legislator did not abolish the concept of separate feminine education in its entirety. It was kept alive in a decree of 15 March 1928 which dealt with the organisation of courses, and defended the diploma as providing recognition for the achievements of girls who had no desire to sit the *baccalauréat* but preferred instead 'to develop the habits which a woman must employ in her home'.[60] The *Revue de l'Enseignement Secondaire des Jeunes Filles*, founded by Camille Sée in 1881, began to appear in a new series in 1927 and continued to promote his ideas.[61] The review, *Famille et Lycée*, even as late as July 1939, was not prepared to accept the complete assimilation of masculine and feminine education.[62] More important, separate *agrégations* continued to be set for women and men, although an *arrêté* of 17 May 1924 did allow women to compete in a masculine examination, if they had been adequately prepared.[63] It was only in 1970 that the female *agrégation* in History and Geography was abolished, and only in 1975 that for the first time the male and female juries in History were united.[64] The reform of 1924 may have represented an inevitable development in the educational system, the logical conclusion of which was to be the fusion of women's and men's higher degrees. But if the First World War contributed to this general evolution, in no way can it be said to have been solely, or even mainly, responsible for it.

Marriage and the family

Given the modesty of women's progress in the wider spheres of
employment and education, one is obliged to conclude that after the
First World War, as before it, the position of women continued to be
defined principally in terms of their role in the family. In the eyes of
many moralists motherhood rather than employment still seemed the
proper goal of women's existence.[65] Last-ditch defenders of bourgeois
values vehemently denied that the decline in the fortunes of the *rentier*
class would lead solid middle-class families, in the provinces at least, to
abandon their pre-war ideals. Rather than allow their daughters to go
out to work, or to marry a worker, the provincial bourgeoisie were said
to be ready to impose any sacrifice upon themselves.[66] According to an
article in the *Revue des Deux-Mondes* survival would be difficult, but was
by no means impossible, especially if daughters took over the tasks
once performed by domestic servants and if the ranks of the bourgeoisie
were renewed by the recruitment of the sons of new-rich peasants.[67]
Apologists for 'woman by the hearth' were therefore not lacking in the
inter-war period. True, they may give the impression of being on the
defensive, but then traditionalists invariably exaggerate the threats to
the values they hold dear.

One index of the continuing prestige of marriage was the stigma
which still attached to the state of female celibacy. A study carried out in
1936 found that the hardships faced by single women were still very real
and that they stood in need of a great deal of sympathy.[68] A more recent
enquiry based on letters written to *La Vie Catholique Illustrée* discovered
that very few women deliberately chose to remain single or considered
celibacy advantageous. Most stressed that life was lonely and hard,
often made more miserable by lack of understanding on the part of
others, including priests. They suffered from the emptiness and silence
in their homes and also from overhearing hurtful remarks. The
majority missed not having children. Indeed, some became pregnant
by design, although this in the end was more likely to add to their
problems. Prejudice against the illegitimate child had not been
elmininated in the bourgeois milieu and such offspring might not
always be grateful to the mothers who had brought them into the
world. The happy ones were those who enjoyed their jobs and
considered that their independence allowed them to achieve more, but
even they had to cope with the lack of companionship and support in
their domestic lives.[69] To end up an 'old maid' was still very much a fate
to be avoided.

There can be little doubt, then, that the First World War magnified
the problems of the single woman in French society. In 1911, the ratio

of females to males in the population was 1.031 to 1. In absolute terms, the female population exceeded the male by 684,000. In 1921, the surplus had risen to 1,904,000, without counting the additional number to be added on after the recovery of Alsace-Lorraine. Correspondingly, the ratio became 1.108 to 1.[70] The number of widows in the population is difficult to calculate but it was probably a minimum of 600,000.[71] Before 1914, the number of widows in the nubile female population had been decreasing, but the war arrested this process. Only in 1936 did the proportion of widows fall below that of 1881, and even then it remained higher than in 1851.[72]

The imbalance of the sexes, however, did not lead to the demise of marriage and the family, as some of the gloomier champions of the cult of domesticity predicted in the immediate aftermath of the war. The women most vulnerable to the disproportion belonged to the generation 1891-5 and 1896-1900. Of the former, 12.5%, and of the latter 11.9% were still single at the age of fifty. In normal times, however, it was reasonable to expect that around 10% of the female population would be unmarried at this age. It would appear, therefore, that despite the losses to the male population occasioned by the war, only an extra 2.5% from the generations most eligible for marriage were constrained to celibacy. What happened was that among native Frenchmen far fewer remained single than one would have expected normally. Some 10% in excess of the average proportion contracted marriage. About 2% married who, without the war, would probably never have done so. Widowers and divorced men played a part, so that the dead men were sometimes replaced by others from their own generation. Above all, a process of substitution took place whereby men who would normally have married widows or divorcees married young girls from the pool of those in the most marriageable generations, while a younger generation of men married older women than normally. Louis Henry has shown that the remarriage of widows in the four generation groups 1876-80 to 1891-5 was frequent between 1919 and 1925, though widows from the generation 1896-1900 were less successful. Thus the marriage of single women was not achieved at the expense of war widows: on the contrary, it was young girls who seem to have been most exposed to celibacy.[73] Nevertheless, the proportion of women of marriageable age who succeeded in marrying rose continually from the mid 1920s. In 1926, 59.30% were married: in 1931 61.70% (higher than in 1911): and in 1936, 65%. In short, the post-war years saw marriage more firmly established than ever.

Whether marriage 'modernised' or not is none of our concern. What may be said is that several new traits could be discerned both in the process of entering marriage and in the matter of husband-wife relations. Probably a young middle-class woman's freedom of choice was widened by the general increase in feminine mobility, which provided more opportunities for meeting a spouse than in the days when she had to wait at home until her parents arranged a desirable match. Dances, as a later survey discovered, probably accounted for many meetings that blossomed into matrimony.[74] 17% of those surveyed admitted to having met at a dance of some sort, whether public or private. A civil servant recalled meeting his wife at the Coliséum ballroom through the accident that they had the first dance together on an evening when few other patrons were present. A romantic police officer had been captivated when dancing a tango while the band played 'The most beautiful tango in the world'. A waiter had met his wife at the annual dance of the Auvergnats of Paris. As Louis Chevalier has shown, provincials resident in Paris tended to seek out friends and acquaintances among people from their native regions.[75] A company director and his wife met at a dance organised by the Young Radicals; a surgeon and his wife at a 'surprise party' when they were both students. Another 15% of the couples in the same survey met through chance circumstances covering a multitude of cases. There was a primary schoolteacher who met a woman in a café, having gone there when he was bored in order to kill time; a doctor who encountered a lady on a ship returning from Algeria, where she had been visiting a brother in the services; a bus driver, who engaged a girl passenger in conversation after she had missed her stop; and so on.

But arranged marriages did not disappear altogether. We have the evidence of Simone de Beauvoir that her friend Zaza was not allowed to marry the man of her choice, but was instead married off to someone she did not love. When she protested to her mother, she received the crushing reply: 'My dear, it is the *man* who loves'.[76] Even in the post-Second World War period, it has been calculated that about 10% of all marriages were arranged by the families concerned. Baptisms, first communions, weddings and other such social gatherings were regarded as promising marriage markets, apart from specific introductions.[77] In the 1920s about a fifth of the marriages celebrated had some kind of contract; thus little change took place between 1913, when the proportion of contracts was 22%, and 1925, when it had fallen slightly to 19.3%.[78] Money continued to be an important consideration in bourgeois marriages after the First World War, indeed it may have become even more important than before 1914. In an era of financial instability, asserted Marcel Prévost, young men were particularly concerned that their marriages should be materially advantageous. Addressing his nephew, he predicted:

For the financial and social advantages that she represents you will marry a young girl who does not repel you, but whom you would not dream of marrying without these advantages.[79]

Romantic love had by no means completely supplanted calculation of interests in marriage formation as a consequence of the First World War.

As regards the relationship between the two spouses, it was assumed in some quarters that the position of the wife would be strengthened vis-à-vis that of her husband in the post-war years. As Jane Misme conjectured, a wife who had learnt to fend for herself would be likely to feel less humble in the home, while a mother who had exercised full paternal powers over her children would be inclined to reflect on the injustice of the law in depriving her of this right in normal times. [80] A Belgian writer visiting Paris in 1926 described girl students as rejoicing in the greater liberty granted them by contemporary mores, which they in no way abused but intended to carry over into marriage when they eventually settled down:

> They cite me, with a surprise mingled with pity, the names of some of their companions who, half through weariness at too solitary a life, half from the need for protection and tenderness, let themselves be married to mediocre men, to whom they have been seen to sacrifice their independence and their most firm intellectual tastes. They declare themselves incapable of a similar abdication and claim to live their lives only with a clear conscience. They will marry late, if necessary: they can wait. In marriage, they will bring neither the submissiveness nor the sentimental demands of their mothers: they will bring a greater awareness of realities, the habit of personal initiative, perhaps a devotion that is perhaps less spontaneous and less disinterested, but often more enlightened and more energetic. [81]

Finally, the demographic fact that, in the post-war years, many wives were older than their husbands may well have helped them achieve real equality within marriage. As Colin Dyer has noted, one result of the dearth of males occasioned by the war was 'a substantial change in the age distribution of newly-wedded husbands'. In 1913, in every 1000 marriages, only 179 brides were older than their grooms: in 1917 the number had risen to 238, after peaking at 278 'in the dismal nuptial year of 1915'. Dyer suggests that with the persistence of this trend in the years following the war, the basis may have been laid for 'the often dominating role of the wife in the French family between the wars and later'. [82] As one contemporary author put it, there could be little doubt that 'in the relations of everday life, married women today possess a situation equal to that of men'. [83] A more recent commentator, in lamenting the encroachments of the state into areas formerly reserved for family life (education, socialisation, care of sick and aged relatives etc.), also draws attention to the increasingly dominant role of mothers consequent upon the decline of paternal authority. [84]

Yet, before celebrating the death of patriarchy and hailing the dawn of the 'new concomitant relationship', we might bear in mind that not all of the evidence points to the possibility that the married bourgeois woman benefited from a new deal in post-First World War France. If the law provides any guide to women's position in the family, the absence of any notable change was striking. The war can in no way be said to have revolutionised women's legal standing. On the contrary, throughout the war the fiction of 'the tacit consent' was maintained, so that a wife continued to exercise authority because her husband was deemed to consent implicitly to the decisions she took on his behalf. [85] A law of 3 July 1915 did permit women to assume full paternal powers in cases where their husbands were demonstrably incapable of acting for themselves, but this was emphatically a temporary measure effective only for the duration of the war. [86]

During the war itself enforced separation could lead to all sorts of problem. It was not uncommon for women to have to appeal to public charity because they could not withdraw funds from a bank without their husbands' authorisation. [87] Thus women continued to suffer from not having full legal capacity. If a Frenchwoman married a Spaniard, for example, she lost her French nationality and could find herself unable to divorce her husband. The death of her husband did not mean that she recovered her French nationality automatically: she had to apply for 'reintegration' and state that she intended to reside permanently in France. [88] A Frenchwoman could not obtain a passport without her husband's consent; [89] nor, despite legislation in 1907, could she necessarily oblige a bank to open an account in her name without her husband's permission. (Maria Vérone knew a colleague at the Bar who had been turned away by a bank.) [90]

It is true that there were some minor improvements in the legal position of women. A law of 20 March 1917 allowed women to be guardians of orphans, though it would be absurd to claim, as one writer does, that this was a revolutionary change. [91] In the matter of guardianship women still did not enjoy complete equality with men, since the husband's permission was still required of a woman who was married at the moment she was to assume custody of the child. [92] A law of 10 August 1927 eventually settled the grievance about nationality in that a Frenchwoman could now retain her own nationality if she married a foreigner. But as Ancel points out, such improvements as were effected in the law amounted only to exceptions to the general rule of incapacity. [93] Married women were not to receive full legal capacity in France until the law of 18 February 1938, and even then wives were still subject to important legal constrictions, since the husband remained the head of the family and could still veto his wife's employment and benefit from the property arrangements under the different types of community. It was not until the law of 13 July 1965 that French women obtained real legal emancipation. The impact of the First World War on the status of women was virtually negligible if measured in terms of the reform of the Civil Code.

Should the law be held to be out of line with social realities, it still cannot be argued that, in practice, relations between husband and wife were invariably characterised by equality. The invaluable memoirs of Simone de Beauvoir, representing as they do the experience of a not untypical bourgeois family, reveal that in her home the predominance of her father remained unchallenged.[94] Her mother, eight years younger than her father, willingly took second place and looked to him for guidance in all intellectual matters. He was to be admired and obeyed, although compensation was provided to her mother through having complete charge of the bodily and moral welfare of the children. Unhappy marriages were probably extremely common, with the wife struggling to make something of a basically unsuccessful match. The mother of Simone de Beauvoir's best friend Zaza had been ordered to marry her husband against her inclinations. She had borne him nine children (he was a pious Catholic) but in instructing her daughter about the experience of sexual relations she used a crudeness of language which suggested that she loathed her husband. As Henri Bordeaux suggests, the First World War was important in exposing the latent discontent among married women and may well have stiffened their resolve to be something more than unpaid domestic servants.[95] Yet a better deal for wives was slow in coming, as more recent opinion polls have discovered. In one survey, more than half of the women interviewed agreed that marriages often worked badly, yet statistics show that only one marriage in ten is broken by divorce.[96] The relative stability of the divorce rate in inter-war France should not be taken to imply that marital relations were usually harmonious. Fears that the children would suffer and that life for the woman outside the family abode would be worse often kept incompatible couples together. Similarly, with regard to sex within marriage, it seems highly improbable to assume that the continuing downward spiral in the French birth rate should be interpreted as primarily a blow struck for the sexual liberation of the married woman. The causes of this decline are complex and in the inter-war period may well be related to the climate of pessimism and fear for the future engendered by the bloodletting in the trenches between 1914 and 1918.[97] As we shall see, as far as the state was concerned, women were not entitled to the right to control their own fertility. True enough, the law was ultimately powerless to influence how couples behaved in the intimacy of their own bedroom, so that contraception continued to be practised to the mutual benefit of man and wife. The point remains nevertheless that in inter-war France there was no lack of signs to indicate the survival of an essentially patriarchal social order.

Chapter VII
THE SOCIAL IMPACT OF WAR: WORKING-CLASS WOMEN

JOHN Williams, writing of the effect of French women's massive participation in munitions work during the First World War, states that, 'for the great majority of France's women, as for those of Britain, 1915 was a year of revolution and liberation'.[1] Such a view is a faithful echo of that of many contemporaries who expressed their belief that in replacing absent male workers women had conquered for themselves a new destiny in the labour force. Although the sight of the *ouvrière* was hardly a novelty in 1914, what was new was to find women workers in large numbers outside the traditionally feminine sectors of the work force, such as domestic service, the clothing industry and textiles. Here, it was felt, was a transformation tantamount to a social revolution.[2] A measure of the working woman's elevated status was the allegedly astronomical wages which they were supposed to be paid for war work. Spokesmen for the depressed *rentier* class commented bitterly on the extravagance with which the new rich working-class women were able to indulge themselves, while the honest bourgeois housewife struggled to make ends meet.[3]

The perspective of the present chapter differs radically from that just outlined. Certainly, as we shall see in the next section, contemporaries were not wrong to point out that the war was responsible for the creation of an entirely new female labour force between 1914 and 1918. But to judge from the evidence of women's contact with the munitions factories, one may well want to question whether warwork was the uplifting or life-enhancing experience which patriotic and feminist propaganda made it out to be. On closer inspection, the material rewards of participation, as calculated in terms of either wage increases or the enactment of social legislation, turn out to be meagre enough. Furthermore, despite important strike movements among women workers in the clothing industry and in the munitions factories, little evidence can be adduced to show that women emerged from the war with a new commitment to militant syndicalism. In short, one can argue plausibly that the war, while leaving some permanent impact upon the pattern of female employment with respect to the kind of jobs available to women, neither engendered a new attitude to work among working women nor raised the status of 'feminine' labour.

131

The new female work force

The initial effect of the outbreak of war was to throw large numbers of women out of work, with Paris, as the centre of the luxury goods industry, particularly hard hit.[4] But as industry revived under the pressure of the need to increase production for the continuation of what seemed to be a war with no end in sight, more and more women eventually found themselves employed in the war factories. As early as March 1915, a resolution passed by the Chamber of Deputies called on the government 'to utilise the feminine labour force to replace the military labour force wherever possible'. In July 1916 this became official government policy, adopted in a circular of the Under-secretary of State for Armaments of 20 July 1916, with the result that the recruitment of women into the labour force became general.[5]

By 1917 almost every conceivable kind of job was being done by women.[6] In industries where they had already been employed in large numbers before the war, for example food, they continued to be taken on to do other jobs which had hitherto been done by men. In newer industries, such as chemicals, the scarcity of labour was also met as far as possible with female workers, although it was recognised that here there were still some tasks for which women were unsuited (for instance, work in oil refineries and in the manufacture of tannic extracts). On the other hand, women were busily employed in soap works, explosives factories and drug factories as well as in gas works. Transport, especially in Paris, was another industry invaded by women in unprecedented numbers. As from 8 August 1914, the Prefect of the Seine authorised the employment of women as conductresses and as drivers. Both the Métro and the railway companies began to employ women as guards or as platform controllers, while on the tramways the uniformed conductress was to become a permanent 'Parisian silhouette'.[7] On the railway networks the percentage of women rose from 8% in 1914 to 13% in 1919.[8]

But it was, of course, for their work in the war factories themselves that women's employment provoked most comment from contemporaries. In France, out of 1,580,459 workers in the war factories, the female component of the labour force rose to 362,879 – that is almost a quarter.[9] In the Paris region, which accounted for about two-fifths of all French war production, women constituted about one third of the labour force in the metal industry.[10] Altogether, some 684,000 women worked in armaments factories at some stage of the war – an impressive figure, even if a smaller total than in Britain, where a million women were eventually mobilised for munitions work.[11] The importance of this contribution has never been in doubt. It was appreciated not least by the military authorities: Joffre, for example, claimed that if women in the war factories had ceased their labours, then France would have lost the war.[12]

The vast majority of the women who made up this labour force in the war factories had no previous comparable experience in industry. For the most part, they were women who either had never worked at all or who had experience of work only outside the industrial sector. After these, the second largest category consisted of women who had quit their jobs in textiles, the clothing industry and other 'feminine' occupations in order to take up war work. Although this point cannot be documented from any comprehensive set of statistics, a number of smaller enquiries give a reasonably clear picture of what was taking place. The most helpful of these is a questionnaire sent out by the Committee on Female Labour* at the Ministry of Armaments in February 1918 to a number of firms who between them employed more than 10,000 women in their war factories.[13] In asking the industrialists what use they would have for their women workers once the war was over, the inquiry also requested information about their backgrounds. A few firms were unable (or unwilling) to reply: Citroën, by far the largest employer of female labour in the survey with 5322 women, did not complete this section of the questionnaire. But other employers were more helpful, even when they could not give precise figures. Thus the General Electrical Company or Orleans, which employed 2400 women, indicated that most had come from a background in commercial professions; while the Beges Paperworks, which had a temporary war factory at Lancey in the Isère where fifty-six women were employed, suggested that the overwhelming majority had previously been housewives. Among the firms which gave specific figures, the Schneider Company which employed ninety women in its two Paris factories stated that none of their workers had any experience of similar employment: twenty of them had worked in other industries, but the other seventy were complete newcomers to industrial work. Likewise, of the 280 women employed by the Decazeville Iron Works, only forty-six had previously worked in the metals industry, while 234 came from a totally non-industrial background. The Taragnat Metal Works in the Loire declared that forty-two out of its forty-four women employees had no previous experience of the industry.

The replies to the questionnaire of the Committee on Female Labour are confirmed by the findings of other enquiries. One private survey carried out in 1917 in a munitions factory employing forty-one women in the process of boring could count only four machine operators and twenty others with any experience of work in factories: the rest were

* This Committee was attached to the Ministry of Munitions and was made up of forty-five people, only ten of whom were women, including politicians, bureaucrats, doctors, academics and a handful of trade unionists. It was supposed to monitor the whole range of problems connected with women's war work.

housewives, apart from one corset-maker and one florist. In the hardening workshop, out of thirty-nine women workers, twenty-nine had been housewives, one a domestic servant, another a gimpler, one a finisher, one a white-collar worker and only the remaining six had any previous factory experience. Of the 337 women on the finishing lathes, 120 had previously been factory workers, while the others included one nurse, sixty-six domestic servants, six trimmers, sixty-eight house-wives and forty-six white-collar workers.[14] In another survey of a shell factory in Lyons employing 4473 women workers (almost 50% of the labour force), only sixteen women had ever operated machines and were likely to have encountered work comparable to the fabrication of shells.[15] These results are consistent with what we know about trends in the female labour force generally. An investigation conducted by the Ministry of Labour into 41,475 establishments which before the war employed 454,642 women, revealed that in July 1918 these firms now employed 533,523 women. Within this general expansion, the increase in the number of women in the metal industry was remarkable, rising from 17,731 in the pre-war period to 119,966 in July 1918, an increase of some 650%. At the same time, numbers in the clothing industry dropped from 98,971 to 90,191. In textiles the decline was from 183,881 to 169,814.[16] Evidently many women in traditional 'feminine' jobs had been attracted into war work, where they were joined by many others without any previous industrial experience.

It was this massive influx of women from non-industrial back-grounds into the war factories which persuaded contemporary observers that some kind of social revolution was well under way. C Duplomb wrote in the *Rennaissance Politique et Parlementaire*:

> Everything gives one to believe that the female labour force will become more general, since experience has shown that women can do tasks which one would never have thought of giving them before the war.[13]

Even in the syndicalist press a writer such as Pierre Hamp saw fit to warn male workers that they would have to come to terms with the new reality of women's increasing participation in industry, despite the unpalatable fact that in the short-term this might allow industrialists to hold down men's wages.[18] This new departure looked all the more decisive with reports from employers of satisfactory returns from their women workers. Industrialists found that the best results were to be obtained by not giving them tasks which involved too much physical force: where they had to engage in the fabrication of heavy pieces or simple labouring their output was considerably less than that of men. But where they were able to specialise in detail, working on tasks which required delicacy and lightness of touch, their performance was generally equal, if not superior, to men's, for instance in sorting and cutting in explosives factories.[19] A survey carried out by the *Union des Métaux*, the journal of the Metalworkers Federation, confirmed this assessment, stressing that in many jobs women's output was identical to men's, although the wages they received were considerably lower.[20] In many eyes equal work if not equal pay was an accomplished fact.

The experience of war work

Proponents of the view that women derived substantial benefits from their contribution to the war effort rarely point out that enthusiasm for their participation was not universally shared among contemporaries. Most often, the tributes to their endeavours were paid by patriotic propagandists, zealous to create the impression of a united nation dedicated exclusively to ensuring the defeat of the enemy.[21] A rather different picture emerges if we turn to the views of male trade unionists and of women workers themselves. From their standpoint, war work looked more like a disaster, submitted to only under duress and intended to last only for the duration of the war itself.

That male syndicalist leaders should have reservations about the employment of women in the war factories is hardly surprising. As we saw in Chapter I, many regarded female labour as a threat to their own position vis-à-vis their employers. In France as in Great Britain the massive expansion of women workers in the munitions factories confronted them with the problem of 'dilution' – the substitution of unskilled or semi-skilled women for skilled men. The replacement of male workers during the war was all the more reprehensible in already anti-feminist syndicalist eyes in that it was female labour which allowed male comrades to be sent off to the slaughter in the trenches. Merrheim, secretary of the Metalworkers Federation, stated this explicitly: 'The aim of intensifying the female labour force entails the consequence of sending men to the slaughter – women ought not to engage in overproduction'.[22] Quite apart from the threat to their own interests and safety, however, male syndicalists expressed genuine concern for the plight of their female colleagues who were often required to labour long and hard at heavy chores which seemed beyond their strength. As F Corcos wrote in *L'Information Ouvrière et Sociale*, the women themselves had not sought this so-called 'liberty' of work, and although they struggled heroically to fulfil their obligations, they knew well enough and openly admitted that they were made for another kind of destiny.[23] Far from being 'emancipated', another syndicalist writer pointed out, women were forced to do all the dirtiest and most menial jobs:

The emancipated woman. But you don't see her at the entrance or the exit of factories, head lowered, shoulders bent, like her male comrade, as if crushed by the filthy skies and the horizons of tar and soot around the explosives works, where she makes you afraid, with her hands and face turned yellow, her colourless hair and the corpse-like look which the handling of explosives gives her.[24]

The author of this article failed to see any process of emancipation. On the contrary, male comrades wept to see the women go off to the factories to be overworked and exploited.

A survey conducted by the Metalworkers Federation deepens this black impression of the condition of women munitions workers.[25] Reports from the local *syndicats* showed that the most common complaint was overwork; the Seine Union of Engineers claimed that women were being forced to do jobs which men would refuse. At Saint-Juéry their night-shift was exhausting. Finishing at 4 am, they had only a few hours' rest because of the need to attend to household chores; they thus returned to work inadequately rested, which gave rise to the numerous accidents and the large number of incorrectly made shells. Other potent sources of grievance were excessively severe discipline and abuses of authority. One woman on night-shift, having finished about 5 am and fallen asleep, was awakened by a brutal kick from her foreman. Informed of the incident, the management took no action, and the foreman continued to show the same attitude towards women workers. Alfred Rosmer summed up the findings of the metalworkers' inquiry in this way:

> Shameful exploitation of children and women, who are treated without consideration, like cheap and plentiful material: night work running to twelve consecutive hours, exhausting tasks etc., conditions which recall the most inhuman practices of the beginning of the Industrial Revolution. They are repeating themselves a century later, under the cover of the democratic war and of the 'Sacred Union'.[26]

The view that work in the war factories took a terrible toll of the health of women workers was by no means confined to the syndicalist press. Even right-wing nationalists were prepared to concede that war work was more likely to bring suffering than liberation, although attempts were made to romanticise the privations of the working woman, as in a fictitious tale published in the *Revue Hebdomadaire*, in which a young girl works herself to death and thus makes the ultimate sacrifice on behalf of the *patrie*.[27] But what lends much more substance to the syndicalist allegations is the testimony of women workers themselves. A petition from the women workers at the Dion factory to Merrheim begged him to take up their cause and described the intolerable fatigue from which they suffered at work:

> Many of us can't sleep, so great are the sufferings we endure and feel in our arms and in our stomachs from this overwork, at the end of our laborious day or night of work

. . . In support of our claims, we can point out that a good number of new employees ask to leave after one night or one or two days, declaring that they don't want to destroy their health doing this slave labour.[28]

At the Wilcoq-Regnault works, of the team involved in a strike on 6 November 1916 (twelve women and ten skilled men), only one woman had been in the factory for as long as six months. She added that her right arm and right hand felt as if they were paralysed and that she had to follow a course of treatment prescribed by her doctor.[29] Instability, in fact, seems to have been a major characteristic of the female labour force in the war factories. A trade union committee concerned with action against the exploitation of women protested that nothing was being done to look into the complaints which they lodged, while their recommendation of a system of three eight-hour shifts was likewise ignored by industrialists. Instead, said their report, women were being allocated to tasks beyond their strength or to dirty, dangerous jobs without the provision of adequate protection. Even one week's work was too much for some.[30] This inability to cope with the physical demands of war work was also noticed by non-trade union commentators, such as Paul Strauss, a politician with a long-standing interest in problems of public health, and Baroness Brincard, wife of the President of the Crédit Lyonnais bank. Mme Brincard cited a factory of the 15e *arrondissement* where only ten women were left out of several hundreds who had started work there seven or eight months previously.[31] Many women thus voted with their feet against the notion that liberation was to be obtained by finding employment in a munitions factory.

Inquiries by the Ministry of Labour inspectorate reinforce the impression of large-scale exploitation. In a survey of 784 factories employing 653,124 workers, of whom 256,992 were women, it was found that in 209 establishments the length of the working day was greater than ten hours in 1916, although this was true of only 155 establishments by 1917. Work was usually done in either one or two shifts, only very rarely in three. At the beginning of the war those on single shift work had normally had to work an 11-12 hour day; by 1917 the average was down to ten hours. In 1916 the proportion of establishments working double shifts of between 10-11 hours was 40%; in 1917 this was down to 20%. But if the length of the working day tended to shorten the longer the war went on, weekly days of rest tended to become more rare. In 1916 the inspectors estimated that on average most women were free on two Sundays a month. With the prolongation of hostilities, industrialists generally cut back on rest hours, limiting them to one day a month (usually Sunday).[32]

The Committee on Female Labour had grave reservations about the night work done by women, which had been increased from the beginning of the war in order to maintain and intensify production. On its strong recommendation, a ministerial circular of 8 July 1916 set out certain limitations on the employment of women at night, banning it to girls under eighteen and making it exceptional and temporary for those aged between eighteen and twenty-one. Ten hours was to be the maximum for all other women workers.[33] An inquiry of June 1917 was instituted to see if these regulations were enforced. 787 establishments were investigated, employing 164,267 women, of whom 58,784 (35.78%) did night work. 1576 (2.68%) of the night workers were girls aged between sixteen and eighteen. In 163 out of the 787 establishments (20.7%) the duration of night work was more than ten hours. In forty-four establishments the night-shift workers worked longer hours than the day-shift workers. The Committee on Female Labour was prepared to accept that these figures represented an improvement, but it reiterated its demand that all girls under eighteen be banned from night work and that the upper limit of ten hours work should in no case be exceeded.[34] Nevertheless, derogations were still likely to be forthcoming for establishments which worked for the National Defence. A decision by the Minister of Armaments in June 1917 forbade the employment of girls under sixteen in the steel works of Firminy, but permitted those over sixteen to be used on the grounds that a 50% reduction in output would result otherwise.[35] At Marseilles, the inspector recommended a temporary derogation for a mechanical constructor who made shells for the *Service des Forges* and needed six women to work on the night shift.[36]

It would seem, therefore, that the statistical evidence goes far towards confirming many of the allegations made by critics of women's war work. In this respect, the figures for industrial accidents involving women are a clear vindication of the charge that their work was not only excessively arduous but also highly dangerous. In 1917 there were some 69,606 reported accidents, of which fifty-nine were fatal, 756 resulted in permanent incapacitation, 67,123 led to temporary incapacity of more than four days while the consequences of the other 1638 were not known.[37] Despite the scale of the problem it was not taken seriously enough by the authorities. Statistics were assembled for different regions but the wider issues they raised were not adequately explored. They provided no basis for the formulation of remedies. The Committee on Female Labour pressed in vain for the investigation of establishments where casualties were particularly heavy, with both day- and night-shifts kept under close scrutiny and accidents studied by the hour, so that perhaps a relationship could be established between accidents and the maximum and minimum points on a curve of fatigue. It also wanted to know which workers were most affected by accidents

– those with or without previous industrial experience.[38] Without knowing the answers to these questions, one may be allowed to conclude that thousands of women must have been relieved to exchange the dangers of industrial life for the comparative safety and tranquility of the home. Far from emancipating women, war work convinced many that such labour was beyond their endurance. This at least was the view of Marcelle Capy, a journalist of bourgeois origins who resigned from the syndicalist newspaper *La Bataille Syndicaliste* in order to take a job in a munitions factory herself and who later co-founded the pacifist and feminist newspaper *La Vague*. On the basis of her own experience she concluded that women had been asked to do tasks for which they simply were not fitted by nature; in future she wanted to see them employed in offices rather than in factories.[39]

The rewards of participation

Viewed in the light of how women actually experienced war work in the munitions factories, the benefits of participation in the war effort were not always readily apparent. Yet by catapulting the question of female labour into the forefront of national priorities the war did lead to some improvements in the condition of working women. The war created a situation where the public was conscious of women's work as never before and where the women themselves could press their claims from a unique bargaining point, knowing how much the country's survival depended on their industrial effort. The opening up of so many new fields of employment to women gave rise to a new mobility in the female labour force and often changed the terms on which they had to confront employers. Doubtless, measures to ameliorate the material situation of working women would have come about anyway, but without the war they would never have become a reality as they did and when they did.

It was between 1914 and 1918, in the first instance, that women's wages rose from the barely subsistence levels of the pre-war period. At first, however, wages fell drastically (until mid-1915) and it was 1916 before any sizable increases in the pay of working women could be noted.[40] For those women who had the fortitude to bear the exhaustion and the dangers of munitions work, there were some compensations, though the legends which grew up of the fabulous sums earned by the *munitionnettes* were wildly inaccurate. The government continually showed itself to be fairly sensitive to the wage demands of women in the war factories and saw to it that regular rises in their rates of pay took place. By 1918 a skilled woman worker in Paris could earn 0.90 francs an hour and an unskilled woman about 0.85 francs; in the provinces these figures were 0.84 francs and 0.80 francs respectively.[41] A decree of 17 January 1917 on conciliation and arbitration stipulated that as regards piece-work done by women, their rates should not be less than men's for identical work. If part of the work had to be done by men the total value of the job was not to be inferior to that which an all-male team would have cost. [42]

On the other hand, several factors were at work to keep the wages of women munitions workers lower than they should have been. Certain industrialists, particularly in the smaller establishments, refused to implement the fixed rate (the *tarif*), while others tried to cheat their workers by manipulating the piece-rates. In some war factories, the wage was made up of so many different elements that it was virtually impossible for a woman to work out how much pay she was entitled to. Despite the decree of 17 January 1917, women nowhere took home the same wages as their male colleagues. It was always argued that the work done by women was never identical to that of men and required the use of much less skill. As we have seen, there was much truth in this argument, for women were set to work after a minimal amount of formal training and usually had to work in a team under the supervision of a skilled male colleague. [43] In consequence the *tarif* always stipulated a rate for men and a rate for women. The gap between these may have narrowed in the course of the war (in the metal industry in Paris a discrepancy of 45% in 1913 was down to 16% in 1916), but invariably women were left at a disadvantage. [44]

In relative terms, it was the lowest paid – those women who had been on starvation wages before 1914 – who did best on the wages front. This was particularly the case in the clothing industry, where a Parisian dressmaker who earned 3fr.50 a day in 1911 could hope to earn 16 francs a day by 1921. [45] Thanks to their successful strike action in the spring of 1917, which we shall consider in detail in the next section, women workers in the clothing industry were able to establish a minimum wage for different categories of worker in each profession. With the laws of supply and demand now operating very much in their favour after the exodus of the war years, dressmakers and others were in a position to drive hard bargains in negotiations with employers, and resorted to industrial action when necessary. [46] It should be stressed that these increases were not brought about by governmental intervention but by trade union action on the part of the workers themselves.

The one group of workers whose earnings were raised by direct government intervention was that of domestic workers. Probably the most unfortunate victims of exploitation in all the labour force they earned on average 0.15 francs – 0.20 francs an hour in 1914. [47] Although the appalling conditions under which they laboured had not gone without observation or protest, no pre-war government enacted legislation to alleviate their situation. Various bills had been introduced in the Chamber of Deputies, first by Albert de Mun, then by Viviani and in 1910, by Honoré. Finally, in 1911, a bill designed to apply only to the clothing industry was introduced and eventually passed by the Chamber in 1913. This provided the basis for the law of 10 July 1915 which established a carefully controlled minimum wage of between 0.25 and 0.40 francs an hour. Despite its pre-war origins, this measure should be seen as a product of the war-time situation, which permitted a legislative triumph over the powerful and intransigent employers' lobby.[48] In practice, however, the law proved difficult to implement. Although the inspectorate readily investigated complaints, individual women workers rarely began actions against their employers, preferring to submit to exploitation rather than risk losing their work. To be successful, complaints usually had to be initiated by professional *syndicats*.[49] Even if striking increases in wages can be observed (in the Bouches-du-Rhône a machinist earning 0.49 francs in 1917 got 0.87 francs in 1918 – a rise of 77%), pay remained very low.[50] A further problem was that the agreed minimum wage in the same profession might vary significantly from region to region. Thus in sewing the department of Meurthe-et-Moselle guaranteed 1fr.50 in 1925, but that of the Vosges only 0.75 francs. Moreover, in three departments no minimum whatsoever could be established.[51]

In the beginning, the law can rightly be criticised as too narrow, applying only to domestic workers in the clothing industry. But of course, this included a lot of women and, more important, it set a precedent which eventually led to its extension to other branches of domestic industry.[52] A decree of 10 August 1922 made it apply to items accessory to the clothing industry, even when the finished product might be destined for completion outside that industry.[53] Perhaps the law's two most serious shortcomings were that the fines imposed on employers were not always sufficiently severe to act as a deterrent and that domestic workers could not claim compensation for industrial accidents.[54]

In general, the pay rises which were awarded during or just after the war represent a considerable advance on the miserable pittances that were so common in the years before. Yet the extent of the progress should not be exaggerated, since it was tempered by two serious qualifications. The first was the steep rise in the cost of living, which did much to obliterate the absolute value of the new salaries. An accurate assessment of the rate of inflation for the whole of France is an impossibility, since regional variations were so great, the Nord and Alsace being the dearest regions and the west the cheapest. But according to the calculations of Lucien March, the cost of living probably doubled between 1914 and 1918 and had virtually quadrupled by 1921.[55] The second qualification touches on a problem which has still to be resolved to this day. The demand for equal pay for equal work never became a reality. The gap between men's wages and those of women closed in the course of the war, especially in the metal industry where a discrepancy of 45% in 1913 was reduded to 16% in Paris in 1916, but it subsequently rose to 21% in 1921 and even reached 40% in Toulouse and 37% at Le Havre.[56] It was 1946 before a French government committed itself to the principle of equal pay for equal work, and even then its existence remained theoretical. In 1964, female manual workers received only 69% of the wages paid to men. Exhortations from the Commission for Social Affairs of the EEC to implement article 119 of the Treaty of Rome (which enshrines the principle of equal pay for equal work) have so far been slow to produce any concrete results.[57]

Higher wages were not the only benefit which working women derived from participation in the war effort. A gain at least as significant as more money was a reduction in the length of the working day. The 'English Week' had long been desired but it was obtained only by recourse to industrial action during the war. To begin with, workers themselves had been hostile to the idea, since the initiative originally came from the Chamber of Commerce – an employers' institution. By 1913, however, opinion had changed and an enquiry by the Labour Office established that a high proportion of working women favoured the reform whereas most of the objections were made by the bosses' organisations. Pre-war attempts to enact legislation in the Chamber of Deputies failed and victory was obtained only after the determined strike of the Parisian dressmakers and their colleagues in the clothing industry in 1917. By the law of 11 June 1917, the 'English Week' was introduced in the clothing industry, though strong pressure had to be exerted by the unions to ensure that it was implemented.[58]

Before the war ended, the demand for the 'English Week' was overtaken by the cry for the eight-hour day. First adopted in France by working-class leaders under the Second Empire, this did not become an important claim until 1888, but even then it remained unrealistic before the ten-hour day had been won. By 1912, Vaillant and other socialist leaders were pressing for ten hours to be reduced to eight, but a motion to this effect in the Chamber was easily defeated. The war put further discussion out of the question. Once hostilities had been concluded, however, it was inevitable that the question would be raised again with renewed urgency. In the world that was to emerge from the chaos and destruction of the war, men looked for more social justice than had existed in the old order and the Peace of Versailles encouraged the adoption of the eight-hour day or the 48-hour week.[59] Under pressure from the CGT, and following the example set by other countries, the French government enacted the law of 23 April 1919 by which each industry was left to find its own way of implementing the principle of the eight-hour day. [60] Thus in dressmaking, agreement was reached on 17 May 1919 after a strike so that the working week was fixed at 48 hours, to be divided into five days of nine hours with three hours' work on Saturdays. [61] Milliners generally preferred to have a similar working week, although an enquiry of 1922 showed that some 22% favoured a system of six days of eight hours. [62] Once again, however, since the law left each industry free to determine its own set of rules, millions of workers, men as well as women, did not benefit from its provisions. Successive governments were unwilling to push employers into complying with the law since ministers like Loucheur feared for its effects on national production. [63]

In addition to higher wages and shorter working hours the war gave rise to a number of welfare measures which benefited working women. Before the First World War the French state had not been prepared to provide for the welfare of workers in the way that Germany, say, had created an elaborate system of social security. French thinking continued to be dominated by the concept of assistance, by which the state undertook to provide help to the needy – medical aid and care of children, the aged and the infirm – provided their indigence could be established. Mutual aid societies were the main working-class safeguard against poverty, though it is true that a number of social services were established to give them support (notably compensation for accidents at work, as prescribed by the law of 8 April 1898, and a pension scheme for workers and peasants, introduced in 1910). Such social legislation, however, did not commit the French state to a new, more positive role in the promotion of welfare, and despite the introduction of several measures during and immediately after the war, this remained the position in the post-war years. [64]

An innovation that can be attributed to the war was the introduction of *dames surintendantes* in 1917. These were a French version of the 'lady superintendents' observed by a delegation of French working women which toured some English war factories at the invitation of Christabel Pankhurst. Their main tasks were to concern themselves with all aspects of the physical and moral welfare of women workers by giving counsel and assistance and by ensuring that all regulations relating to the protection of female labour were strictly observed. [65] Feminine hygiene was another major preoccupation. The Committee on Female Labour pressed for the setting up of refectories in factories to ensure that meals were taken under hygienic conditions and by an *arrêté* of 10 August 1917 the government responded by making funds available to firms prepared to take the initiative in this field. Special canteens, however, continued to be run primarily by charitable organisations. A decree of 23 October 1917 laid down that seats had to be provided wherever it was possible for a woman to work seated and in all other cases benches had to be available for use at certain specified times. Other measures tried to eliminate health hazards from, say, toxic poisoning in chemical factories, and accidents caused by dangerous machines. To fight against venereal disease, dispensaries were also set up in some factories employing large numbers of women to allow them to consult a doctor after work – a facility which was apparently much appreciated. [66]

On the whole the war did not promote a far-reaching programme of welfare legislation to improve the lot of working women. But at least every effort was made by the factory inspectorate to guarantee that such legislation as did exist was rigorously enforced. Allegations in a newspaper such as *Humanité* were diligently investigated, and in the process often shown to be inaccurate. For instance, in November 1924 it was alleged that the Gervais factory was managed by a 'brute' who made women work nine and ten hours a day and dismissed them for the most trivial offences. [67] Because he employed two negresses as foremen, the other workers were supposed to have to work under conditions of excessive heat in the summer on the grounds that this was good for the black women's skin. This latter charge was completely refuted in the inspector's report, which also established that hygiene in the factory was good. It was true that the women workers did have to work hard, but since they were not covered by the terms of the law of 1919 on the eight-hour day their hours were not illegal. Also, if they succeeded in finishing a certain amount of work, they were allowed to go home early. [68] Elsewhere it was the inspectorate itself which brought to light violations of the social legislation regulating women's labour. In a chemicals factory in the south of France an inspector discovered exploitation on a scale such as he had never seen. Women were made to do heavy manual tasks and to work night-shifts in contravention of the law of 1893 in an atmosphere of toxic fumes and fearful heat. His intervention, approved by the Minister of Labour, put a stop to all of these abuses. [69] In general, the Minister turned a deaf ear to employers' pleas to be allowed to let women do night work. A glass factory, which had been able to obtain a derogation for the war years, was informed that this could not be extended to peacetime. Proceedings were started against the management when an inspector visited the factory during the night of 7 July 1920 and found three teenage girls and four women all employed on the night-shift. [70] Permission was granted only in very exceptional circumstances, as at the Loriol factory, which alone in France made certain salts useful for treating tuberculosis. [71] Altogether, the vigilance of the inspectorate did much to raise the post-war condition of women workers far above the level of abject misery and exploitation that had persisted throughout the nineteenth century.

The commitment to militancy

Having reviewed the ways in which the material situation of working women was improved by participation in the war effort, we must consider, finally, whether these advances were accompanied by a change of attitude on the part of women themselves towards their position in the labour force. Can it be argued that women workers emerged from their experience of work during the war with a new spirit of militancy or sense of syndical solidarity?

Some of the evidence seems to point in this direction. For the first two years of the war, French labour relations reflected the harmony engendered by the ideal of the 'Sacred Union'. From the autumn of 1916, however, ripples of discontent produced sporadic strike action until in May-June 1917 a great wave of strikes was unleashed in a number of different industries, including the munitions factories. After further intermittent outbreaks in late 1917 and early 1918, the climax of industrial unrest came in the form of the massive strike campaign of Spring 1918, orchestrated by certain syndicalist militants in the hope of imposing peace and social revolution by means of a general strike. Before the war ended further strikes broke out in September and October 1918, notably in the Parisian clothing industry. These movements have been extensively studied by Mme Annie Kriegel in her dauntingly impressive work *Aux origines du communisme français*. But perhaps because she is mainly interested in the degree to which these strikes were politically motivated, Mme Kriegel does not dwell extensively on the fact that some of the most active and important participants in several of the most serious strikes in France between 1914 and 1918 were to be found among women workers.

This new militancy, contrasting sharply with women's pre-war syndical activity, was most evident in the clothing industry. It was here, in one of the traditionally 'feminine' industries, that the ferment of Spring 1917 was first apparent, affecting the dressmakers to start with and then spreading throughout the garment industry. At the same time, the strikes which took place in the war factories, lasting until July 1917, were due for the most part to women workers. One study calculates that between 1915 and 1918, some 50,000 women were involved in strikes in the war factories of the department of the Seine.[72] That militant action should occur in these two industries was a direct result of the impact of the war on the female labour force in each case. As we have seen, large numbers of women deserted the clothing industry in order to find better paid jobs in munitions; consequently, within the clothing industry, once trade began to revive, skilled labour was at a premium and dressmakers and milliners found themselves in a strong position to bargain with their employers. With wages still lagging behind prices, they had every incentive to adopt a militant stance by

1917.[73] As for women in the war factories, despite their relatively high pay, the harsh conditions which have already been described were sufficient to foster considerable discontent. Above all, the steep rise in the cost of living hit all women hard. Young single girls in the clothing industry who had never been paid a living wage began to agitate for fairer remuneration for their labour. Married women in the munitions factories, desperately trying to provide for themselves and their families while their husbands were away at the Front, were driven to strike for a wage that would support themselves and their children. To the Head of the *Renseignements Généraux* at the Prefecture of Police the fact that women were 'notoriously at a disadvantage from the point of view of wages' went far towards explaining their massive participation in the strike movement in the first half of 1917.[74]

In 1915 the plight of the woman worker in the clothing industry was extremely serious. Bosses paid the lowest possible wages, the so-called 'war-rate'.[75] *Humanité* drew attention to other abuses: a certain Mme Protat, whose workers made earth sacks, would not provide heating in her establishment and was prepared to pay only 1fr.40 for finished articles, with a deduction of 50 centimes for every needle broken. A woman who should have received 5 francs might thus be paid only 3fr.50.[76] Discontent with such exploitation had been building up for some time before it exploded in the general movement of May–June 1917. In January 1917 the women of the Maison Agnès asked for a rise of 1 franc a day. When the management retracted after agreeing, reducing their offer to 0.50 francs for first hands and 0.25 for seconds, the girls went on strike.[77] Another strike took place in the Maison Bernard, where some workers struck successfully for the restoration of pre-wartime rates.[78] Dressmakers generally gave their approval to agitation conducted by male militants such as Millerat and Rey for wage increases to keep pace with the rise in the cost of living.[79]

It was finally a dispute at the Maison Jenny on the Champs Elysées which launched the general outbreak of strikes throughout the clothing industry.[80] On 11 May 1917, two women workers were told that they were to be made redundant on Saturday afternoons. Refusing to accept this, they went on strike and called on the others to join them in demanding a real 'English Week', without any reduction in their weekly wage packets. In addition they demanded a cost of living bonus of 1 franc a day. By the following day the conflict had spread to most fashion houses and by 14 May about 200 women were on strike. According to *Humanité* they were all in buoyant spirits and created a kind of carnival atmosphere in their street demonstrations:

Mid-day. On the grands boulevards a long cortège is advancing. It's the Parisian dressmakers with their blouses fragrant with lilacs and lilies of the valley: they run, they jump, they sing, they laugh, and yet it is neither the feast of St Catherine nor of mid-Lent: it is the war. [81]

Laborious negotiations were opened at the Ministry of the Interior where Malvy received both the workers' and the bosses' delegations, at first separately and then together. On the workers' side the male leaders, Millerat and Rey, were ready to accept the Minister's word that a law would be passed to make the 'English Week' general in all fashion houses. This offer, however, was not good enough for the women workers, about 10,000 of whom from some thirty houses were now on strike. At a mass meeting, to great applause, a young girl worker insisted that they should stay out until the 'English Week' had been conceded. [82] The head of the bosses' union, M Aine, seemed amiable and anxious for a settlement, agreeing to the principle of the 'English Week' and prepared to concede a cost of living bonus of 0.75 francs. On this basis, the dressmakers agreed to end their strike on 19 May – but at the last minute M Aine's terms were repudiated by the other bosses. The strike therefore went on, gathering increased momentum as it was joined by milliners, corset-makers and girl workers from shirt-making and furs. In the face of this determination, the employers reluctantly gave in on 22 May. The dressmakers' demands for a cost of living rise of 1 franc a day, the 'English Week' and no victimisations over the strike were met in full and they returned to work on 23 May. [83]

But the general agitation in other corporations did not die down. On the contrary, the strike movement continued to swell right through the rest of May and into June, spreading into the provinces. By 24 May the milliners had clarified their aims: 100 francs a month for top hands, 75 francs for seconds and 50 francs for small ones; a cost of living payment of 30 francs a month, and a special bonus for workers in houses which did not supply their employees with their mid-day meal. [84] In ready-made clothes the demands were for pre-war wages; a bonus of 1 franc a day; the retention of the nine-hour day; the abolition of fines for late arrival and of the necessity to provide one's own thread; and, inevitably, the 'English Week'. [85] The female personnel of a number of banks also began to join the movement, while a threat to strike by the temporary auxiliary women workers at the Ministry of Finance was taken sufficiently seriously for their demands to be met without recourse to militant action. [86] Women workers in the food industry and in cardboard and paper also became involved. [87] *Humanité* claimed that it was almost impossible to keep up their reports of industrial action, usually brought to a successful conclusion. [88]

The milliners proved to be every bit as intransigent as the dressmakers. Even when the bosses conceded almost all of their demands, certain women in high fashion stayed out until their precise

conditions were met.[89] Most interestingly, their stand was supported with admirable solidarity by the women workers of ready-made clothes: all agreed to give a contribution from their own wages to allow the women workers in high fashion to fight to the finish.[90] For the remainder of the war, it was the clothing industry generally which set the pace in strike activity among the female labour force. Victory in May-June 1917 did not spell the end of agitation. At the end of September 1917 trouble flared up among the male and female tailors for women, who for some time had been demanding the suppression of piecework, a minimum weekly wage of 90 francs and the application of the 'English Week'.[91] The dressmakers wanted the abolition of the strict discipline enforced in their workshops, double time for *veillées*, and a minimum wage for each category of worker.[92] Male and female cutters in men's ready-made clothes demanded the 'English Week', a minimum weekly wage of 75 francs and the application of the principle of equal pay for equal work.[93] Men and women workers in men's civilian ready-made clothes demanded the 'English Week', double time for any work which might have to be undertaken on Saturday afternoons, and a 25% rise for domestic workers, to compensate them for having to furnish their own materials.[94] Evidently, the success of the first strike movement had inspired the leaders to obtain the 'English Week' for all categories of work in the clothing industry. The police suggested that the main instigators of the dissension were outsiders – foreigners and professional revolutionaries.[95] There were even rumours that the agitation was the work of German *agents-provocateurs*; in some workshops it was whispered that the authorities were ready to have strikers shot down.[96] Such talk can be dismissed as having no foundation in reality. The strikes by the cutters and makers of ready-made clothes were over specific economic grievances. The workers were not wholly successful but most got at least some kind of pay rise.[97]

More agitation took place during March 1918, mainly among the makers of ready-made clothes. About 1200 came out on strike in support of a wage increase, having rejected the employers' offer of an extra 0.10 francs a day on top of their cost of living bonus. The dispute ended in compromise.[98] Far more significant, however, was the launching of a second great wave of strikes in the clothing industry in September-October 1918. The main source of the conflict was the soaring cost of living and consequently the widespread feeling that the beneficial effects of the award of 1917 had been wiped out.[99] In August the General Union of Clothing Workers of the Seine began to hold meetings to plan a campaign for a higher cost of living bonus – 3 francs a day was now thought to be an acceptable figure.[100] At the same time, concern was expressed about what to do about the diminution in the working day, in some cases to eight hours, which meant substantial cuts in weekly wages. [101] The syndicalist leaders were also conscious of the need to defend themselves against political smears, notably the charge that they were unpatriotic. [102] By mid-September, after a series of mass-meetings, women workers in the clothing industry were spoiling for another big strike to demonstrate their determination. [103] A proposal by Maréchal, the secretary of the Shirtmakers and Seamstresses Union, to wait to see what could be obtained by intervention by the Minister of Labour was rejected by an audience of 3,000 workers (most of them women) with cries of: 'We don't want to wait any more, we want a strike'. [104] Once again, reluctantly, syndicalist leaders were pushed into organising strike action by pressure from rank and file women workers. [105]

Once again the dressmakers took the lead. The strike began on 21 September and by 24 September 8000 workers had come out. Over twenty arrests were made for 'attempts at enticing', those in question being taken off for identity checks and then released. [106] The employers proposed to grant the 3 francs bonus if the workers returned to their places immediately, leaving other matters open to future negotiations. Some corporations were disposed to accept these conditions: the corset-workers and those of the Belle Jardinière, for instance, both went back to work. [107] The dressmakers, however, were intransigent on the issue of the eight-hour day, which they had come to see as the only viable solution to the problem of the reduction in working hours. [108] The Confédération Générale du Travail, having taken up their case, put it to Prime Minister Clemenceau that since the workers were producing as much in eight hours as they had formerly in ten, they not unreasonably wanted to receive the same wages. [109] After Clemenceau had told the employers' delegation that they would have to make sacrifices, the bosses agreed to offer a package which included the 3 francs bonus, the setting up of cheap restaurants and further talks. More corporations found these proposals acceptable and went back to work; but once more the women in high fashion, backed by those in embroidery, said they would return only when the employers gave in on the eight-hour day. This intransigence alarmed the male syndicalist leaders who had conducted the negotiations with the government and considered that they had made good progress. Jouhaux, secretary of the CGT, insisted that it was a mistake to think that the eight-hour day could be won as easily as the 'English Week'. Since it would require new methods of production and much study by the workers' and bosses' organisations, it could not simply be introduced overnight by ministerial decree. [110] A good number of dissenting voices were raised against him which urged the continuation of the strike and a similar attempt by Millerat, a top official in the clothing workers union, to persuade the women to resume work was decisively rejected, mainly as the result of the arguments of women militants.[111] Deadlock persisted and Millerat, almost in despair, was heard insinuating that the implacable stand of the women workers was due to sinister machinations by male revolutionaries from the railway and building unions.[112] It took a speech by Maréchal at another meeting two days later to convince the women that the whole question of the eight-hour day and its implications was to be discussed both nationally and internationally in the immediate future, and that no more was to be gained from the prolongation of the strike.[113] Once again, however, the *cousettes* had shown remarkable tenacity in holding out for a fortnight after others had accepted terms.[114]

The strikes of women in the clothing industry, on the whole, made a favourable impact on public opinion. Even the reactionary *Action Française* wrote complacently in 1917 about 'this pretty and short strike' while *L'Eclair* described it as a strike which was 'very rue de la Paix', characterised by 'style, gracefulness and smartness'. Strikes by women workers in the war factories, on the other hand, were regarded in a very different light. *L'Eclair* talked about 'treason' and *Le Temps* about 'a crime against the *patrie*'.[115] Both right-wing nationalists and the authorities were afraid that a cut in the production of munitions might affect the performance of French troops at the Front. They also suspected that the strikes might have a deeper political aim, namely to bring about an end to the war and to create a revolutionary situation out of the general confusion. What made the crisis seem all the more alarming was the outbreak of mutinies in the French army after the failure of the Nivelle offensive in spring of 1917. The possibility that a contagious defeatism could spread the disease of mutiny at the Front was not one which the police or the patriotic propagandists were slow to develop.

In fact it is unnecessary to resort to politics to explain the outbreak of the strike wave of 1917 among the female labour force in the war factories. Even before the mass movement of May–June 1917, there had been some protests about pay and conditions.[116] As in the clothing industry, the strike movement of 1917 was triggered off by a fairly trivial incident, namely the dismissal of five women workers from the Salmson establishment at Boulogne-Billancourt for absenting themselves without permission on Whit Monday.[117] Although these were not the only workers to have taken the day off, they were the only ones to be sacked and they therefore sought support among the 200 women employed at the Iris Lamp factory at Issy as well as among various unemployed women and washerwomen of the Boulogne area. Having unsuccessfully tried to persuade their former colleagues to come out in sympathy with them, the women then made their way to another aeroplane factory, Hanriot's, at Billancourt and rounded up 150 women workers (possibly against their will) who went with them to the Bureau du Travail. There a list of grievances was formulated, calling for an hourly wage of 1.50 francs, the 'English Week' and no work on Sundays – although the Hanriot workers repudiated these demands once they were able to return to work.[118]

At this point, according to the police report, certain outside elements began to move in on the strike and to egg on the women leaders. On 30 May, a crowd of about 1000 women arrived at the Salmson factory, with the five dismissed women at their head, one of them carrying a red flag. When they invaded the factory, the bosses reacted by sending everyone home, male and female, with the result that more workers joined the strikers in their attempts to generalise the stoppage in the area. Some 2500 women at the important Renault works downed their tools in sympathy and there began to develop an atmosphere charged with rumours and talk of intrigues. The *poilus*, it was said, would return as soon as the production of arms in munitions factories was ended. The butchers in Paris were alleged to be poisoning their meat. Outside the Renault factory, it was whispered that the whole strike movement was being led by Germans and strange cars and suspicious characters were seen (on investigation, however, these seem to have been a weird group of deaf and dumb friends 'with special morals', i.e. homosexuals).[119]

Alarm was aroused among the authorities because some women workers were heard to shout, 'Down with war!' and because a number of soldiers seemed to be prepared to associate themselves with the movement and even to share the anti-war sentiments.[120] A banner was seized which read on one side 'We want our *poilus*' and on the other 'We want the "English Week" '.[121] In front of the barracks at Reuilly, there were shouts of 'The draft-dodgers to the front and our husbands will come back' and 'Long live the *poilus*'.[122] Stories were put around that mutineers at the Front were on the point of coming back home to support their womenfolk and that in incidents at Saint-Etienne, 200 women had been shot down by colonial soldiers, since French troops would not obey the order to fire.[123] The Head of the Service des Renseignements Généraux was concerned that pacifist-minded individuals who had abstained from activity during the agitation of the *midinettes*, in the knowledge that they would have little influence 'in the relatively refined milieu of millinery and dressmaking', would now see opportunities to exploit the effervescence in the war factories.[124] For the most part, these elements belonged to the Committee of Syndicalist Defence (CDS), a section of the Committee for the Resumption of International Relations (CRRI), though there were others.[125] All of these agitators were men and according to the report, ready to throw their influence behind 'veritable revolutionary demonstrations on the public highway'.[126] Other foreigners were alleged to have tried to stir up the women not only to continue their strike but also to sabotage the factories and prevent soldiers leaving for the Front by picketing the Gare du Nord and the Gare de l'Est.[127]

Yet further inquiries into the origins and development of the strikes in the munitions factories soon reassured the authorities that the women strikers were not party to the defeatist campaign.[128] To begin with, none of the five dismissed women had any previous experience of political or syndical action. The police tried to belittle their motives, claiming that they were activated purely by discontent at their dismissal. Marie-Louise Pouchet, born in 1886, was married with one child. Her husband had been called up and since the beginning of the war she had been employed in munitions work. Her file made her out to be 'aggressive' and 'insolent' and one of the most ardent picketers. But the most that could be said against her was that she received at her home 'several individuals, apparently workmen, who are understood to be lovers'. Marguerite Testud, seven years younger and also married with one child and her husband mobilised (though he had 'disappeared'), was reckoned to be 'a not very serious or assiduous worker'. She also had numerous visits from soldiers and workers but she again could not be connected with any revolutionary organisations. Pauline Danton, yet another with a mobilised husband and one child, was the one seen carrying the red flag, but the police decided that probably this did not have any great significance. Her private conduct conformed to police notions of what was 'good'. The fourth, Lucie Richard, was the youngest, aged twenty-three and single, although she usually slept with her lover. She was thought to be anxious to get back to work. On the fifth woman, Lucie Porche, thirty-five, divorced and with two children the police had very little information. Among other ring-leaders was Caroline Martin, born in 1881, single and living with her mother. The police found it hard to account for the presence of such a respectable woman in a strike movement (she had a brother who was a journalist on the Catholic newspaper *La Croix*) and could only suggest that she was weak and easily led. Even more disconcerting was the presence of Louise Piat, a woman of about forty, whose husband was a prisoner-of-war and who was known to be of good character. By contrast, they were ready to believe anything about Louise Waternel, a widow of thirty-two, whom they described as an 'exaltée'. A former washerwoman now working for Renault, she had lived with a man before the war which made it perfectly comprehensible to the police why she should have been extremely active in the picketing.

Clearly, as far as the police were concerned, any deviation from the model of bourgeois marriage or any kind of questioning attitude to authority was tantamount to subversion of the state. Their files on the leading militants tell us little about the real character of the women concerned but a great deal about ruling-class paranoia at the threat of social disorder. What does emerge from the police reports, however, is the fact that, as in pre-industrial times, intolerable economic pressures could galvanise women into militant action, with the strike (or in the case of Glaswegian women in 1915, a rent strike) replacing the bread riot. The fact that so many of the principal strike leaders were breadwinners made dismissal from employment little short of a disaster. Had the police been endowed with a little more imagination, they would have understood why more or less mature and responsible women could display the militancy they did in demanding reinstatement. Significantly, agitation was most serious among the least well-paid workers,[129] though the participation in the movement of some women from establishments where pay was high (for example the Maisons Darracq and La Gallia at Suresnes) indicates that grievances among the female labour force were by no means confined to their financial remuneration but might relate also to questions of their material conditions or factory discipline.[130] In the end, therefore, it is hardly surprising that the Head of the Service of General Information concluded his report by repudiating suggestions that the *munitionnettes* were doing the work of the enemy: it was neither the Germans nor the Revolution which had stirred them into industrial action but rather, as with their comrades in the garment industry, the deteriorating economic situation.[131]

To be sure, the strikes did have their ugly side. In some places violence flared in the course of the confrontations, as at the Aéronautique factory, where two dismissed women workers led a movement to occupy the factory and intimidated other women workers who were not prepared to support them: force had to be used to expel the invaders from the premises.[132] Altogether, some 390 arrests were made over the course of the strike movement, and unlike those in the clothing industry, they resulted in prosecutions.[133] At certain establishments a more overtly political note did creep into the women's action, as at the Delaunay-Belleville factory where 2800 women came out because they thought it had become a refuge for draft-dodgers, and at some firms in Montreuil, Suresnes and the Pré St Gervais, where a handful of pacifist agitators received some encouragement from the ranks of women workers.[134] But in general the ferment subsided quickly. By 2 June almost all of the aviation factories were working at full strength, with the workers having accepted increases of between 0.10 francs and 0.15 francs an hour.[135] By 21 June all the troubles were over, their non-defeatist nature noted in bitter comments by committed pacifists, who probably underestimated their revolutionary potential precisely because they were strikes involving mainly women and their economic grievances. A disheartened soldier, writing on 27 May 1917, was under no illusion that there was any connection between the military and economic crises, observing that instead of asking for the 'English Week' and a pay rise women would have done better to demand peace. [136]

The non-revolutionary intentions of women strikers was clearly revealed in the Spring of 1918, when they kept their own demands separate from the movement built up by syndicalist militants to end the war by means of a general strike. Masterminded by the CDS, a body made up of pacifist anarcho-syndicalists whose imaginations had been fired by the success of the Bolshevik Revolution, the defeatist campaign of 1918 had been set in motion by violent agitations in the Loire area in December 1917. Following the arrest of Andrieu, secretary of the Metalworkers Union of Firminy, Péricat, secretary of the CDS organised demonstrations and protests which he hoped would escalate into a revolutionary general strike. When it broke, the wave of strikes in the metal industries of the Loire amounted, in the words of Annie Kriegel, to 'a mass political strike, an insurrectionary strike which awoke Blanquist echoes of the revolutionary appeal to the most authentic proletarian forces'. [137] Women workers, however, had nothing to do with the mounting of this campaign, though inevitably some got caught up in the general agitation. At St Etienne in May 1918 a procession of strikers consisting mainly of women and young men made its way to the station of Châteaucreux to prevent the departure of those of military age from the classes of 1910, 1911 and 1912. Another group of women and young girls clashed with mounted police when they carried banners and red flags to protest outside the Manufacture Nationale d'Armes. [138] Significant as these protests were as an indication of increasing war weariness among women and outrage at the operation of the conscription laws which attempted to recall the younger classes to the Front, it is difficult to see the mass involvement of women in a great concerted movement of disaffection. Likewise, the male revolutionaries failed to exploit the ferment in the clothing industry to their own ends, though not completely through want of trying. In September 1918 Sirolle of the railwaymen's union told the girls from dressmaking, furs and embroidery that the railwaymen were following their action with interest and approval, and that he was happy to put himself before them as one of those who were called 'defeatists'. Having tried to conjure up in their minds a picture of the horrors of war, he insisted that the real villains were not the draft-dodgers but the arms merchants who were making vast profits out of the misery of others. [139] His speech was greeted with loud applause, but it remained true nevertheless that at mass meetings of *midinettes* on strike it was rare to find speakers airing political rather than economic grievances.

In the metal industry, after May-June 1917 as before, the strike activity of women workers was prompted mainly by disputes over wages. In September 1917, there were flashes of militancy in the Clément and Farman aviation factories where 'the women workers seemed particularly agitated'.[140] Their demand for equal pay with male workers was also taken up at the Panhard and Renault factories but the protests subsided a week later.[141] In November 1917 all the 270 women employed by the Hispano-Suiza factory at Bois-Colombes stopped work in support of a pay claim and a cost of living bonus.[142] In December 250 women workers at the Société Anonyme des Ateliers de Constructions Electriques du Nord et de l'Est refused to work until the management paid immediately a cost of living allowance promised since September.[143] The female personnel at the Panhard and Knyff works at Gentilly successfully struck for a full 1 franc bonus instead of the 0.90 francs with which their bosses had tried to placate them.[144] Some twenty women at the Otto factory rejected all attempts at compromise by the management over the issue of equal pay for equal work, preferring to quit rather than go back to work as most of their co-strikers showed themselves ready to do.[145] At the Caudron establishment five women blacklegs were attacked and had their hair pulled by other women strikers.[146]

Women could be intransigent, too, on other, non-economic issues. At Peugeot's in Levallois Perret both male and female workers, who had to work every second Sunday, demanded that every Sunday should be free and proposed to walk out at 17.00 hours instead of 19.00 hours every fortnight until they obtained satisfaction.[147] In the Citroën factory the behaviour of foremen towards women was a special grievance among a number of complaints.[148] At another establishment three women were dismissed for their endless baiting of a foreman but two of them had to be reinstated after the personnel staged a solidarity 'folded arms' strike on their behalf.[149] The woman who actually hit him, however, was not taken on again, since she had a record of similar aggressive behaviour at the Panhard factory, where she was nicknamed 'La Boxeuse'.[150] On the other hand, there were times when women seemed unwilling to become involved in militant action of any sort. During a dispute at Nieuport's over the representation of union delegates, some women made it clear that they had no wish to join any strike movement for the moment and it was decided that they would not be compromised if action did have to be taken.[151] Elsewhere, in certain drinking establishments, women were overheard saying that various male strike leaders were 'disgusting people' who earned fat wages while their own husbands went off to be killed for 0.25 francs a day.[152]

All in all, the industrial action of women employed in the war factories was not as consistently militant as that of the dressmakers and other women workers in the clothing industry.[153] Certainly, they could be stung into challenging their employers – often successfully – but their action was usually spontaneous and shortlived. They also lacked the capacity to organise and therefore most often took their grievances to the male trade union leaders. Thus, even at meetings where women constituted a majority of the audience, the principal speakers were always men. If, as happened occasionally, a woman spoke, as at the meeting of strikers from the Otto factory on 8 March 1918 at the Bureau du Travail, it was most likely to be to pledge support to mobilised male workers, no matter what they decided.[154] Women were often the subject of debate at such meetings, rather than participants. Again and again they would be told how they were exploited and how the road to salvation lay through syndical organisation. Their help in sustaining strikes was greatly appreciated. But not only did they nowhere emerge as converts to the doctrines of revolutionary syndicalism but more importantly their participation in union membership proved to be transitory. Certainly, in the course of the great strikes in the metal industry in 1917, women flocked to join trade unions to the extent that in Paris they probably constituted about 30% of the membership, a proportion almost exactly comparable to their numbers in the labour force as a whole. Put another way, about 12% of all women workers in metallurgy in the Paris area belonged to a *syndicat* – a vast improvement on the pre-war figure of less than 2%.[155] Altogether, by 1920, with some 239,000 members, women made up 15% of the total number of *syndiqués* as against 8.7% in 1914.[156] But this impressive wartime achievement was not sustained in the post-war period, and cannot therefore be seen as a breakthrough to a new level of syndicalist consciousness. Following the defeat of the great strike movement of the spring of 1920 and the tendency towards schism which eventually split the CGT and the new, communist dominated CGTU, union membership in general declined catastrophically, and the number of women unionists dwindled to a mere 32,000 in 1932 in the CGT and the CGTU combined.[157] Male comrades who were in favour of enlarging the syndical role of women could not conceal their disappointment with the poor response. As one militant pointed out, they seemed to have learned nothing from the war:

> The same narrowness of views, the same softness aborts their better instincts: they follow in the wake of men and projects devised by men, they don't make even the slightest impression of their originality.[158]

Outside of the clothing industry, there is little evidence of a heightened sense of militancy among women workers as a result of the First World War.

The post-war sexual division of labour

Surveys carried out by the Ministry of Labour leave no room for doubt that the mobilisation of women for war work had a significant impact upon the structure of the female industrial labour force. An inquiry of July 1917 revealed that, whereas women were to be found in fewer numbers in such industries as textiles and clothing, they had greatly multiplied in industries such as chemicals (up 64% from pre-war days) and metals (where a staggering 913% rise was registered).[159] Clearly, what happened during the war was that women abandoned the traditionally feminine sectors and found employment in areas hitherto occupied primarily by men.

These developments, however, need to be understood in the context of economic trends which pre-dated the war. Essentially, they accompanied and possibly accelerated the change towards an economy in which older industries such as textiles declined while new industries such as chemicals, electricity and light engineering, along with the tertiary sector as a whole, underwent rapid expansion. The evolution of the female labour force reflected the general movement. Thus, while domestics accounted for 17.7% of all working women (outside agriculture) in 1906, they comprised 14.8% in 1921 and 15.1% in 1936.[160] In 1921, the textiles industry employed 270,000 fewer women than it had done in 1906 (a drop of 18%, although it should be noted that the years between 1921 and 1926 saw something of a recovery, with another 61,000 being hired). In the clothing industry, almost 55,000 women left between 1906 and 1921, followed by a further 162,000 between 1921 and 1926.[161] By contrast, the number of female white-collar workers in the tertiary sector shot up from 344,000 in 1906 to 855,000 in 1921, and 1,034,000 in 1936 (respectively 7.9%, 18.4% and 23.5% of the total female work force).[162]

Looked at from the point of view of the work available to women, the changing employment pattern can be seen to have consolidated the sexual division of labour which came into existence in the nineteenth century as a concomitant of the rise of industrial capitalism. More than ever under the 'family consumer economy' (as Scott and Tilly call it) work was constituted essentially by labour carried on outside the home in return for a wage. For married women who wanted (or needed) to contribute to the family budget the option of engaging in domestic work became more and more remote (one important consequence of the decline in the clothing industry). Rather, they had to join the ranks of the wider, wage-earning labour force. Thus the category of women workers classifiable as 'small employers and isolated workers' accounted for 35.9% of all working women in 1906, but could muster only 26.7% in 1921 and 19% in 1936 (in other words, a decline of nearly 50% over thirty years).[163] In 1906, 20.2% of all married women in the population had non-agricultural jobs. Of these, 13.3% could be classified as 'independents' (heads of firms, small employers and isolated workers) while 6.9% were wage-earners. By 1936, the overall proportion of married women who worked had declined to 18.7%, but of these only 8.1% were 'independents' while 10.6% were wage-earners. [164] If one looks simply at the two categories *ouvrières* (industrial workers) and *employées* (white-collar workers), one sees that the proportion of married women in the population who engaged in these sectors increased by 74% between 1906 and 1936. [165] There can be no question that one of the most striking social realities of the period was the massive incursion of French married women into paid employment outside the home. Equally significant, however, is the fact that the overall proportion of married women with jobs declined (from 20.2% in 1906 to 18.7%). [166] The more emphatic dichotomy between home and work made the problem of how to reconcile the maternal role with economic participation all the greater, and the vast majority of French women seem to have come down on the side of domesticity, as in the pre-war period.

War work itself was by no means inconsistent with the pre-war situation in which, ideally, married women refrained from economic activity in the wider sphere unless family circumstances made it necessary. The wartime mobilisation of women should be regarded precisely as the kind of expedient (albeit on a grand scale) likely to require the temporary employment of women. In the absence of the principal breadwinner housewives found themselves obliged to provide for their families, while young girls and single women who previously had difficulty in finding work outside the traditionally feminine sectors profited from the opportunity to obtain employment in the relatively higher paid industries which were producing for the war effort. In replacing the absent male workers, however, the new women workers did not go far along the road towards achieving a new position of equality with men in the world of work. In the munitions factories, singled out by contemporaries as nurseries of female emancipation, women generally worked only at the least skilled jobs and required the supervision of a male worker. True, as the war wore on, women were employed at tasks which involved a certain level of skill, such as fitting, handling steam engines, oxyacetylene welding and many others. In addition, they were given various tasks of inspection – checking car parts, light shells, grenades, cables and precision instruments. Thanks to the introduction of new labour-saving machinery, industrialists were able to adapt their methods of production to allow women to replace men at jobs which had previously called for the expenditure of considerable physical effort. Thus in munitions factories, conveyor belts and special pulley blocks were devised to bring heavy pieces of metal to the lathes where women worked. But while women could be successfully employed at these semi-skilled jobs, they had to rely on a skilled male worker to see to the maintenance and repair of the machines. Every team of eight or ten women workers had to have its male toolmaker, who was needed to do specialised jobs such as sharpening tools and who had acquired his skill only after a long apprenticeship. Women workers in the war factories were never given the chance to acquire such skills, but rather were set to work as quickly as possible and after only the most elementary training.[167] Thus even if during the war women moved away from traditionally feminine jobs they ended by taking up new feminine unskilled or semi-skilled industrial work which reinforced their inferior status vis-à-vis their skilled male colleagues.[168]

Moreover, the fact that women had proved themselves capable of taking over almost any kind of job during the war did not guarantee that they would continue to occupy these new stations once the war was over. For thousands of women who wanted to carry on earning a wage the opportunity was not always available in the post-war period. With the return of peace many employers began to preach the virtues of domesticity and sought to get rid of their women workers, to make way for the returning men.[169] Likewise the government, recently so desperate to recruit women into the labour force, now reconverted to the domestic ideology and gave its full support to propaganda which exhorted women to return to their hearths. Redundancy payments were offered to women as an extra inducement to leave their jobs.[170] So incompetent was the handling of these dismissals and voluntary redundancies that a government circular of 24 January 1919 was forced to admit that thousands of women had been 'victimised in shocking conditions'.[171] By April 1919 the Metalworkers Federation reckoned that some 500,000 women had left their industry, while a feminist inquiry conducted at Puteaux found that two-thirds of the women workers employed there during the war had taken their bonus and quit.[172]

In large measure the problems which confronted the female labour force as a result of demobilisation stemmed from the reluctance of most employers to reorganise their plant or to rationalise their work force. The exigencies of wartime had led to the introduction of the Taylor System in a number of war factories and to a switch to mass production at the Citroën plants. But even Renault, who was in general an admirer of American methods of scientific management, was unable to introduce Taylorism wholesale, although some progress was made at his Billancourt factory. Most French businessmen, however, had no desire to adopt a new technological approach, while politicians such as Herriot who expressed some interest rarely did anything practical. The replies to the questionnaire sent out by the Committee on Female Labour in 1918 showed that only employers like Citroën and Renault who were fired by American example could see any future for women in their peacetime labour force. A number of firms stated that they wanted to keep a certain percentage of their female staff: Peugeot calculated in terms of 50%, Pillon and Co. 80%. The planemakers Henri Lepante said that they were prepared to keep some women if a demand for cars replaced the demand for planes during the war: but in any case women had failed to penetrate aeronautics factories in any significant numbers between 1914 and 1918. Some establishments, like the Industrial Telephone Company, were quite explicit about their desire to see women replaced by men as soon as possible. The Decazeville Iron Works considered that there was no place for women in heavy industry, except perhaps as cleaners or office workers, while the metallurgy firm of Bonvillain and Ronceray thought that only women with very special reasons should be considered for employment.[173]

Yet not all the blame can be laid at the doorstep of the employers, for it can hardly be said that the war produced a radical transformation in the attitude of male workers towards women's work. As we have already seen, on the eve of the war the Couriau Affair had served notice on the syndicalist movement that it had to clarify its position on the question of female labour and female participation in trade unions. The largescale participation of women in war work lent the matter new urgency, but the extensive debate to which this gave rise did not result in a clear cut repudiation of traditionalist conceptions of the role of women in society among male trade unionists. On the contrary, their long-held suspicion that manual labour was detrimental to women's health and to family life was often reinforced, as was their belief that women's work could be used by employers to keep down men's wages. Hence at the congress of the transport workers, one delegate explained that female labour was tolerated only because of the exceptional circumstances produced by the war; in the future, women's place would be elsewhere. Another delegate admitted frankly that in Lyons women were not allowed to join the union, although he claimed that this made no difference to the efforts it was prepared to make on their behalf to improve wages and working conditions. Unanimously, the congress adopted a resolution which proclaimed that women's work was only a temporary consequence of the war and that jobs occupied by women should be given back to male comrades on their demobilisation.[174] In the printers' union, the *Fédération du Livre*, traditionally one of the most ardent opponents of women's work, some members showed a reluctant awareness of the need to bow before new realities. Fernand Mammale, a member of the *Comité Central du Livre*, prepared a report which, while insisting that women workers had only been employed because of the dearth of men, recognised nevertheless that the scale of the slaughter meant that women's services would still be required before the war was over. Conflict between male and female workers, however, still seemed to him a distinct possibility.[175] A conference which discussed the question was in broad agreement with Mammale's conclusions. The central committee declared unanimously that it saw women's 'natural and social mission' as being to devote themselves to their families; it should be possible for a husband to earn enough to provide for the upkeep of the whole household. At the same time, the conference recognised that many women would be obliged to earn their own living as a result of the disastrous losses of the war, but it feared that their remuneration would be a mere pittance and that they would be subjected to exploitation. A compromise solution seemed to be to accept the resolution of the Bordeaux Congress of 1910, which would accept female labour provided it did not reduce male wages: that is, women should be paid at the *tarif syndical*, with equal pay for equal work, though the big question of the female working day still had to be decided.[176] Much the same line was taken by Keufer, secretary of the *Fédération du Livre*, in his report to the congress of 1919. Here it was decided to admit women to the trade but only under certain strict conditions. First, the number of female apprentices was never to be more than that of male apprentice compositors; secondly, in printing works where there were no female compositors, women should only be taken on in the proportion of one woman to five men; and finally there must be no deviation from the principle of equal pay for equal work.[177]

The same type of thinking pervaded the official outlook of the *Fédération des Métaux*. Its commission on the woman question was headed by the anti-feminist Lenoir, who had never made any secret of his view that women's place was in the home.[178] Not surprisingly, the resolution adopted by Congress in 1918 proclaimed that 'the systematic introduction of women into the workshop is in absolute opposition to the creation and existence of the home and the family'. The husband alone must be the breadwinner, for all too often women were not paid a real wage, but only a trifling token which barely allowed the family to keep pace with the cost of living. In addition women's work augured ill for the future of the race. On the other hand, the federal committee promised to do its utmost on behalf of women who were obliged to work. It wanted an absolute ban on night work, a maximum working day of eight hours, and equal pay for equal work. Most of all, it exhorted women to join the male syndicats as the best means possible of furthering their cause.[179] In this way, in both the printing and the metal industries, the war finally overcame the old corporatist prejudices of pre-war days. Yet many misgivings remained among the ranks of male workers on the subject of female labour and the limited degree of their concessions can be measured by the conspicuous absence of women delegates at syndicalist congresses. Thus no woman was a delegate to the congress of the Metalworkers Federation before 1936. On the eve of the Second World War only in two federations (food and clothing, both long recognised as feminine sectors) were women to be found in positions of authority at the national level.[180] The militant primary school teachers who formed a third of the membership of the Fédération Unitaire de l'Enseignement were very exceptional: and even they encountered intransigent male opposition when they tried to extend their action to the communist dominated Confédération du Travail Unitaire.[181] The CGT itself gave no clear lead in trying to recruit women workers to the cause of militant syndicalism. Marie Guillot, one of the few women activists privileged to speak at its National Congress in 1918, called for more places to be opened up for women on both its executive and its delegations. She also wanted to see a Secretariat for Female Labour established within the Confederation.[182] Male delegates were prepared to pay no more than lip-service to such proposals. This complacency on the part of the CGT was bitterly criticised by Jeanne Bouvier, who accused it of being interested in women workers only to make up the numbers of union membership, but not to struggle on their behalf.[183] The sexual division of labour in France had no stauncher friend than the French trade union movement.

Chapter VIII
AFTER THE WAR: THE DURABILITY OF THE DOUBLE STANDARD

IF the arguments in the two previous chapters are correct, it would appear that the First World War cannot be held to have overthrown the ideology of domesticity. It remains to be seen whether the war made any inroads upon the pre-war ally of domesticity, the double standard of morality. According to contemporaries, it most certainly had: as we shall see below, many commentators considered that a revolution had been effected in sexual mores and that a 'new woman', freed from the constraints of traditional (bourgeois) morality, had made her appearance. Once again, however, our appraisal of the situation will differ markedly from that of contemporaries.

The 'new woman' and the old morality
Probably the main reason for the new image of women in the post-war period was the fact that, thanks to changes in fashion, they looked different. The role of women during the war had required new types of costume, allowing greater freedom of movement, and this more functional conception of dress had led to shorter skirts, unaccentuated waists, with corsets replaced by suspender belts, flat breasts and a vogue for slim, boyish figures. Short, straight, close-cropped hair emphasised this *garçonne* look, which was developed by fashion designers such as Chanel in their white silk shirts and men's ties, made to match their tailored suits. Other influences also conspired to produce the new look: dances like the Charleston demanded short skirts, while the stars of the music hall and the cinema, such as Josephine Baker, Greta Garbo, and the Dolly sisters, all suggested new fashions of dress and behaviour.[1] Women clearly had a new image in the immediate post-war period and contemporaries can hardly be blamed if they took fashion to be only the external manifestation of more profound changes.

Thus, for many gloomy commentators, the new fashions announced an era of moral decadence, for looser morals could not but be the natural concomitant of looser dress. One male traditionalist objected that it was bad enough that girls should make themselves look like boys by cutting their hair short, 'but it is another matter when they attempt to appear with as few clothes on as possible'. In his view, skirts were just about tolerable as long as the girl remained standing, but if she sat down, rode a bicycle, went upstairs or stooped to pick something up, decency was violated and men were scandalised.[2] Novelist Marcel Prévost thought that post-war bathing costumes were particularly indecent. He lamented the passing of the kind with long trousers going down below the knee and with a belted tunic 'which would have preserved the chastity of Diana'.[3] Church leaders, always particularly sensitive to feminine dress, were well to the fore in denouncing the new trends. The popes themselves gave the lead. Benedict XV told Italian women in 1919 that feminine dress was disgraceful and was bound to have pernicious effects upon society because men would be provoked to evil: it was astounding, he said, that some brazen women even dared to wear the new dresses to church.[4] Pius XI expressed his worries about the influence of the craze for sport upon dress, and gave a stern warning that extreme care had to be taken to avoid things not conducive to modesty and virtue.[5] In keeping with the line from Rome, members of the French hierarchy also turned their attention to the grave matter of female dress. In a pastoral letter of 1926, the Bishop of Angers condemned the latest fashions and laid down the correct clothes to be worn on different social occasions. As the following extract shows, the prelate had obviously reflected at great length on the female figure:

> For all ceremonies in church a high-necked dress should be worn. It should have long sleeves and should come down well below the knees. At marriage ceremonies the bride and bridesmaids should at most wear a slight *décolletage à la vièrge*: they should never have their arms bare or covered merely with a scarf.
>
> In town, dresses should not cling closely to the body, they should have sleeves to the elbow, and the skirt should end distinctly below the knee. At most, a *décolletage en rond*, not loose, but neatly fastened, and not below the collar bone. Open work stockings must never be worn. In the evening, the *décolletage*, which must always be close-fitting, may only be a little lower than the collar bone. Dresses must not be skin-tight, must have at least small sleeves, and must be two hand-breadths below the knee.
>
> At dances, gloves should be worn always. No dances which involve close bodily contact should be indulged in.
>
> At the seaside, the scanty bathing suit should be discarded in favour of the fuller bathing dresses formerly worn. Sun-bathing and games on the shore in bathing costume are prohibited.
>
> Girls over ten years of age should wear long stockings and dresses which cover the knees.[6]

No doubt, such ecclesiastical exhortations had some impact upon the more pious of the female faithful. As an arbiter of fashion, however, the Church could not compete with Chanel. The revolution in female dress clearly failed to abolish prudery and prurience, but it did permit women to cast off the unhealthy 'feminine' outfits which they had been obliged to wear in the years before 1914, and in so doing created a general aura of emancipation around women in the immediate post-war years.

Fashion was by no means the only pointer to the emergence of a new woman. A greater freedom of movement outside the home, particularly among bourgeois women, further served to convey the impression that the liberation of women was at hand. Here again commentators such as Marcel Prévost pointed to the war as the source of the transformation, since it was the war which gave young girls the right to go out on their own unchaperoned, a right still denied by most of their mothers in 1914. The crucial breakthrough was the right to visit the sick and wounded in hospital, and this in turn had been responsible for another major development – a new, freer and more intimate association of the sexes. Comforting the heroic war-wounded or going out with valiant *poilus* during their leave, girls had put their relationships with men on a new footing. Prévost was especially struck by the number of romantic attachments which blossomed in the hospitals:

> It is in this place of physical misery, among the groans in the odour of blood and iodine, that the new communion of young men and young girls was established. That alone eliminates any notion of decline or perversion.[7]

Young girls could no longer be innocent and ignorant as they used to be. As Prévost pointed out to his niece, the contrast with her own adolescence could not have been more marked. Dressed in the drab clothes demanded by her *pension*, allowed out only twice a week (on Sundays after mass and on Wednesday afternoon), she had never come into contact with the other sex save at select balls where vigilant chaperoning was performed by the mothers. To go out alone into the street had been unthinkable, while even in the vacations she was expected to remain close to her mother, so that all she saw and heard could be strictly supervised. For Prévost, the new post-war familiarity between the sexes went much further than the 'Americanisation' of mores that had been taking place since 1900. A lot of the respect that still existed before the war had been lost, and the new trend seemed irreversible. In the estimation of Dr Toulouse, 'war is necessarily a school of sexual liberty'. Enforced separation and the ever-present threat of sudden death had created the conditions for a transformation of moral standards.[8]

Contemporary evidence for a revolution in sexual mores, it should be said, is not dependent solely upon the anxieties of apologists for traditional bourgeois morality. The new woman also had her passionate advocates, among whom could be numbered militant feminists like Louise Bodin. To her mind it was neither fair nor realistic to expect those girls who would not be fortunate enough to find a husband in the post-war period to refrain from seeking sexual pleasure or the experience of love.[9] Even some spokesmen for traditional moral standards came round to the same view. Thus Martin de Torina, a staunch champion of the sanctity of the family and a militant anti-Malthusian, precisely because he was troubled by France's declining population which was bound to deteriorate further on account of war losses, wrote a book to encourage unmarried women to have children and called on (bourgeois) society to show a new respect for the unmarried mother.[10] Perhaps the most fully developed image of the new woman, however, was the heroine of Victor Margueritte's novel, *La Garçonne (The Bachelor Girl)*.[11] For the French reading public, Monique Lerbier came to epitomise the female revolt against the double standard. Having left home in disgust after discovering that her *fiancé* continued to keep a mistress, she abandons herself to a life of vice, indulging in multiple love affairs, lesbianism, masochism and drugs. The novel was an immediate best-seller. Published in July 1922, it sold 20,000 copies in four days. By the end of the year its sales were in the region of 300,000. By 1929, it had sold over a million copies in France alone and had been translated into a dozen languages, including English. Of its mass readership, then, there can be no doubt. A recent student of the work, Mlle A-M Sohn, calculates that between 12% and 25% of the adult male population must have read the book, this proportion being considerably higher in the bourgeois class.[12]

The phenomenal sale of the novel represents a *succès de scandale*. Despite its far from subversive ending (the heroine eventually marries an open-minded engineer to whom the virginity of his bride is unimportant and who thinks that women should merely have the same sexual opportunities as men) officialdom condemned the book as an outrage. Margueritte was stripped of his Legion of Honour and a film based on the novel was banned by the censor on the grounds that it was 'a deplorable defamation of the character of the young French girl'.[13] Mlle Sohn has argued that *La Garçonne* created such a scandal because it crystallised the fears of the French middle classes regarding the evolution in the position of women, particularly with respect to sexual mores, attributable to the First World War. Margueritte's bachelor girl, it is suggested, corresponded to a social reality. This argument is far from convincing. Even if one looks only at other literary evidence, it becomes clear that the double standard still had its defenders in post-war France. In the works of Montherlant, for example, aggressive *machismo* is omnipresent. In *Pity for Women* the hero Costals is the epitome of male chauvinism.[14] No one woman can ever satisfy him, nor has he any hope of establishing a loving, lasting relationship. The women in his life are those whom he does not love but whom he pursues through 'a blend of affection and desire'. A man can be perfectly happy without a woman, but the reverse is not true, and women are dreamers, watching and waiting for the right man to come into their lives. Education in a woman is unimportant; attraction purely sensual. The Goncourts themselves could not have been more condescending. Montherlant may have been more intransigent than most (as befitted a fascist homosexual), but literature furnishes many other examples of male-female relations conducted on the basis of the double standard. Maurice Badel's novel *Jérôme*, for instance, (awarded the Prix Goncourt in 1926) depicts a hero who rates himself highly as a Latin-style womaniser yet finds himself impotent when confronted with a genuinely emancipated Norwegian girl. Her frank, straightforward attitude to love-making is alien to the acceptance of a double standard where women have to be pursued and conquered. [15]

On balance proponents of the new morality seem to have been outnumbered by the traditionalists. Thus Louise Bodin was not a typical representative of the view of the mainstream feminists on the question of sexual mores. Just as these were not slow to dissociate themselves from Margueritte's claim to have written a 'feminist' novel in *La Garçonne*, so too Jane Misme attacked another novelist, Léon Frapié, for advocating the right of unmarried women to become mothers in his work *Les filles à marier*.[16] To admit unmarried motherhood, Mme Misme insisted, was to strike a deadly blow at the institution of marriage, while to bring a child into the world without two parents to rear it was a crime against both the child and society. Another contributor to Jane Misme's newspaper *La Française* put the case against sexual liberation, advising young women to remain 'good friends' with men, and to avoid lowering themselves to the level of masculine morality.[17]

The literature on the subject of sex education provides further evidence for the durability of the double standard. Ignorance about sex was unlikely to be removed by many of the books published about it. Thus, the old horror stories about masturbation were still being peddled in 1918, as in Dr Alibert's work *The Vices of Love: Self-Abuse among Women*.[18] In post-war France, however widespread the practice was (something the historian will never know), masturbation was not regarded as 'the regulated release of emotional tension', as Havelock Ellis calls it, but rather as a secret vice.[19] Frank, straightforward sex education books for girls were very rare. A few did exist, such as Dr Bourgas' *Le Droit à l'Amour pour la Femme*, which consciously set out to enlighten women on how to increase the pleasure they derived from sex.[20] Dr Eynon ridiculed the idealised language used by clerics and moralisers when describing the technicalities of sexual relations.[21] An anonymous writer deplored the reluctance of parents to explain the facts of life to their daughters, especially when most girls were no longer innocent and succeeded in gaining at least some vague notions on the subject. These, he thought, should be made more precise long before their wedding day.[22] Such opinions, however, were not typical of the literature (in any case limited) available on sex education. Dr H Abrand advised parents to answer their children's questions frankly but to avoid going into the details. They must be spared the awfulness of the full truth and be content to know that love involved a union of bodies as well as of souls. Even the best-informed of young girls, for instance medical students, should never be completely knowledgeable before the completion of marriage, otherwise 'she will be shocked, wounded in one of her most beautiful attributes, her modesty'.[23] Such was also the viewpoint of Dr Georges Surbled, who wrote that the 'legitimate curiosity' of a girl should be satisfied by an explanation that told her that an intimate linking of bodies permitted a man's seed to fertilise a woman's egg in order to produce a child, for this act only took place within marriage ('the nest of love') and for the purpose of procreation.[24] For a doctor, Surbled showed a somewhat surprising repugnance to the human body. He warned girls undergoing puberty not to be misled by the materialists who claimed that their sex organs were noble; rather, these were always 'a symbol of our fall and the object of our shame'.[25] St Jerome and the misogynist Fathers of the Church could hardly have been more severe.

The idea of public instruction in sexual matters in the schools was particularly abhorrent to clerical writers. I de Recalde (the pseydonym of a secular priest from Troyes) violently denounced the pamphlet produced by the Jesuit-run *Action Populaire* for daring to describe not only the reproductive organs of plants but even those of human beings – and all in the vernacular! (These 'most offensive' passages the author turned into Latin in his citations.) Such tracts which claimed that instruction in 'sexual initiation' might educate children in purity were the cause of immense harm, stimulating the imagination in the same way as bad books and obscene films. As Recalde pointed out, the principle of sex education in schools had been vigorously rejected by the General Assembly of Cardinals and Archbishops in France in a statement of 28 February 1923:

> The Assembly rejects the procedure of what is called sex education which is based on science alone outside of all religious morality. Again it emphatically diapproves of public or collective methods of initiation, either by schools or by books, or by pictures or lectures. It declares that this initiation belongs to the father and mother or, in their absence, to persons who have their complete confidence.[26]

The *Association du Mariage Chrétien* took the same line. The Jesuit R P Ganay, summing up the conclusions of an exchange of opinion among Christian parents, doctors, organisers of charities as well as priests, moral theologians and educators, rejected 'scientific initiation', that is in the course of teaching in the natural sciences:

> This education would then be collective, neutral from the point of view of religious morality and exclusively anatomical and physiological in kind, which is to say that this education would be disastrous.[27]

In the post-war period, then, one is struck more by the persistence of traditional ideals than by the emergence of a new order of sexual mores. Attachment to the stereotype of the modest, virginal young girl was still strong, notably among medical men. Doctors like Abrand might admit that previous generations had been wrong to maintain girls in almost total ignorance about the nature of sexual relations, but now that some of the barriers to knowledge had been removed it was argued that more than ever mothers should watch vigilantly over the conversations and companions of their daughters to ensure that standards of purity did not fall. Good parents would also closely supervise the reading material of young girls, in which task they would be helped immensely by the availability of publications such as M Bethléem's *Romans à lire et à proscrire* and the *Revue des Lectures*.[28] A common assumption was that young men looking around for a wife appreciated seriousness rather than the frivolity of the *mondaine* who spent all of her time dressing up to excess, and going off to dances. According to Dr Georges Surbled, those girls who flirted and encouraged dangerous familiarities, flaunting themselves in the cafés, in the theatre and other public places, smoking and even seeking out men to satisfy their thirst for pleasure, were in no way to be emulated. Rather, girls should be 'well-behaved, prudent and modest'; modest above all, for 'a woman without modesty is a woman without a sex, without virtue, beyond the pale'.[29] Needless to say, virginity must be preserved for the future husband: 'that will be the richest, the most handsome wedding present that you could make him, a royal gift'.[30] Such advice was proferred by female as well as male moralists. Jacqueline Veulette, who undertook to counsel girls on how to go about acquiring a husband, insisted on the necessity of being pure of soul, which meant no drinking, flirting or smoking:

> Young girls ought to convince themselves of one thing: namely that the serious young man, worthy of making an excellent husband later, seeks in them a modesty that is real and without false shame, and that he respects them all the more to the extent that they know how to refuse him all the unhealthy familiarities which too many, alas, bestow indecently.[31]

In the moralists' model of femininity, the attribute of beauty came a very close second to chastity in the order of priorities. Any girl, no matter how ugly, should be able to make herself attractive by the judicious application of make-up and good dress sense. To quote once more from the self-appointed authority Jacqueline Veulette:

> All the feminine art is to know how to show to advantage all the physical qualities which one possesses and there are no girls so lacking in looks that they are incapable of seducing the man whom they want to love them. To counter the imperfection of forms it suffices to have a little practical intelligence and coquetry, which easily disguise blemishes to the eye of the loved one.[32]

Provided a girl looked after her health, beautification was no problem, and many manuals were available with advice on both. Dr Monin's *Hygiène de la Beauté* was typical in that its express intention was to inform women how to make themselves easy on the eye for men. (It was also very successful: by 1922, when a new edition was published, 20,000 copies had been sold and the book had been translated into six languages.)[33] But as well as a good appearance, it was necessary that she should show herself eager to please: her manners had to be gentle and agreeable. M Emile Fenouillet, whose basic assumption seems to have been that all women desperately need husbands while men can afford to be selective, advised girls that they should use every conceivable ruse they could think of in order to make themselves indispensable to men and to flatter their sense of vanity. True, he did indicate that in some respects times had changed. No longer, he said, must a girl remain at home, hoping that one day the right man would come to her door; nor should she expect to find him at a ball or dance, since the days when a man might fall for the first pretty face he saw were long since past. The onus was now on a girl to go out looking for a husband, to seek one out for herself without waiting for her family to arrange one for her, and the best place to find him was at work. 'Work is the best means of finding the best husband', he concluded pontifically. They should even be prepared to speak to strangers – in trains, on ships, sometimes in the streets:

> In the streets, don't always show a face like those of the saints in wood of primitive art to the man who looks at you with a frank astonishment, who follows you, who even approaches you. Today men are in a hurry, their haste is not always a sign of wicked intentions: words murmured with a real fervour are easy enough to recognise . . .![34]

M Fenouillet's counsel was certainly novel as regards the *methods* girls should employ in order to find a husband, but with regard to the qualities they should possess in order to press their claims, it in no way abandons the traditional values of the male gallant.

It would appear that, on closer examination, the revolution in sexual mores disappears from view. Even the *jeune fille sportive* cannot really be seen as a sign of more emancipated times. The tennis star Suzanne

Lenglen may have been the idol of many girls but in general sport in France did not enjoy anything like the prestige it did in, say, England or the USA. Time for sports was notably absent from the curricula of the lycées of both boys and girls. According to Franck L Schoell, a French *agrégé* teaching in California and anxious to explain the role of women in French society to 'Anglo-Saxons', tennis was not taken seriously, except possibly by fat girls trying to get their weight down. Cycling, fashionable in 1895 when elegant young ladies could be seen riding their bicycles in the Bois de Boulogne, had become merely a form of exercise for the *petite bourgeoisie*.[35] 'Excessive' sport was distrusted by the beauticians on the grounds that women's figures might lose their essentially feminine contours. Dr Monin was of the opinion that housework was the best form of exercise they could do, since this both developed harmoniously all their muscles and also allowed them to remain women.[36] An enquiry held among doctors and physiologists on the suitability of sports for women, inconclusive in itself, is revealing about attitudes. All agreed that women's health required exercise and fresh air, but even if some were capable at excelling at particular sports, these were 'exceptions, almost objects of curiosity'.[37] A woman's organism was not made for the intensive muscular effort and the attentiveness and concentration required for success in sport:

In reality, women do little sport, and those who appear to take up sports are more likely only going through the motions, trying to cause a temporary sensation; thus when driving they soon hand over the steering wheel to their male companion.[38]

Running was bad for girls in their view, which ruled out all athletics. Swimming, on the other hand, was good, as was tennis. Cycling had to be done in moderation, while driving cars was dangerous. Thus it would appear that a new involvement in sport is notably lacking as an index by which to measure the greater degree of freedom women were supposed to enjoy as a result of the war.

In real life the numbers of genuinely emancipated women were few. The bohemians of Montparnasse could qualify. Kiki (Alice Prin), Jeanne Léger, wife of the painter, Soutine ('the most moving incarnation of Montparnasse's excessive and cosmopolitan bohemian-ism, the Rembrandt of the *abbattoirs*'), Youki, a young blonde Walloon, Régina Badet, a stripper convicted several times for appearing nude who would do belly dances with a pearl in her navel to the accompaniment of an invisible orchestra, all these might be said to have given Paris some of the flavour of the American 'Roaring Twenties'. 1925 was in a sense the jazz age, the time of audacious sexual exploits, *actes gratuits* and inexplicable suicides, a time given over to frenetic hedonism after the privations of war.[39] But Montparnasse was not

France or for that matter Paris, and it no more represented the characteristic behaviour of French women than Toulouse-Lautrec's dancers and prostitutes characterised the role of women in the *belle époque*. In any case Bohemianism was not new, even if the Montparnos showed that *la bohème parisienne* could move with the times.

Moving on the fringes of this world, girl students like Simone de Beauvoir might enjoy an intoxicating sense of freedom when taken round the bars and cafés of Montparnasse by male friends. But on her own admission their wild nights out were far from acceptable to bourgeois parents and could even leave her with a sense of guilt. For long she retained a reticence about sexual relations and a conventional belief in chastity that would last until the great, momentous sequel to a white wedding. Sexually uninhibited and promiscuous women such as Sartre's friend Camille rather shocked her.[40] Indeed, Simone de Beauvoir's recollections about her upbringing provide a unique insight into the moral standards on which a girl of good family continued to be reared.[41] Born the daughter of a Parisian lawyer in 1908, Mme de Beauvoir remembers her father as almost a caricature of the right-thinking bourgeois, despite his taste for acting. An unbeliever himself, he nevertheless respected the Church and was horrified by the lay state created by the Republicans. Without actually becoming a member of *Action Française*, he subscribed to its nationalism, xenophobia and anti-semitism, and naturally never doubted the guilt of Dreyfus. For him, the family was the basis of all morality. Exalting women's role as mother, he demanded a strict fidelity from wives and spotless chastity from young girls, though he was prepared to overlook sexual weakness in men. Thus one of his best friends who was 'living in sin' with a mistress could still be received at home, though it was unthinkable that the woman herself should ever cross the threshold. Mme de Beauvoir's pious mother, eight years younger than her husband, accepted such situations in men's lives but categorised women as either 'respectable' or 'loose'.

The First World War may have damaged her parents' position in a material sense, but it in no way caused them to make a drastic reappraisal of the moral values which they sought to inculcate in their daughters. The youthful Simone soon learned that there were subjects which she must not mention and books which she must not read, and her mother snatched a copy of *Claudine à l'école* away from her maid. Discussion of these forbidden subjects was not always possible even between her peers; one girl at her school was expelled for indulging in 'evil conversations'. Her sexual education consisted in a haphazard piecing together of fragments of information gleaned from friends, and her mother was still content to leave her with the impression that babies came out of the anus. Nor did her mother prepare her for the onset of menstruation. Enlightenment came finally only when she read the forbidden books – Bourget, Daudet, Prévost, Maupassant, the Goncourts – though even then she remained hazy about the precise nature of the sex act.

In short, the double standard of morality survived the war relatively unscathed. The most serious blow against it remained the law of 1912 which permitted paternity suits, but its narrowness of scope meant that aggrieved women might not always obtain justice. Thus a domestic servant who got to know one of her neighbours, a clerical worker, on the seventh floor of their apartment block and, after talk of marriage, became pregnant by him, was unable to bring a paternity suit against the father when he abandoned her. In the eyes of the law, they had not cohabited, nor had she written proof of her lover's intention to marry (not surprisingly, since she was illiterate).[42] Nevertheless, it should be noted that in principle the law did not demand cohabitation, provided continuity and regularity of sexual relations could be established over a period of time. The point was that these relations had to be 'notorious' that is, known to the neighbourhood, and not clandestine.[43] On the other hand, the Penal Code continued to regard the adultery of the wife as a much more serious offence than that of the husband. For at least some women, the alternative to the role of housewife continued to be that of mistress, as may be seen in the careers of the women in the lives of some of the leading literary and political figures of the Third Republic. As depicted in the anecdotal history of P B Ghensi, these women owed their advancement to the status of their lovers. Mme Berthe Cerny of the Théâtre Français might teach Aristide Briand to speak properly and help him lose his common accent, and Alfred Edwards, the financier and press-baron, might be persuaded to promote one of his protégées in the pages of *Le Matin*, but for the women concerned their success was merely the traditional kind obtained by the courtesan.[44]

Some writers, however, did recognise that it was unfair to demand one standard for women and another for men. For Dr Toulouse, as for the mainstream feminists, the answer to the two moralities question was to persuade men to adopt the chastity required of women.[45] Two other members of the medical profession who shared his viewpoint were Dr Robert Chable and the prolific Dr Georges Surbled, who made an extraordinary impassioned plea to his many (male) readers:

> Young men, before all else have concern for the honour and dignity of life. Offer to your *fiancée* a superb wedding basket, fill it with dahlias, roses, lilacs, carnations, gardenias of the most shining whiteness, but, above all, place there the immaculate flower of your virginity![46]

Such suggestions, it would appear, fell upon deaf ears. An illuminating fragment of evidence here is provided by the case of a workman called Jaudry, who had actually wanted to remain that very rare bird, a male virgin. An idealist, he confessed in an extraordinary private letter to Jane Misme that he had wanted to keep himself for the chaste maiden of his dreams, despite the fact that 'I was not backward and I was troubled a great deal by desire: that was a torment'. Until the age of twenty-five, he kept to his resolutions, refusing even to go to dance-halls, 'considering them places of perversion and moral defloration more than of healthy recreation'. Finally he met a girl he liked and started to court her. Great was his horror, however, when he discovered that she was an unmarried mother and had no inhibitions about wanting to sleep with him. The point of the story is not so much that the girl was sexually emancipated – this had long been true in the working class – but rather that she was astonished at Jaudry's own sexual reticence. Taunting him for talking to her like a priest, she told him that it was too silly for words to think that he had never gone to bed with a woman. Thus Jane Misme, in his view, was wrong to write an article suggesting that men should remain continent, for it was neither appreciated nor expected. He had abandoned his ideals and no longer restrained himself, though the streets of Paris filled him with disgust. [47] The trouble with Jaudry was that he had bourgeois standards for working-class women. For men in the bourgeois class, the existence of lower-class women with freer sexual morals was indispensable for the maintenance of the chastity of their daughters and sisters. Simone de Beauvoir's cousin Jacques did not share Jaudry's scruples but rather followed the classic pattern in losing his virginity to a woman of the popular classes before going on to make a successful match with a girl from his own social milieu. [48] Recent opinion polls suggest that such attitudes continue to exist even today, with male adultery enjoying widespread tolerance within the bourgeois class. [49]

Prostitution: the triumph of neo-regulationism

The ultimate sanction of the double standard, the system of regulated prostitution, survived the war more or less intact and continued to find protectors to shield it from the mounting abolitionist onslaught. As we have seen, all forms of prostitution had boomed during the war itself. But, after the armistice, the number of houses and of girls continued on the decline that was clearly discernible even before 1914: in a situation of acute housing shortage, the police were reluctant to grant permission for the opening of new houses because of the scandal that might ensue if priority over families was given to prostitutes. Thus post-war Paris was left with thirty tolerated houses and 270 *maisons de rendez-vous* which ministered to roughly one million men a year. [50] The number of registered prostitutes – 5283 in 1918 – dropped to 4813 in 1922 and was down to 4145 in 1924.[51] Of course the number of non-registered prostitutes remained very much higher: although, as ever, precise figures are not available, some indication of the extent of clandestine prostitution can be derived from the fact that of the 2322 prostitutes who appeared before the Prefecture of Police in 1924, only 740 were registered.[52] Yet at no stage did it ever seem likely that governments would dismantle the regulatory system. On the contrary, as in the years leading up to the war, they were concerned rather with how to make it function more successfully, as was confirmed by a circular of the Ministry of the Interior in June 1919 which suggested, on the recommendation of Dr Faivre, that the principle be retained and applied in the manner most conducive to the promotion of public health.[53] Another report by Dr Faivre advocated the establishment of centres for the treatment of venereal diseases, while the creation of a new Ministry of Hygiene established a new governmental institution through which the problem of prostitution could be tackled.[54] The war thus guaranteed the victory of neo-regulationism.

Doctors continued to form the vanguard of the neo-regulatory lobby. In an impressive medical thesis N-M Boiron argued strongly in favour of regulation. As always, the crucial consideration was public hygiene: since a prostitute could infect up to forty-five men a day with syphilis she had to be subjected to sanitary control. The existing régime, he maintained, did guarantee that soliciting and public provocations to debauchery were punished, even if the system did not always work as well as it might. The fault for this lay mainly with the municipal authorities, who often failed to devote enough attention to the problem.[55] The Englishwoman Ettie Rout, whose sterling wartime services in a Parisian tolerated house we have already noticed, wrote enthusiastically about the regulated system. According to her, very few of the girls ever became pregnant or contracted disease, thanks to the effectiveness of medical supervision. The principal method was the application of Vaseline and soap and water afterwards, with urination after each connection, but she herself, having learned of an antiseptic tablet prepared in Germany, was keen to develop Chinosol tablets whose results seem to have been satisfactory.[56] Another to defend the principle of regulation was Armand Villette, arguing that in addition to considerations of public health, the existing system served both to keep down the number of prostitutes and also to make possible their rehabilitation by having them sent back to their families.[57]

Some pro-regulationists, including Villette, denied that the life of a registered prostitute was intolerable. Marcel Rogeat cited a letter signed by eight prostitutes who claimed to be happy with their lot. Hélène, who drafted the letter, said that she had two children at boarding school and sent them money every week: if she were to live outside the *maison* she would face all kinds of problem whereas inside she was relatively free from worry. Rogeat added that the prophylactic measures were good, and that brothels played an important social role in providing an outlet for male frustrations. A case in point was that of a schoolboy who attacked and killed a cleaning woman and a *concierge* in 1934: according to Rogeat, the youth would not have been driven to these crimes if his parents had seen fit to take him to a brothel! Another with this viewpoint was F Jean-Desthieux, who argued that prostitution was as old as humanity itself and would disappear only with the end of the human race. Since it was well known that in wartime the military authorities had organised 'veritable infirmaries of debauchery', he saw no reason why civilian officials could not honourably provide similar facilities in peacetime, when the services of prostitutes were no less valuable, preventing 'the multiplication of rapes, passions, crimes, murders of every sort'.[59]

The regulationists did not have it all their own way in the post-war period. Bodies interested in moral reform, spearheaded by feminist and temperance organisations, launched considerable abolitionist campaigns. In the post-war period the most prominent abolitionist society was the *Union Temporaire contre la Prostitution Réglementée et la Traite des Femmes*, whose secretary-general was Mme Legrand-Falco.[60] At the provincial level, a particularly effective pressure group was the *Association Dauphinoise d'Hygiène Morale*, a multi-party, non-sectarian body headed by Dr Hermite, a surgeon and president of the local Radical-Socialist party. Their efforts were rewarded in June 1930 when the Municipal Council of Grenoble issued a decree suppressing regulation.[61] Paul Gemähling, a Professor at the University of Strasbourg, was another crusading abolitionist who succeeded in arousing public indignation among respectable citizens over incidents such as those surrounding a gymanstics festival in Strasbourg in the summer of 1925. For three successive nights young athletes made their way to the brothel quarter, where large crowds, including many minors, turned out to see them. Twenty worthy citizens drew up a petition protesting against the regulated system for its corruption of the nation's youth.[62] The new League of Nations also gave a substantial fillip to the abolitionist cause by its inquiry into the white slave trade in 1924, which issued in a strong condemnation of it in a report of 1927.[63]

It was always the abolitionists' contention that, apart from moral considerations and arguments relating to the dignity of women, the regulatory system never worked as it was supposed to. Increasingly fewer prostitutes bothered to enrol with the police, so that the system failed to maintain public order and safeguard public health in the manner claimed for it by its defenders. On the contrary, the system maintained important links with organised crime and the underworld, a fact which further explained police opposition to the abolitionists, since brothels were regarded as highly useful sources of information. The medical inspection of prostitutes was frequently inadequate, with the result that brothels served to endanger rather than to preserve public hygiene. Mme Legrand-Falco cited the case of one house where thirty-two cases of syphilis were contracted in two months. Finally, the system conferred excessive powers on the Vice Squad, whose members were notoriously corrupt. [64]

Yet, however persuasive their arguments, the abolitionists failed to carry the day in the period after the First World War. Despite a measure of success at the local level (like Grenoble, the municipalities of Mulhouse (1927) and Roubaix (1930) also closed down their brothels) no legislation against regulation was enacted at the national level until after the Second World War. [65] A bill introduced in the Chamber in 1936 by Henri Sellier, mayor of Suresnes deputy and minister, was defeated in the Senate in 1937, a defeat attributed by the abolitionists to the successful machinations of the brothel keepers syndicate. (It was alleged that they raised 50 million francs to buy support from the press, politicians and medical opinion.)[66] Only after the humiliating experience of Vichy and German occupation, when many of the leading Paris brothels were deeply compromised by their collaboration with the Nazis, did a climate of opinion develop which was favourable to abolition, now championed by Marthe Richard and the new Christian Democrat party MRP (regulation was abolished by the law of 13 April 1946). [67] In the inter-war period, France remained a country which officially made provision for the sexual indulgence of men on a different standard than that permitted to women.

Chapter IX
AFTER THE WAR: THE FATE OF FEMINISM

WITH the end of the War in sight, the prospects of the French feminist movement looked auspicious. Thanks to women's contribution to the war effort (and here of course feminists had been well to the fore) it was widely expected that fitting recognition would take the form of legislation to introduce the female suffrage, which, as we have seen, had become the movement's main demand in the years before 1914. A typical prediction was that of Gaston Rageot:

> Among all the novelties which this war, disrupting the old world to create a better one, will provoke, the most striking, perhaps, and the most lasting, will be furnished by the advent of women to national life.[1]

In like manner, the socialist deputy Bracke wrote that all the arguments used against women's suffrage collapsed in the face of their wartime achievements.[2] Naturally the feminists themselves looked forward to the imminent realisation of their hopes. Marguerite Durand, in a front page article in *L'Oeuvre*, stated the case for a new deal for women in the post-war period.[3] Suzanne Grinberg, female barrister and feminist, after sounding out the views of a number of parliamentarians in 1917, was optimistic about the chances of a bill to introduce women's suffrage.[4] Even opponents of votes for women were moved to advocate the suffrage for widows and female relations of those who had fallen in battle (an idea first suggested by the novelist and prophet of integral nationalism Maurice Barrès).[5]

These forecasts of an impending feminist victory appeared to be vindicated in May 1919, when the Chamber of Deputies debated the question of women's suffrage. Time and again in the course of the deliberations politicians of all parties returned to the theme that women were entitled to the vote as a reward for their endeavours on the home front, 'a gesture of justice and recognition', Jules Siegfried called it.[6] The turning point in the debate was a speech by the ex-socialist and former prime minister René Viviani, who eloquently summed up all the principal arguments in favour of women's emancipation, stressing their war record, their special talent for solving moral and social problems, and the example of other countries which increasingly recognised the political rights of women.[7] To his call for the immediate introduction of suffrage equality for women, the Chamber of Deputies responded by voting in favour of the bill by a majority of 344 to 97. The feminist lobby was jubilant. Lucie Colliard, one of the militant schoolteachers persecuted under the Clemenceau régime for anti-war activities, spoke for many when she wrote:

> At last we are going to have it, this ballot paper desired for such a long time. For the old gentlemen of the Senate, led by the sound arguments and eloquence of Louis Marin, will not dare to do less than their colleagues in the Chamber. [8]

Unfortunately for the feminists, however, all the celebrations proved premature. The 'old gentlemen of the Senate' did indeed do less than their colleagues in the Chamber. Having procrastinated until November 1922 before debating the bill passed by the Chamber, the senators threw it out by the narrow margin of 156 votes to 134. [9] Their discussions allowed most of the hoary arguments against women's suffrage to be aired. Some members took the view that the bill would undermine the already dwindling powers of the husband and head of the family: others claimed that women neither wanted the vote nor had any talent for politics. But the crucial argument against the bill was put by its *rapporteur* in the Senate, Alexandre Bérard, when he objected that it invited clerical rule and was likely to imperil republican institutions. [10] For the remainder of the Third Republic's lifetime, the spectre of clericalism was raised by aged senators of the Radical-Socialist party to defeat further attempts to achieve the political enfranchisement of women. A bill sponsored by the right-wing deputy Louis Marin to give women the vote in municipal elections was passed by the Chamber but thrown out by the Senate in 1927. In 1928, the senators passed a resolution to have no further debates on the subject of women's suffrage. In 1931 the deputies again carried a suffrage bill (by 319 votes to 1) without producing any change of heart in the Senate. [11] If the issue of women's suffrage is any criterion, it is difficult to sustain the thesis that the First World War destroyed 'all the old arguments about women's proper place in the community'. [12]

Public opinion and women's suffrage

Post-war France remained a basically stable and conservative society. The peasantry continued to be by far the largest single class in the population: and very few of the inhabitants of rural or small town France showed any enthusiasm for social or political experimentation. The publicity which the issue of women's suffrage received during and immediately after the war should not be allowed to obscure the mixture of indifference, suspicion and hostility with which the cause of women's rights was still viewed in the provinces, as the feminists themselves well knew. In many places feminism was associated in the popular mentality with the excesses of the English suffragettes. Thus, in the Charente-Inférieure for example, even when the local women sympathised with the suffrage cause they were afraid to identify with it openly.[13] In general, it was only in the towns that the feminists met with any success. Up and down the country they were able to establish committees and hold meetings but most often they preached to the converted. Their newspapers were unknown to the reading public, appearing only in limited editions and available only by subscription. Even the celebrated *Fronde* was unable to attract a circulation of more than 5600 in its heyday.[14] Marguerite Durand reckoned it collapsed because it was 'judged too bourgeois by the socialists, too serious by the Parisians, too Parisian by the provinces'.[15] No doubt her explanation is over-facile but it does have the merit of pointing out the enormous difficulties confronting the French feminists in their attempts to strike a sympathetic chord among the general public. When the well-known journalist Louise Weiss attempted to relaunch the suffrage crusade in the 1930s, she encountered the same apathy and ignorance which had greeted the earlier campaigns. As she put it:

> In 1934 the peasants remained open-mouthed when I spoke to them about the vote, the workers laughed, women in commerce shrugged their shoulders and bourgeois women repulsed me in horror.[16]

The anti-feminists in France did not constitute an organised lobby, but their jibes represent the kind of prejudices which blocked the advance of feminism. The old accusation that feminists were ugly, man-hating dragonesses, renegades from the true mission of their sex, was, if anything, reinforced in the aftermath of the First World War, given the demand for women to fulfil their traditional role as mothers and thus to participate in the work of rebuilding the population. In the eyes of some, feminism was still an outlet for single women who were either frustrated or demented.[17] Another favourite anti-feminist argument was the charge that feminism was an un-French phenomenon, flourishing only in Protestant and Anglo-Saxon countries. (One man was awarded a doctorate in law by the University of Paris for writing a thesis on the character of feminism which had this hypothesis as one of its cardinal points.)[18] The view that feminism was incompatible with femininity seems to have been popular with a number of literary women, who claimed that feminists mistakenly wanted to cultivate women's minds at the expense of their emotions.[19] Other contributors to the debate expressed fears about the type of role women might play if admitted to the political arena and recalled the excesses of the *tricoteuses* of the Revolution and the *pétroleuses* of the

Commune.[20] In themselves, these anti-feminist arguments counted for little and could easily be refuted by the superior intellectual armour of the feminists. But, like the clerical bogey constantly evoked by the senators of the Radical party at the prospect of enfranchising women, such crude and atavistic prejudices were only the outward symptoms of a deep-seated antipathy to change. Reason and justice might be on the side of the feminists but they still had to reckon with the force of massive social inertia in the 'stalemate society'.[21]

Certainly, then, the climate of public opinion in France as a whole was not conducive to the easy passage of a parliamentary bill introducing women's suffrage. On the other hand, it would be a mistake to exaggerate the extent to which the principal demand of the feminists had to yield to the force of anti-feminist pressure at the grass-roots. Public opinion was not so exercised by the spectre of votes for women that the enactment of the female suffrage bill was simply unthinkable. It is hardly sufficient to argue, as the anti-feminists did, that women were not entitled to the vote because there was no popular clamour for it. After all, when universal male suffrage was introduced in 1848 this was not in response to any widespread agitation among the majority of the male population. Similarly, no militant suffrage campaign was to precede the extension of the franchise to French women in 1945. Had women received the vote in 1919 – as seemed a distinct possibility – it is scarcely to be imagined that millions of Frenchwomen would have been so horrified as to have removed themselves from the electoral roll.

On the contrary, if the results of mock ballots in the national press can be trusted, thousands of women revealed a positive desire to vote. On the model of the poll conducted by *Le Journal* in 1914, *Excelsior* obtained 34,952 ballot papers in response to their mock election among women in Paris and the department of the Seine in 1919.[22] *L'Oeuvre*, now under the direction of Gustave Téry, who had earlier been responsible for the *Journal* ballot and who opened his pages to feminist contributors such as Jane Misme and Maria Vérone (he was also vice president of the LFDF), organised a ballot of a slightly different kind to try to gauge how the female vote in a Parisian constituency would have affected the eventual outcome of the elections in 1919. Over 12,000 women voted, though had their votes counted the *Bloc National* would still have come out on top.[23] In 1922, *Le Journal* itself held another referendum among its female readers in which some 224,155 women declared themselves in favour of the suffrage with only 1288 against.[24] Even if these polls should be construed essentially as publicity stunts on the part of enterprising press barons to try to increase sales among women, they furnish evidence nevertheless that women's suffrage was a cause which enjoyed not inconsiderable support in public opinion. As an enterprise, the female suffrage campaign was no more doomed to failure in France than it was predestined for success in Britain and America. If votes for women did not become a reality in France after the First World War, this was only partly because of its limited appeal to the majority of Frenchmen and Frenchwomen. More fundamental to the defeat of women's suffrage was the attitude of the male political establishment and the weakness of the feminist movement itself.

Politicians and women's suffrage

On the surface, the failure of the women's suffrage campaign appears attributable to the Senate's fears that votes for women would in reality turn out to be votes for the Catholic Church and therefore for those right-wing and anti-republican groups to whom the Church gave its political allegiance. Feminists said as much at the time and subsequently this view has come to represent the orthodox version of why the feminist movement in France was never able to enjoy the same success as equivalent movements in Protestant countries such as Britain, the USA or Holland. As Richard Evans put it in his recent comparative study of feminist movements in Europe, America and Australasia, the main problem in France was not the system of government but rather the Catholic Church.[25] François Goguel, one of the most distinguished students of the political history of the Third Republic, has likewise advanced the view that it was French conservatives who showed the greatest enthusiasm for women's suffrage as a way of dishing the Left.[26] Such judgements, however, too readily endorse the validity of the anti-clerical case. As the present author has had occasion to point out at length elsewhere, clericals and anti-clericals were fundamentally agreed that women's proper place in society was in the home.[27] In the nineteenth century, anti-clericals were at least as hostile to the cause of women's rights as was the Catholic Church. It therefore seems inappropriate to accuse the anti-clerical senators of the Radical Party of 'betraying' the feminist movement in the inter-war years, since the politicians in question were never feminists in the first place.

The French Radical Party's devotion to the cause of anti-clericalism in the years after the First World War is testimony not so much to the reality of the clerical threat as to their own refusal to come to terms with the twentieth century. With the separation of Church and state in 1905, the essential goal of nineteenth-century anti-clericalism had been reached. Certainly, the clerical problem did not disappear overnight: but by the 1920s it had become difficult to sustain the view that clericalism was still the enemy *par excellence* of the Republic.[28] For many Radicals, however, anti-clericalism was not without its uses. First of all, it provided the one unifying tendency which could hold together an immensely variegated, opportunist and largely undisciplined political party. Secondly, it served as an excuse to delay the implementation of political and social reform. Occupying the politicial centre, the Radicals represented the interests of 'static France', the small businessmen, shopkeepers, artisans and peasants who were determined to resist the encroachments of big business and big government. Once a force on the extreme left of the French political spectrum, Radicalism had developed into the creed of the new 'establishment' which was determined to preserve the existing order against the machinations of extremists whether of the Left or of the Right. Radical politicians therefore had an essentially negative concept of government in that they participated in cabinets more to deprive dangerous rivals of office than to carry out any positive programme of action. Politics was about the defence of the *status quo*.[29] Given that Radical support was essential for the formation of any government (for the political system was such that coalitions were necessary in order to ensure a parliamentary majority) it is perhaps not altogether surprising that the question of votes for women made little headway in inter-war France.

Characteristically, to preserve at least the semblance of standing for progress and reform – for if their pocket books were on the Right, their hearts were on the Left – the Radicals did not reject the idea of the female suffrage outright. The party rather used equivocal language expressing its desire to see the 'progressive accession' of women to political rights. At its congress of 1924 a resolution was passed in favour of making women eligible to vote in the municipal elections of 1929, but by 1927 it was again prevaricating on the issue, calling for further study of its implications.[30] The party was not without its champions of women's political emancipation. In the pre-1914 period, Beauquier, deputy for the Doubs and friend of Marguerite Durand, was the convenor of a parliamentary group for the defence of women's rights. One of the main spokesmen for women's suffrage in the Senate was Louis Martin, senator for the Var (1909-36), while Justin Godart, a close collaborator of Herriot, first as deputy, then as senator for the Rhône, was regarded as another friend of the women's movement. Support for the suffragists, however, was not always sincere. For example, Chautemps spoke in favour of the female franchise at the Radical Congress of 1927, yet he had voted against the suffrage bill in 1922.[31] In general, the Radicals were solidly opposed to any extension of the franchise to women: thus of the 104 votes against Bracke's suffrage motion of 1935, 94 were cast by Radicals and Radical-Socialists.[32]

Ultimately, then, the cause of women's suffrage in France became one of the casualties of the Third Republic's immobilism. The greybeard senators of the Radical party were by no means the only exponents of such politics, nor were they the only people to attach less than compelling importance to the issue of votes for women. The fact is that although politicians might sympathise with the justice of the feminists' demands as private individuals, on becoming cabinet ministers they were not prepared to stake the existence of any French government of the inter-war period on the issue of the promotion of women's suffrage. Thus in 1922, despite being on record as an advocate of votes for women, prime minister Poincaré made no attempt to influence the outcome of the deliberations in the Senate. Herriot, a partisan of at least municipal voting rights for women and premier at the time of the *Bloc des Gauches* government in 1924, also failed to act on behalf of the feminists once in office.[33] Even Léon Blum, first ever socialist prime minister and head of the Popular Front coalition which took power in 1936, shrank from introducing equal political rights for women and tried to palliate the feminists by appointing three women to junior ministerial posts. Taken as a whole, from the days of the Commune to those of the Popular Front, the leadership of the Third Republic showed symptoms of an extreme neurosis about the imminent possibility of social strife and therefore acted as though political and social stability enjoyed only the most fragile and parlous existence. In the 1930s, the external threat from Nazi Germany combined with the internal dangers from Fascism and Communism served only to strengthen the case against the introduction of a major political reform like women's suffrage.

Fundamentally then, women's suffrage was resisted within the political élite because of exaggerated fears about the consequences for the future security of the régime. In so far as they contributed to such fears, the old clerical-anti-clerical antagonisms had their part to play in destroying the feminists' hopes. Yet, paradoxically, women's suffrage was ultimately defeated not because it was recognised as being an issue of momentous importance, one that was too hot for the Third Republic to handle, but rather because it was regarded as being of little importance within the all-male political establishment. In France universal male suffrage had existed since 1848, and consequently franchise reform had ceased to be a major political issue (apart from the type of electoral system which should be used to represent the votes of the male electorate). In Britain, by contrast, the question of the right to vote was far from settled even by the Third Reform Act of 1884,[34] while in America women suffragists were fortunate in being able to hitch their cause to the larger and more successful bandwagons of Populism and Progressivism (and, in the South, to the defence of white supremacy).[35] French politicians might pay lip-service to the desirability and inevitability of female suffrage but in practice they had no incentive to push the issue in parliament.

This may be seen most clearly in the case of the socialists, who, in principle, were the party most devoted to women's rights. Even before the war they had been the first political party to admit women members. Several prominent socialists (notably Marcel Sembat and Ernest Tarbouriech) had close connections with the LFDF, while Bracke, the socialist deputy for the Seine and later for the Nord, was perhaps the most consistent parliamentary champion of votes for women throughout the life of the Third Republic. Seventy-three out of seventy-six socialist deputies signed the Dussaussoy-Buisson suffrage bill.[36] Yet, in reality, the commitment of the socialists to women's suffrage was a good deal less than total. As we saw in Chapter I, socialist (and syndicalist) leaders espoused the cause of women largely for propaganda purposes in order to make political capital out of depicting proletarian women as the victims of an unjust and corrupt bourgeois order. Certainly, to maintain their progressive image (even more of a necessity for them than for the Radicals) socialists were obliged to include political equality for women in their party manifestos. In practice, however, they did next to nothing to bring this about. They offered few signs of encouragement to women who wished to join their organisations, as Madeleine Pelletier discovered.[37] Moreover, as Charles Sowerwine has pointed out, the socialists were far more preoccupied with the question of proportional representation than with that of women's suffrage. In 1912, when PR seemed close to being realised, the socialists rejected feminist appeals to link this issue to that of women's suffrage.[38] If they continued to act as the principal spokesmen for the female suffrage in parliament in the post-war period, they did so because first of all it was a useful way of accusing bourgeois governments of being politically and socially retrogressive, and secondly, because they were secure in the knowledge that no bill passed by the Chamber of Deputies would ever succeed in obtaining a majority in the Senate, dominated as it was by Radicals. In general, the French Left answered the call for women's suffrage with varying degrees of hypocrisy, cynicism, apathy and boredom.

Feminists and Women's Suffrage

If the French feminists suffered defeat at the hands of a male political establishment which shrank from the controversy and uncertainty surrounding women's suffrage, they themselves did little to convince parliaments of the urgency of their cause. As a pressure group, the mainstream feminists were an abysmal flop. They never considered recourse to the massive lobbying conducted by American women between 1916 and 1918 and still less did they contemplate the kind of action employed by the militant suffragettes in England.

Far from radicalising the mainstream feminists, the First World War served to illustrate their timidity. Their enthusiastic support of the war effort has already been related. The charge of pacifism levelled with some justice at elements in the American woman's movement, could hardly be brought to bear against the principal women's organisations in France. [39] After 1918, as before 1914, their programme continued to demand a mixture of legal, political and moral reform: full civil capacity for married women, equal suffrage rights, the abolition of the regulated system of prostitution, a sustained attack on other social evils like alcoholism, tuberculosis and depopulation, and, of course, equal opportunities for women in employment. [40] Continuity in personnel was equally evident: just as many of the pre-war male politicians continued to dominate political life in the inter-war period, so the leading lights of the feminist movement – Avril de Sante-Croix, Cécile Brunschvicg, Maria Vérone, Jane Misme – were all women who had come to feminism in the years before 1914. When they were joined by new groups, these, if anything, were more conservative than the original organisations. The most notable addition to the mainstream movement was the National Union for the Women's Vote (*Union Nationale pour le Vote des Femmes*) founded in 1925 and headed first by Mme Levert-Chotard and then, after 1931, by the duchesse de la Rochefoucauld. Its membership reads like a roll-call of the French aristocracy and its influence was almost exclusively in conservative Catholic circles among women who had some previous experience of charitable work. From the outset, it consciously repudiated 'foreign' methods of propaganda and promised to maintain a 'correct' attitude even towards its adversaries. [41] The close personal connections which some feminist leaders enjoyed with members of the Radical Party also inclined the movement towards excessive toleration about their alleged anxiety about clerical influences on the female vote. [42]

The best way forward was still considered to be the rational deliberations and attendant favourable publicity of feminist congresses, a tactic which culminated in the staging of a female Estates-General in 1929 with the intention of refuting the allegation that women did not want to vote. [43] Yet in 1925 the UFSF seemes to have realised that its moderation had not been rewarded by any parliamentary action and drew up a protest accusing the authorities of taking advantage of their peaceful disposition. [44] Mme Odette Simon, a woman barrister, concluded that women in Latin countries had been too decorous and too afraid of ridicule in their campaigns for the suffrage: they ought instead to follow the example of English and American women as regards the intensity, extent and tenacity of their propaganda, though any 'complete imitation of the suffragettes would run the risk of damaging French women'. [45]

Occasionally, some of the mainstream feminists tried slightly bolder tactics. In 1923 some went around with a sticker in their hats saying 'Women must Vote', which in the eyes of a correspondent in *La*

Française was a 'decisive gesture' and a very daring act for a respectable woman.[46] Maria Vérone had the hare-brained idea of spying on brothels in the hope of catching senators as they came out and shaming them into supporting the female franchise.[47] She also called for an enquiry into the private lives of senators, with a view to establishing that those senators most opposed to women's suffrage were guilty of keeping mistresses and therefore not qualified to speak on questions which affected mothers and their families.[48] Another device was to lead a drunk man around the Luxembourg Palace with shouts of 'Look, here's someone with the right to vote'.[49] Such antics were patently not so much sensational as absurd, and revealed the bankruptcy of thinking in the feminist camp as regards getting themselves taken seriously by politicians and the public.

It is little wonder, therefore, that the French feminists remained an isolated and ineffectual lobby. Jane Misme herself had to admit that the movement lacked popular appeal and contained a large number of dilettantes, an élite of female intellectuals who have been and still are more often profiteers from, rather than supporters of, feminism'.[50] Another feminist also complained of careerism and the takeover attempts of society women who wished to make a name for themselves and their own particular côterie.[51] The truth was that mainstream feminism in France was the monopoly of a handful of upper-class women who were out of touch with the mass of the female population.

Radical feminism was even more of a cause without disciples. In March 1918 the *Comité d'Action Suffragiste*, a group which brought together women with socialist and syndicalist connections, could boast of only 2.70 francs in the bank; a collection taken up after one meeting raised the princely sum of 6 francs.[52] In February 1919 the indefatigable Hélène Brion started another newspaper, *La Lutte Féministe*, which took as its motto the injunction 'Woman, dare to be' and described itself as the 'unique and rigorously independent organ of integral feminism'.[53] But, as Brion herself complained, except for a handful of left-wing newspapers, no one took any notice of her journal's existence.[54] In so far as the radicals had a single forum, it was provided by *La Voix des Femmes*, which had first appeared in 1917 under the direction of Colette Reynaud, and whose feminist society of the same name, founded in 1920, gave the militants an opportunity to coordinate their activities.[55]

The radical sisters, however, did not find collaboration easy and quarrelled over the road to be trodden to reach the feminist goal. Militant suffrage activity, in the aftermath of the First World War and the Russian Revolution, seems to have lost much of its appeal. Instead, several of the leading radicals (including Madeleine Pelletier, Hélène Brion and Marianne Rauze) were for a time captivated by Communism, with its prospect of a completely regenerate society in which equal rights for women would inevitably be recognised. Some militants were to find a permanent home in the French Communist Party and the PCF in its turn, like the SFIO in the pre-war period, put up ineligible women candidates in a number of elections.[56] Disenchantment with both the Party and the Soviet Union sent other members of the advance guard in search of other causes with which to identify, the most favoured being that of pacifism. Marcelle Capy and Marianne Rauze both turned to the peace movement after their flirtation with Communism, though Hélène Brion, it is true, found more consolation in spiritualism. *La Voix des Femmes* itself was largely instrumental in establishing the League of Women against War (*Ligue des Femmes contre la Guerre*) in 1921, an organisation whose 500 members were pledged, in the event of war, never to support the national cause by social action on the home front.[57] After 1918, radical feminism in France, having fragmented into obscure and isolated sects, all but disappeared from view.

In the light of the general indifference of public opinion regarding the question of women's suffrage, the reluctance of political leaders to embark on reform, and the feeble nature of the feminist movement itself, it seems difficult to agree that the First World War destroyed all the old ideas about women's proper place in society. As in so many other respects, the war raised hopes of a breakthrough which in the end did not materialise. The feminist campaign and women's activities during the war itself may have prepared public opinion to anticipate change, but without the consent of the male political establishment no reforms could be carried in the legislature. Certainly, the cause of women's suffrage in France was not helped by the historical accident that universal male suffrage had existed since 1848. Unlike their British or American counterparts French feminists lacked the opportunity of a larger reform movement with which to associate themselves. Yet, ultimately, the British and American suffragettes had recognised the need to bring powerful pressure to bear on their political masters, and if at the decisive moment in 1917 the British suffragettes were quiescent, the threat of renewed militancy was always there in the background. By contrast, French feminists shared the impression of the Third Republic's politicians that, in the light of France's turbulent history since the days of the Revolution, the fragile nature of national unity ought not to be put to the test: hence their unwillingness to unleash a militant suffrage crusade. Their tame cooperation with the régime, however, brought only token recognition from the *République des camarades*. The tiny numbers and sectarian tendencies of the radicals, on the other hand, nullified their claims to be taken seriously. Despite the confident predictions of contemporaries at the time of the First World War, it should come as no surprise to the historian that French women remained without the vote throughout the inter-war period.

CONCLUSION: THE CONSOLIDATION OF DOMESTICITY

At the outset of the Third Republic domesticity was both the prevalent ideal and the essential social reality of the condition of French women who lived in an urban environment. When the régime foundered in 1940, despite the greater educational and job opportunities available to middle-class and working-class women alike, the doctrine of separate spheres had not been seriously undermined, either in theory or in practice. On the contrary, the First World War ultimately served to consolidate the domestic ideology in two major respects.

First, the appalling loss of French manpower (some 1,350,000 Frenchmen were slaughtered in the trenches) confronted a nation already undergoing a long-term decline in its birth rate with the spectre of depopulation. The response of the French state to this frightening prospect, with its stark implications for the future of France as a great power, was to throw its very considerable weight behind the pro-natalist campaign to try to turn French women into baby machines. In 1919 the newly created Ministry of Health gave official recognition to the pro-natalist organisations by establishing a Conseil Supérieur de la Natalité. Punitive legislation was introduced in an attempt to crush the neo-Malthusians who preached the virtues of family planning. A law passed on 31 July 1920 prescribed one to six months imprisonment and a fine of 100-500 francs for anyone convicted of disseminating birth control propaganda or facilitating the use of contraceptives. Another law of 27 March 1923 aimed at curbing abortions. Anyone who procured an abortion for a woman was liable to a prison sentence of between one to five years, while doctors, midwives or others who carried out the operation also faced the same penalty. A woman who obtained an abortion was herself liable to between six months and two years imprisonment and a fine of between 100 and 200 francs.[1] As far as the legislators were concerned the role of women as wives and mothers was more than ever considered to be their paramount contribution to society. The culmination of this pro-natalist policy was to be the introduction of the Family Code on the eve of the Second World War. By the decree-law of 29 July 1939 the state offered financial inducements to women who fulfilled their maternal role. An allowance was to be paid to couples who produced their first child within two years of marriage, with further bonuses payable on the birth of subsequent children.[2] All of the régimes which succeeded the Third Republic, it may be said, have persevered with this policy of trying to make maternity a financially attractive proposition. Proudhon would doubtless have approved.

Secondly, by requiring the mobilisation of female labour on an unprecedented scale, the war graphically highlighted the dichotomy between home and work existing in an economy characterised by the sexual division of labour fostered by the advent of capitalism. The problem of how to reconcile women's productive and maternal roles was not a new one but the war lent it a new urgency. Catholic conservatives belonging to the school of Le Play deplored the threat to morality and the future of the race represented by women's war work. As one of their number claimed, it was necessary to mount a crusade to persuade as many women as possible to return to their homes.[3] Another, who showed a greater appreciation of the dilemma by recognising the role which female labour could play in the post-war work of reconstruction, proposed that the family should be put into the workshop and the workshop into the home: in other words, factories should be equipped with crèches and playrooms for children, while domestic industry should be given every encouragement.[4] Part-time work for women was proposed as another possible solution (a suggestion which met with a certain amount of feminist support).[5] Other commentators were more intransigent, invoking medical opinion to the effect that babies born to working mothers were less normal than those born to full-time housewives. Doctors were in fact divided about the effects of munitions work upon women. Some argued that war work encouraged contraception and abortion in that it made women so obsessed with earning money that they were not prepared to have children. Other doctors, notably Dr Bonnaire, a member of the Committee on Female Labour and the official medical spokesman for the Ministry of Armaments, denied these allegations and stressed the importance of women's contribution to the national defence.[7]

On the eve of the First World War the French state had done very little to resolve the problem of the working mother. A law of 29 November 1909 guaranteed that women would not lose their jobs as a result of giving birth. Certain decrees on hygiene and other matters also dealt with maternity: for instance that of 28 December 1909, which banned women from loading or carrying any weights in the three weeks following a confinement. Another law of 12 June 1913 went further and prohibited women from any work whatsoever for four weeks after the birth of a child and also insisted on their stopping a fortnight before the expected confinement. Financial assistance was provided for women workers during this time by a law of 30 July 1913, but only if they were 'without resources', something it was often difficult to establish. There was also the question of when the money ought to be paid: a pregnant worker might stop work and find that the child did not arrive after two weeks, but if her allowance were cut off to ensure that she did not work for four weeks after delivery, she might be deprived of financial support at the crucial juncture. In any case, the sums they received were paltry (between 0.50 francs and 1.50 francs a day). [8]

The war intensified the pressure on the state to come up with a better solution. The most militant pro-natalists, headed by Professor Pinard, strongly urged governments to exclude all pregnant women from the labour force and to pay them instead a daily allowance of 6 francs. Senator Paul Strauss, president of the League Against Infant Mortality, and more sensitive to the claims of the *patrie*, advocated less drastic action, proposing that only a specified number of arduous and dangerous jobs should be closed to pregnant women and that measures such as the introduction of crèches be brought in to facilitate the task of the working mother. It was basically the latter option which the Ministry of Armaments adopted. Having issued instructions that pregnant women should not be turned away by employers and that their wages should not be less than those of other workers, it proceeded to lay down (by a law of 5 August 1917) that women should have the right to feed their children at work twice a day, morning and afternoon, without loss of wages. Supplementary legislation of 26 October 1919 guaranteed that women benefiting from existing maternity arrangements would qualify for a further allowance of 15 francs a day from the state for a year after giving birth. [9]

These laws, far from guaranteeing the future of the working mother, soon proved to be only a stop-gap solution to the problem of how to render work and maternity compatible. Only a very small number of munitions factories bothered to comply with the law of 1917. Even where crèches and feeding facilities were available it would appear that many women were reluctant to take advantage of them, preferring to feed their children at home. [10] This can only have strengthened the hand of the many industrialists who objected to such institutions on the grounds of their cost and who, in any case, as we have seen, had no plans to keep on their female wartime labour force after demobilisation. Like the state itself, most employers envisaged a future in which women's primary role would be to bring children into the world. In the bitter words of two neo-Malthusian propagandists:

> The rights of women increase. But what is their great duty: to give birth, to give birth again, always to give birth . . . Should a woman refuse to give birth she no longer

deserves her rights . . . The price of woman is the child. Childless by choice, she falls to the rank of the prostitute, the whore whose organs are only instruments, obscene playthings, instead of remaining the venerable matrix of all the future centuries.[11]

Well into the twentieth century, the Proudhonist antithesis of housewife and harlot retains its relevance for the historian of women's place in French society.

Abbreviations used in the Notes

APP	Archives de la Préfecture de Police
AN	Archives Nationales
Annales ESC	Annales Economies, Sociétés, Civilisations
art., arts., art. cit.	article, articles, article already cited
BMD	Bibliotheque Marguerite Durand
BMT	Bulletin du Ministère du Travail
CGT	Confédération Générale du Travail
CNFF	Conseil National des Femmes Françaises
IFHS	Institut Français d'Histoire Sociale
GT	Gazette des Tribuneaux
J.O.	Journal Officiel
UFSF	Union Française pour le Suffrage des Femmes
UNVF	Union Nationale pour le Vote des Femmes

Notes

Introduction

1. T Zeldin, *France 1848-1945*, 2 vols., (Oxford University Press 1973-7) vol.1 *Ambition, Love and Politics*.
2. The formula 'courtisane ou ménagère' comes from P J Proudhon, *Contradictions économiques. La propriété*. vol.II, (1846), p.197. See also *id., De la justice dans la Révolution et dans l'Eglise*, (1858) and *La pornocratie, ou les femmes dans les temps modernes*, (1875).
3. J Daric, *L'Activité professionnelle des femmes en France*, (Institut National d'Etudes Démographiques, cahier no.5, 1947), p.15.
4. Mrs F Trollope, *Paris and the Parisians in 1835*, (1836), vol. 2, p.93.
5. L Sanua, *Figures féminines, 1909-1939*, (1942), pp.41-2.

6   *Le Crapouillot*, no. 29, 'La Belle Epoque'.
7   The notion of a 'masculinist system', formulated by feminist pioneers of the mid-nineteenth century, is developed by P K Bidelman, *The Feminist Movement in France: the Formative Years 1858-1889*, (PhD Michigan State, 1975).
8   E Shorter, *The Making of the Modern Family*, (Basic Books, Inc. 1975): P Branca, *Women in Europe Since 1750*, (Croom Helm 1978).
9   T Judt, 'A Clown in Regal Purple: Social History and the Historians', *History Workshop*, no.7, Spring 1979, pp.66–94.
10   For a classic Marxist view, see A Bebel, *Women in the Past, Present and Future*, (1893); also J Fréville, *Les femmes et le communisme. Anthologie des grandes textes du marxisme*, (1951). A representative contemporary feminist view is J Mitchell, *Woman's Estate*, (Penguin, 1971).
11   S Verdeau, *L'Accession des femmes aux fonctions publiques*, (Law thesis, Toulouse, 1942), p.36.
12   M Collinet, *L'Ouvrier français. Essai sur la condition ouvrière 1900-1950*, (1951).
13   P Grimal (ed), *Histoire mondiale de la femme*, vol. IV, pp.160-1.
14   J Williams, *The Home Fronts. Britain, France and Germany 1014-1918*, (Constable, 1972), p.2.
15   A Marwick, *War and Social Change in the Twentieth Century*, (MacMillan, 1974), p.77.
16   See E Weber, *Peasants into Frenchmen: the Modernisation of Rural France*, (Chatto and Windus, 1977), esp. ch.11.

Chapter I

1   cf. the Roman epitaph *casta vixit, lanam fecit, domum servavit*.
2   *Le Ménagier de Paris*, ed. and transl. E Power as *The Goodman of Paris*, c. 1393, (London 1928).
3   Pierre Le Moyne, *La Galerie des femmes fortes*, (1647), cited by Carolyn C Lougee, *Le Paradis des Femmes. Women, Salons and Social Stratification in Seventeenth Century France*, (Princeton University Press, New Jersey, 1976), p.63.
4   C Hall, 'The Early Formation of Victorian Domestic Ideology' in S Burman (ed), *Fit Work For Women*, (Croom Helm, 1979).
5   Abbé de Gibergues, *Les devoirs des hommes envers les femmes, instructions aux hommes du monde prêchées à St Philippe-du-Roule et à St Augustin*, (1903).
6   On the origins and development of the Catholic attitude, see R R Ruether (ed), *Religion and Sexism. Images of Women in the Jewish and Christian Traditions*, (1974), and J T Noonan, *Contraception. A History of Its Treatment by the Catholic Theologians and Canonists*, (Harvard University Press, Cambridge, Mass. 1965).
7   Gibergues, *op. cit.*
8   For a general discussion of Catholic and conservative thinking on women and the family in the early nineteenth century, see R Deniel, *Une image de la famille et de la société sous la Restauration*, (1965).
9   Mme de Rémusat, *Essai sur l'éducation des femmes*, (1824); P Guizot, *Lettres de famille sur l'éducation*, (1824). These and other manuals are discussed in B C Pope, 'Maternal Education in France, 1815-1848', *Western Society for French History*, Proceedings of the Third Annual Meeting, Dec. 4-6, 1975.
10   Aimé Martin, *The Education of Mothers of Families or the Civilisation of the Human Race by Women*, (transl. 1860).
11   See Introduction, n.2.
12   J Michelet, *L'Amour*, (1858).
13   J Michelet, *Du prêtre, de la femme et de la famille*, (1845). See also T Zeldin, 'The Conflict of Moralities', in Zeldin (ed), *Conflicts in French Society: Anti-clericalism,*

Education and Morals in the Nineteenth Century, (Allen and Unwin, 1970).

14 J Ferry, *Discours sur l'éducation; l'égalité d'éducation*, (1870).

15 P Grimanelli, *La femme et le positivisme*, (1905).

16 E J Hobsbawm, *The Age of Capital 1848-1875*, (Weidenfeld and Nicolson 1975), p.3.

17 For a stimulating discussion of the bourgeoisie and bourgeois values, see T Zeldin, *France 1848-1945*, (Oxford University Press, 2 vols, 1973-7), vol.I, *Ambition, Love and Politics*.

18 J Simon, *La femme au vingtième siècle*, (1892), p.67.

19 Mme Romieu, *La femme au dix-neuvième siècle*, (1859), pp.28-9.

20 *L'Assiette au Beurre*, 15 Oct. 1912.

21 Zeldin, *France 1848-1945*, vol.II, *Intellect, Taste and Anxiety* pp.669-71.

22 *ibid.*, pp.668-9.

23 D Lesueur, *L'evolution féminine: ses résultats économiques*, (1900), p.5.

24 Cited by Madeleine Guilbert, *Les femmes et l'organisation syndicale avant 1914*, (1966), p.407.

25 *ibid.*, p.408.

26 *ibid.*, p.410.

27 P Gemähling, *Travailleurs au rabais. La lutte contre les sous-concurrences ouvrières*, (1910), p.150ff.

28 This account of the Couriau Affair is based on Guilbert, *op. cit.*, and a paper to be published by C Sowerwine, 'Socialists, Syndicalists and Women: The Couriau Affair'. I am most grateful to Dr Sowerwine for allowing me to see an early draft of his article.

29 M Perrot, 'L'éloge de la ménagère dans le discours des ouvriers français au XIXe siècle', *Romantisme*, 13-14, 1976, pp.105-21. This paragraph draws heavily on Mme Perrot's very useful article.

30 See H Medick, 'The proto-industrial family economy: the structural function of household and family during the transition from peasant society to industrial capitalism', *Social History*, vol.I, no.3, Oct. 1976, pp.291-316 and especially Louise A Tilly and Joan W Scott, *Women, Work and Family*, (Holt, Rinehart and Winston 1978).

31 E J Hobsbawm, 'Man and Woman in Socialist Iconography', *History Workshop*, no.6, Autumn 1978, pp.121-38. For criticism of various aspects of this article see M Agulhon, 'On Political Allegory: a Reply to Eric Hobsbawn', *History Workshop*, no.8, Autumn 1979, pp.167-73 and S Alexander, A Davin and E Hostettler, 'Labouring Women: a Reply to Eric Hobsbawm', *ibid.* pp.174-82.

32 Christiane Dufrancatel, 'La femme imaginaire des hommes: politique idéologie et imaginaire dans le mouvement ouvrier', in *L'Histoire sans qualités*, (Editions Galilée 1979).

33 L Chevalier, *Labouring Classes and Dangerous Classes in Paris During the First Half of the Nineteenth Century*, transl. F Jellinek, (Routledge and Kegan Paul 1973); and J Roberts, *The Paris Commune From the Right* (Longman, 1973 *English Historical Review*, Supplement no.6).

34 P Gemähling, *op. cit.*, p.150ff.

35 A McLaren, 'Sex and Socialism: the Opposition of the French Left to Birth Control in the Nineteenth Century', *Journal of the History of Ideas*, vol.37, 1976, pp.475-92. See also F Ronsin, 'La classe ouvrière et le néo-malthusianisme avant 1914', *Le Mouvement Social*, Jan.-March 1979, pp.85-117.

36 H Balzac, *The Physiology of Marriage*, (Eng. edn. 1904), pp.48-9.

37 L Fiaux, *La femme, le mariage et le divorce. Etude de physiologie et de sociologie*, (1880), p.306.

38 E Grenadou, *Paysan Français* (Le Seuil 1966) pp.49-50.

39   K Thomas, 'The Double Standard', *Journal of the History of Ideas*, vol.20, 1959, pp.195-216.
40   Fiaux, *op. cit.*, pp.94, 112. cf. C N Degler, 'What ought to be and what was: women's sexuality in the nineteenth century', *American Historical Review*, 79, Dec. 1974, pp.1468-91.
41   Penal Code, arts. 324, 336-9.
42   GT, 26 June 1847.
43   GT, 4 Feb. 1880.
44   GT, 11 March 1880.
45   GT, 5-6,7,8 April 1880.
46   GT, 24 July 1913.
47   GT, 20 March 1914.
48   GT, 2, 3-4 Jan. 1914.
49   Mme Romieu, *op. cit.*, p.13.
50   E Faguet, *Le féminisme*, (1907), p.272. See also E Goblot, *La barrière et le niveau*, (1925) which discusses the customs and practices by which the bourgeoisie distinguished itself from other social classes.
51   cf. the novel by René Boylesve, *La jeune fille bien-élevée*, (1912).
52   Goblot, *op. cit.*
53   M Prévost, *Lettres à Françoise*, (1902), pp.192-3.
54   F de Céez, *En attendant l'avenir: aux jeunes filles*, (1905), pp.47-8.
55   Y Delatour, *Les effets de la guerre sur la situation de la Française d'après la press féminine 1914-1918*, (Maîtrise, Paris, 1965), p.13.
56   M Prévost, *Les demi-vierges*, (1894).
57   F de Céez, *op. cit.*, p.3.
58   A McLaren, 'Some Secular Attitudes Towards Sexual Behaviour in France 1760-1860', *French Historical Studies*, Autumn 1974, pp.604-25.
59   On Tissot, see McLaren, 'Secular Attitudes'; Dr Rozier, *Des habitudes secrètes, ou de l'onanisme chez les femmes*, (1825).
60   B. Lecache, *Séverine*, (1930), p.27.
61   *L'Assiette au Beurre*, 2 May 1908.
62   F Henriques, *Prostitution and Society*, (1962-8), vol.III, p.231.
63   Dr O Commenge, *La prostitution clandestine à Paris*, (1897).
64   The essential work on prostitution is now A Corbin, *Les filles de noce: misère sexuelle et prostitution au 19e et 20e siècles*, (Aubier 1978). See also J J Servais and J P Laurend, *Histoire et dossier de la prostitution*, (1967).
65   A J B Parent du Châtelet, *De la prostitution dans la ville de Paris considérée sous le rapport de l'hygiène publique, de la morale et de l'administration*, (2 vols., 1836).
66   C J Lecour, *La prostitution à Paris et à Londres 1789-1871*, (1877), p.254.
67   A Flexner, *Prostitution en Europe*, (1914), pp.180-1.
68   Corbin, *op. cit.*, p.36ff.
69   *ibid.* pp.50-1.
70   Commenge, *op. cit.*, p.338.
71   E Zola, *Nana*, (1880).
72   G Darien, *Le Voleur*, (republished 1955). See the illuminating discussion of Darien in R C Cobb, *A Second Identity*, (Oxford University Press, 1969).
73   Corbin, *op. cit.*, p.362ff.
74   J Butler, *Personal Reminiscences of a Great Crusade*, (1896).
75   Corbin, *op. cit.*, p.315ff; Y Guyot, *La prostitution*, (1882); and L Andrieux, *Souvenirs d'un préfet de police*, 2 vols., (1885).
76   cf. *La Fronde* 22 Jan. 1898 and 24 Feb. 1898.
77   L Fiaux, *La police des moeurs devant la commission extra-parlementaire du régime des moeurs*, 3 vols., (1907-10); Corbin, *op. cit.*, p.466.

78   Corbin, *op. cit.*, p.669ff.
79   Numerous works set out the legal position of women in France. See for instance M Ostrogorski, *The Rights of Women*, (1893) and M Ancel (ed), *La condition de la femme dans la société contemporaine*, (1938). A lucid attack on the Civil Code can be found in T Stanton (ed), *The Woman Question in Europe*, (1884). A guide to the technicalities of the different types of marriage contract is J Monnet, *Le contrat de mariage et son utilité*, (1924). See also P Moissinac, *Le contrat de mariage de séparation de biens*, (2nd edn. 1924) and A Eyquem, *Le régime dotal: son histoire, son évolution et ses transformations au 19e siècle sous l'influence de la jurisprudence et du notariat*, (1903).
80   P Granotier, *L'autorité du mari sur la personne de la femme et la doctrine féministe*, (Law thesis, Grenoble 1909).
81   A Daumard, *Les bourgeois de Paris au 19e siècle*, (1970), p.192.
82   R Dereux, *Le budget matrimonial*, (Law thesis, Lille, 1923), pp.68–9.
83   A Rouast, 'La transformation de la famille en France depuis la Révolution', in *Sociologie comparée de la famille contemporaine*, (Centre National de la Recherche Scientifique 1955) and M Rouquet, *L'évolution du droit de la famille vers l'individualisme*, (1909).
84   E Acomb, *The French Laic Laws 1879-1889: the First Anti-clerical Campaign of the Third Republic*, (New York, 1941), pp.193-202.
85   P Margueritte, 'L'évolution de la morale et de l'amour', *La Revue*, 1 Aug. 1907, pp.329-37.
86   A Valensi, *L'Application de la loi du divorce en France*, (Law thesis, Montpellier, 1905). cf. R Phillips, 'Women and family breakdown in eighteenth century France: Rouen 1780-1800', *Social History*, vol.I, no.2, May 1976, pp.197-218.
87   GT, 19 Feb. 1914.
88   John T Noonan, *Power to Dissolve: Lawyers and Marriages in the Courts of the Roman Curia*, (Havard University Press, 1972).
89   GT, 3 April 1914, 14 March 1914.
90   GT, 27-8 April 1914.
91   GT, 14 March 1914.
92   Branca, *op. cit.*, p.161.
93   A Damez, *Le libre salaire de la femme mariée et le mouvement féministe*, (Law thesis, Paris 1905).
94   Moissinac, *op. cit.*, p.1ff.
95   Granotier, *op. cit.*, p.169ff.
96   *ibid.*, p.226.

Chapter II

1   Shorter, *The Making of the Modern Family*, (Fontana edn. 1977).
2   Branca, *Women in Europe since 1750*, p.45 n.1.
3   *ibid.*, p.89.
4   See, for instance, the plays of Augier and Scribe. S B John has an interesting chapter on this subject in J Cruickshank (ed), *French Literature and its Background*, vol.V, *The Late Nineteenth Century*, (1969).
5   Mme Romieu, *La Femme au dix-neuvième siècle*, p.21.
6   Maria Deraismes, 'Comment on se marie aujourd'hui', *Le Nain Jaune* 14 March 1866.
7   cf. *L'Assiette au Beurre*, 12 March 1904.
8   P Bureau, *L'Indiscipline des moeurs*, (1927), p.60. See also Zeldin, vol.I, p.288ff. for a discussion of the importance of financial arrangements in marriage. According to P Moissinac, *Le contrat de mariage de separation des biens* pp.5-6, 82, 346, marriages of the 287,179 which were celebrated in 1898 had some form of contract.

9   See A Tolédano, *La Vie de famille sous la restauration et la monarchie de juillet*, (1943), pp.94-5 for examples.

10   *Le Crapouillot*, no.19, 'Les bonnes manières', discusses marriage etiquette in detail.

11   R Pillorget, *La tige et le rameau. Familles anglaises et françaises 16e-18e siècles*, (Calmann-Levy 1979).

12   C de Ribbe, *La vie domestique, ses modèles et ses règles d'après des documents originaux*, (1877), p.165ff.

13   L Stone, *The Family, Sex and Marriage in England 1500-1800*, (Weidenfeld and Nicolson, 1977). See the review by E P Thompson, 'Happy Families', *New Society*, 8 Sept. 1977.

14   *La Fronde*, 4 March 1898.

15   cf. the satirical sketch of a day in the life of 'a lady of rank' by E C Grenville-Murray, *High Life in France under the Republic: Social and Satirical Sketches in Paris and the Provinces*, (1884).

16   B Dangennes, *Ce que toute femme moderne doit savoir*, (n.d.), p.31.

17   E Goblot, *La Barrière et le niveau* discusses the different customs and practices by which the bourgeoisie distinguished itself from other social classes.

18   Branca, *op. cit.*, T McBride, *The Domestic Revolution: The Modernisation of Household Service in England and France 1820-1920*, (Croom Helm 1976).

19   McBride, *op. cit.*, pp.19-20.

20   A Valette, *La journée de la petite ménagère*, (1883).

21   One of the pioneers of domestic science was A Moll-Weiss. See her *Le livre du foyer*, (1912).

22   Cited by Maria Martin, *La Fronde*, 23 Feb. 1898.

23   On medical developments generally, see Branca, *op. cit.*, p.122ff. On wet nursing, see G D Sussman, 'The Wet Nursing Business in Nineteenth-Century France', *French Historical Studies*, vol.9, no.2, 1975, pp.304-28.

24   L Delzons, *La famille française et son évolution*, (1913).

25   J Michael Phayer, *Sexual Liberation and Religion in Nineteenth Century Europe*, (Croom Helm 1977).

26   E Shorter, 'Female Emancipation, Birth Control and Fertility in European History', *American Historical Review*, vol.78, no.3, June 1973, pp.605-40.

27   Branca, *op. cit.*, p.90.

28   cf. P Bouvier, S J, *Les décisions du Saint-Siège et le devoir des confesseurs. Circa abusum matrimonii* (1925): Père Féline, *Catéchisme des gens mariés*, (1880 edn.); J Hoppenot, S J, *Petit catéchisme du mariage*, (1920 edn.).

29   J L Flandrin, *Families in Former Times: Kinship, Household and Sexuality*, (Cambridge University Press 1979).

30   Zeldin, vol.I, p.303.

31   On the theology of marriage see John T Noonan, *Contraception: a History of its Treatment by the Catholic Theologians and Canonists*, (Cambridge University Press 1965). On the sexual mores of Montaillou, see E Leroy Ladurie, *Montaillou*, (Penguin edn. 1980).

32   G Droz, *Monsieur, Madame et Bébé*, (1866).

33   Zeldin, vol.I, pp.296-7.

34   C N Degler, 'What ought to be and what was: women's sexuality in the nineteenth century', *American Historical Review*, vol.79, Dec. 1974, pp.1468-91.

35   E J Hobsbawm, *The Age of Capital*, p.234.

36   Branca, *op. cit.*, p.128.

37   On medieval contraception, see the forthcoming article by my colleague P P A Biller, 'Birth Control in the West in the 13th and 14th centuries'. I am very grateful to Dr Biller for allowing me to see a pre-publication copy of his article. For the Ariès thesis, see P Ariès, 'Interprétation pour une histoire des mentalités',

in H Bergues (ed) *La prévention des naissances dans la famille: ses origines dans les temps modernes*, (Institut National d'Etudes Démographiques, Travaux et Documents, Cahier no.35. 1960).

38   See J Dupaquier and M Lachiver, 'Sur les débuts de la contraception en France ou les deux malthusianismes', *Annales E.S.C.*, vol.24, 1969, pp.1391-1406; J J Spengler, *France Faces Depopulation*, (1938) and *id.* 'Birth Prevention in France', *Marriage Hygiene*, vol.3, no.1, Aug. 1936, pp.67-76.

39   On Robin, see D V Glass, *Population Policies and Movements in Europe*, (1940); F Ronsin, 'La classe ouvrière et le néomalthusianisme: l'exemple français avant 1914', *Le Mouvement Social*, Jan.-May 1979, no.106, pp.85-117; AN F7 12652: publications obscènes.

40   Branca, *op. cit.*, p.128.

41   Shorter, *Modern Family*, p.113ff.

42   Branca, *op. cit.*, p.129ff.

43   J Daric, *L'activité professionnelle des femmes en France*, pp. 15 and 36.

44   L R Villermé, *Tableau de l'état physique et moral des ouvriers employés dans les manufactures de coton, de laine et de soie*, 2 vols, (1840); E Buret, *De la misère des classes laborieuses en Angleterre et en France*, (1840); J Blanqui, *Des classes laborieuses en Angleterre et en France pendant l'année 1848*, (1849). An excellent introduction to these and similar enquiries is M Perrot, *Enquêtes sur la condition ouvrière en France au dix-neuvième siècle*, (1972).

45   Quoted in J Simon, *L'Ouvrière*, (1861), p.iv.

46   J Simon, *La femme au vingtième siècle*, p.81ff.

47   A Audiganne, *Les populations ouvrières et les industries de la France*, 2 vols., (2nd ed. 1860), vol.1, pp.68-9.

48   *ibid.*

49   M Pelletier, *Philosophie sociale: Les opinions, les partis, les classes*, (1912), p.142.

50   Branca, *op. cit.*, p.135.

51   Daric, *op. cit.* p.154.

52   Joan W Scott and Louise Tilly, 'Women's Work and the Family in Nineteenth Century Europe', *Comparative Studies in Society and History*, vol.17, Jan. 1975, pp.36-64.

53   M Gemähling, *Le salaire féminin*, (1912), pp.35-36.

54   *ibid.*

55   H Medick, 'The proto-industrial family economy: the structural function of household and family during the transition from peasant society to industrial capitalism', *Social History*, vol.1, no.3, Oct. 1976, pp.291-316.

56   O Hufton, 'Women and the Family Economy in 18th Century France', *French Historical Studies*, Spring 1975, pp.1-22.

57   W R Reddy, 'Family and Factory: French Linen Workers in the Belle Epoque', *Journal of Social History*, Winter 1975, pp.102-12. See also P Leroy-Beaulieu, *Le travail des femmes au dix-neuvième siècle*, (1873).

58   L Tilly and J Scott, *Women, Work and Family*.

59   Daric, *op. cit.*, p.80.

60   P Stearns, *Lives of Labour: Work in a Maturing Industrial Society*, (Croom Helm 1975), p.80.

61   *Cost of Living in French Towns. Report of an Enquiry by the Board of Trade into Working Class Rents, Housing and Retail Prices, together with the Rates of Wages in Certain Occupations in the Principal Industrial Towns of France*, (1909), p.xvi.

62   Tilly and Scott, *Women, Work and the Family*, pp.91-92.

63   *ibid.*, p.167.

64   *ibid.*

65   A McLaren, 'Abortion in France: Women and the Regulation of Family Size

1800–1914', *French Historical Studies*, vol.10, Spring 1978, pp.461–85.

66   F Ronsin, 'La classe ouvrière et le néo-malthusianisme'

67   Tilly and Scott, *Women, Work and Family*, p.123.

68   cf. Stearns, *op. cit.*

69   G Mény, *La lutte contre le sweating-system*, (Law thesis, Paris 1910), p.21. See in general M Gulbert and V Isambert-Jamati, *Travail féminin et travail à domicile*, (1956).

70   *Enquête sur la travail à domicile dans l'industrie de la lingerie*, (Office du Travail 1913), vol.I, p.727.

71   *Enquête sur le travail à domicile dans l'industrie de la fleur artificielle*, (Office du Travail, 1913).

72   cf. Buret, *op. cit.*, p.417, where he observed 'concubinage has become the normal state in the working classes'. Villermé, *op. cit.*, vol.I, pp.31–2 commented on the dissolute morals of the cotton workers of the east of France. See also Audiganne, *op. cit.*

73   J-V Daubié, *La femme pauvre au dix-neuvième siècle*, 3 vols. (2nd edn. 1870), vol.II, pp.98–9. According to her the Society of St François Régis legalised more than 100,000 unions in thirty years.

74   L Chevalier, *Labouring Classes and Dangerous Classes*.

75   Branca, *op. cit.*, p.90.

76   *ibid.*

77   Phayer, *op. cit.*, p.63.

78   Flandrin, *Families in Former Times*.

79   H Leyret, *En plein faubourg. (Moeurs ouvrières)*, (1895), p.122ff.

80   *ibid.*

81   M Frey, 'Du mariage et du concubinage dans les classes populaires à Paris (1846–1847)', *Annales ESC*, July-Aug. 1978, pp.803–29.

82   Villermé, *op. cit.*, vol.I, p.123; Simon, *op. cit.*, p.150.

83   C Dufrancatel, 'La femme imaginaire des hommes'.

84   R Michaud, *J'avais vingt ans. Un jeune ouvrier au début du siècle* (1967). For Lille in the 1830s see Villermé, vol.I., pp.81–3.

85   M Halbwachs, *La classe ouvrière et les niveaux de vie. Recherches sur la hiérarchie des besoins dans les sociétés industrielles contemporaines*, (1913).

86   All the nineteenth-century commentators note the working-class penchant for drink. See for example J Lefort, *Etudes sur la moralisation et le bien-être des classes ouvrières: intempérance et misère*, (1875).

Chapter III

1   P-M Duhet, *Les femmes et la Révolution*, (Colin: Collection Archives 1971).

2   cf. E Thomas, *Les femmes de 1848*, (1948).

3   The National Council of French Women, the principal organisation of the mainstream feminist movement, had a permanent committee on education. *La Fronde*, the first feminist daily newspaper in France, had a special correspondent to write on educational issues.

4   F Mayeur, *L'Education des filles au 19e siècle*, (Hachette 1979) is now the best introduction. See also E Charrier, *L'evolution intellectuelle féminine*, (1931) and A Prost, *Histoire de l'enseignement en France*, (1968).

5   Charrier, *op. cit.*

6   The most comprehensive treatment is F Mayeur, *L'Enseignement secondaire des jeunes filles 1867-1924*, (Thèse pour le doctorat d'état des lettres et sciences humaines, 2 vols., University of Paris IV, Paris-Sorbonne, 1975). Mme Mayeur's thesis has been published as *L'Enseignement secondaire des jeunes filles sous la Troisième République*, (Presses de la Fondation Nationale des Sciences Politiques

1977). See also O Gréard, *Education et instruction: enseignement secondaire*, vol.I, (1887).

7 Zeldin, *France 1848-1945*, vol.II, ch.4.

8 Mayeur, *L'education des filles*, p.21.

9 AN F17 8753-8755. See also C Sée, *Lycées et collèges de jeunes filles* (1884), pp.6-7 and S A Horvath, 'Victor Duruy and the Controversy over Secondary Education for Girls', *French Historical Studies*, vol.IX, Spring 1975.

10 Mgr F Dupanloup, *M Duruy et l'éducation des filles: lettre à un de ses collègues*, (1867) pp.15-16.

11 Mgr F Dupanloup, *Seconde lettre sur M Duruy et l'éducation des filles*, (1867), p.19.

12 AN F17 8753.

13 Sée, *op. cit.*, pp.7-8.

14 *ibid.* and AN F17 8753.

15 AN F17 8755. Duruy approved a speech along these lines given by the mayor of St Mihiel.

16 Sée, *op. cit.*, p.60.

17 J Ferry, *Discours sur l'égalité d'éducation*, (1870).

18 Zeldin, vol.II, p.153.

19 Tilly and Scott, *Woman, Work and Family*, p.178.

20 Sée, *op. cit.*, p.157ff., p.192.

21 AN F17 8757. Académie d'Aix: Rector to Minister of Education, 21 July 1885.

22 AN F17 14187. Le Mans: Report of Mayor to Municipal Council, 24 Dec. 1900.

23 AN F17 8770. Académie de Toulouse: Inspector to Rector, 2 Aug. 1886.

24 AN F17 8758. Académie d'Aix: Inspector to Minister of Education, 16 Aug. 1886.

25 AN F17 8763. Académie de Douai: Rector to Minister of Education, 14 Aug. 1886.

26 AN F17 14187: Minister's letter 20 March 1888 and note 1887.

27 Mayeur, thesis, p.543ff. See also G Coireault, *Les cinquantes premières années de l'enseignement secondaire féminin, 1880-1930*, (Thèse complémentaire, Poitiers, 1940), p.77.

28 Mayeur, thesis, p.894.

29 Coireault, *op. cit.*, p.29.

30 *ibid.*, pp.129-30.

31 Charrier, *op. cit.*, p.143ff.

32 L Weiss, *Mémoires d'une européenne 1893-1919*, (1968), vol.I, pp.139-41.

33 Weiss, *op. cit.*, p.93.

34 P Kergomard, 'La féminisation de l'enseignement primaire', *La Fronde*, 18 Feb. 1898.

35 I Berger, *Lettres d'institutrices rurales d'autrefois, rédigées à la suite de l'enquête de Fracisque Sarcey en 1897*, (n.d.). This is a marvellous collection of autobiographical statements.

36 *Autorité*, 16 April 1893, (cutting in AN F17 9399).

37 Berger, *op. cit.*, pp.1-11.

38 J Ozouf, 'Les instituteurs de la Manche au début du XX siècle', *Revue d'Histoire Moderne et Contemporaine*, 13, 1966, pp.95-114.

39 *La Fronde*, 16 Dec. 1897.

40 Berger, *op. cit.*, pp.54-7.

41 *La Fronde*, 25 Dec. 1897.

42 G Vincent, 'Les professeurs de l'enseignement secondaire dans la société de la Belle Epoque', *Revue d'Histoire Moderne et Contemporaine*, 13, 1966, pp.49-86.

43 Mayeur, thesis, p.553ff.

44 F Clark, *The Position of Women in Contemporary France*, (1937).

45 Phrase used by Aline Valette, *La Fronde*, 17 Feb. 1898.

46   J Bouvier, *Histoire des dames employées dans les postes, télégraphes et téléphones de 1714 à 1929*, (1930).
47   M Guilbert, 'L'évolution des effectifs du travail féminin en France depuis 1866', *Revue Française du Travail*, Sept. 1947, 764ff.
48   M Guilbert, *Les fonctions des femmes dans l'industrie*, (1966), p.59.
49   Guilbert, *op. cit.*, p.768.
50   Mlle T Razous, *Guide pratique des femmes et des jeunes filles dans le choix d'une profession*, (1910), pp.311-12.
51   Guilbert, *art. cit.*, p.768.
52   A Bonnefoy, *Place aux femmes! Les carrières féminines administratives et libérales*, (1914), pp.89-91.
53   R Guillou, *La Française dans ses quatre ages*, (3rd edn., 1911), pp.83-4; Gibon, *op. cit.*
54   F de Donville, *Guide pour les professions des femmes*, (1894), p.18.
55   Gibon, *op cit.*
56   Charrier, *op. cit.*, p.242ff. P Kergomard, 'Les écoles professionnelles de filles', *La Fronde*, 20 May 1898.
57   Mme G Regnal, *Comment la femme peut gagner sa vie*, (1908).
58   Razous, *op. cit.*, p.ii.
59   J Bouvier, *Mes mémoires: où 59 années d'activité industrielle, sociale et intellectuelle d'une ouvrière*, (1936).
60   *ibid.*, p.27.
61   J Vallier, *Le travail des femmes dans l'industrie française*, (Law thesis, Grenoble 1899).
62   'Le travail féminin à Paris, avant et depuis la guerre dans les industries du vêtement', BMT, Oct.-Dec. 1925, pp.348-9.
63   C Milhaud, *L'Ouvrière en France*, (1907), p.17.
64   *ibid.*, p.18.
65   BMT, *art. cit.*, p.351.
66   L and M Bonneff, *Les métiers qui tuent: enquête auprès des syndicats ouvriers sur les maladies professionnelles*, (n.d.), p.35.
67   Milhaud, *op. cit.*, pp.41-2. cf. AN F22 514, reports of factory inspectors on the temperature in factories plus related pamphlets, esp. P Boulin, *Les milieux chauds et humides dans l'industrie textile*, (n.d.).
68   Milhaud, *op. cit.*, pp.42-3.
69   *ibid.*, pp.70, 74.
70   *ibid.*, pp.75-6. cf. AN F22 512/513, Hygiène des travailleurs.
71   *Journal Officiel (Chambre des députés)*, 17 Feb. 1914.
72   K Schirmacher, *Le travail des femmes en France (Musée Social: mémoires et documents)*, May 1902.
73   Milhaud, *op. cit.*, pp.27-8.
74   M Guilbert, *Les femmes et l'organisation syndicale avant 1914*, (1966), p.21.
75   O Uzanne, *La femme à Paris, nos contemporaines*, (1894), pp.93-4; J Bouvier, *op. cit.*, pp.60-1.
76   BMT, Oct.-Dec. 1925, *art. cit.*, p.349.
77   Bouvier, *op. cit.*, p.52.
78   BMT, *art. cit.*, pp.349-50.
79   Milhaud, *op. cit.*, pp.79-81.
80   BMT, Oct.-Dec. 1925, pp.351-2.
81   AN F22 439: report of Mme Maître, 13 June 1911.
82   BMT, Oct.-Dec. 1925, p.352.
83   BMT, Jan.-March 1926, pp.1-24.
84   *ibid.*, p.7.
85   C Benoist, *Les ouvrières de l'aiguille à Paris*, (1895), p.33.

86   *ibid.*, pp.114–15.
87   BMT, Jan.–March 1926, p.10.
88   Bouvier, *op. cit.*, pp.53–4.
89   L Chevalier, *Les Parisiens*, (1967).
90   See E Zola, *Au bonheur des dames*, (1871) which forms the basis of an interesting study by F Parent-Lardeur, *Les demoiselles de magasin*, (1970). See also A Laine, *Les demoiselles de magasin à Paris*, (Law thesis, Paris, 1911) and C Lesellier, 'Employées de grand magasins à Paris avant 1914', *Le Mouvement Social*, Oct.–Dec. 1978, (the whole issue is devoted to the theme of women's work in nineteenth-century France).
91   Laine, *op. cit.*, pp.51–2.
92   *ibid.*, p.43ff.
93   *ibid.*, pp.58–9.
94   *ibid.*, pp.79–81.
95   *ibid.* p.88, quoting C Chessyon, 'Du rôle et de l'avenir de la petite et de la grande industrie', *Journal des Economistes*, Nov. 1884, p.314.
96   *ibid.*, p.92–3.
97   *Enquête sur le travail à domicile dans l'industrie de la lingerie*, vol.I, Paris, (Office du Travail, 1907), pp.648–9.
98   *ibid.*, pp.649–50.
99   *ibid.*, pp.658–9.
100 *ibid.*, pp.661–2.
101 *ibid.*, p.727ff.
102 *Enquête sur le travail à domicile dans l'industrie de la lingerie, t. II. Cher, Allier, Loir-et-Cher, Indre, Maine-et-Loire, Sarthe.* (Office du Travail, 1908) pp.234–6.
103 *ibid.*, pp.362–3.
104 *ibid.*, p.651.
105 *Enquête sur le travail à domicile dans l'industrie de la lingerie, t. III. Seine-Inférieure, Oise, Aisne, Somme, Pas-de-Calais, Nord, Meuse, Meurthe-et-Moselle, Vosges,* (Office du Travail, 1913).
106 *Enquête sur le travail à domicile dans l'industrie de la fleur artificielle,* (Office du Travail, 1913.)
107 Louis Bonnevay, *Les ouvrières lyonnaises travaillant à domicile* (1896), pp.78–80.
108 Quoted by Mény, *op. cit.*, p.97.
109 Uzanne, *op. cit.*, has colourful descriptions of these professions.
110 J Simon, *op. cit.*, pp.84–7.
111 Uzanne, *op. cit.*
112 T Zeldin, *France 1848-1945*, (1977), vol.II, p.943.
113 M Cusenier, *Les domestiques en France*, (Law thesis, Paris 1912), p.17.
114 T McBride, *The Domestic Revolution: The Modernisation of Household Service in England and France, 1820-1920*, (1976), pp.34–5.
115 McBride, *op. cit.*, cf. M Mittre, *Des domestiques en France dans leurs rapports avec l'économie sociale, le bonheur domestique, les lois civiles*, (1867), p.50.
116 Uzanne, *op. cit.*, p.63ff.
117 M Vilain, 'Les gens de maison', *La Fronde*, 14 March 1898.
118 Uzanne, *op. cit.*
119 Cusenier, *op. cit.*, p.165ff.
120 Bouvier, *op. cit.*, p.34.
121 Mittre, *op. cit.*, p.25.
122 Mme Romieu, *La femme au dix-neuvième siècle*, (1859), p.165.
123 F Fournier, *Des domestiques d'aujourd'hui*, (1877), pp.2–3. cf. E Legouvé, 'Les domestiques d'autrefois et ceux d'aujourd'hui', *Revue des cours littéraires*, 13 March 1869; C de Ribbe, *Les domestiques dans la famille*, (1862), p.14.

124   Legouvé, *op. cit.*
125   Cusenier, *op. cit.*, p.84.
126   *ibid.*, pp.90–2.
127   Bouvier, *op. cit.*, pp.38–9.
128   Fournier, *op. cit.*, pp.18–19.
129   O Mirbeau, *Le journal d'une femme de chambre*, (1900).
130   Cusenier, *op. cit.*, p.77ff.
131   *ibid.* p.304ff., and E Chauvet, *Le travail: études morales: les domestiques*, (Caen 1896).
132   Cusenier, *op. cit.*, p.123ff.
133   Mirbeau, *op. cit.*
134   Cusenier, *op. cit.* p.273.
135   Dr O Commenge, *La prostitution clandestine à Paris*, (1897), p.338.
136   GT, 10 Feb. 1914.
137   GT, 18 Feb. 1885.
138   GT, 4 March 1880.
139   GT, 7 March 1880.
140   GT, 17 April 1880.
141   GT, 7 Jan. 1880.
142   GT 18 July 1913.
143   GT, 4,5,6 Aug. 1913.
144   GT, 9 Jan. 1914.

Chapter IV

1   See in general J Abray, 'Feminism in the French Revolution', *American Historical Review*, 80, Feb. 1975, pp.43–62; A Dessens, *Les revendications des droits de la femme au point de vue politique, civil, économique pendant la Révolution*, (Law thesis, Toulouse, 1905); and L Lacour, *Trois femmes de la Révolution*, (1900).

2   A Rossi (ed), *The Feminist Papers from Adams to de Beauvoir*, (1973), discusses the stimulus given to feminist ideas by the Enlightenment.

3   See also Condorcet, *Lettres d'un bourgeois de New Haven à un citoyen de Virginie*; (1787); and *Essai sur la constitution et les fonctions des assemblées provinciales*, (1788).

4   All these pamphlets and petitions are discussed by P-M Duhet, *Les femmes et la Révolution*, (1971).

5   Olympe de Gouges (1748–93); real name Marie Gonze. Born in Montauban, the daughter of a butcher. Married an army officer, 1765. Went to Paris, where she established herself as a playwright. A moderate revolutionary who admired Mirabeau.

6   S H Lyttle, 'The Second Sex (September 1793)', *Journal of Modern History*, 27, 1955, pp.14–26; R B Rose, *The Enragés: Socialists of the Revolution?*, (1965), reviewed by R C Cobb, *A Second Identity*, (1969).

7   Lacour, *op. cit.*

8   R C Cobb, *Reactions to the French Revolution*, (OUP, 1972). See also O Hufton, 'Women in Revolution, 1789–1796', *Past and Present*, 53, 1971, pp.90–108.

9   C Patureau-Mireaud, *De la femme et de son rôle dans la société d'après les ecrits saint-simoniens, exposé analytique*, (Politics thesis, Limoges, 1910).

10   C Thiébaux, *Le féminisme et les socialistes depuis Saint-Simon jusqu'à nos jours*, (Law thesis, Paris 1906).

11   C Demar, *Appel d'une femme au peuple sur l'affranchissement de la femme*, (1833).

12   Thiébaux, *op. cit.*; M Thibert, *Le féminisme dans le socialisme français de 1830 à 1850*, (Law thesis, Paris 1926).

13   J Tixerant, *Le féminisme à l'époque de 1848 dans l'ordre politique et dans l'ordre économique*, (Law thesis, Paris 1908).

14   E Sullerot, *Histoire de la presse feminine en France des origines à 1848*, (1966).
15   J-L Puech, *La vie et l'oeuvre de Flora Tristan*, (1925) and E Thomas, *Les femmes de 1848*, (1948).
16   E Sullerot, 'Journaux féminins et lutte ouvrière (1848-49)', *Etudes présentées à Jacques Godechot. Bibliothèque de la Révolution de 1848*. Vol.XXIII, (1966).
17   E Niboyet, *Le vrai livre des femmes*, (1863).
18   Thomas, *Les femmes de 1848*, (1948).
19   E Thomas, *Pauline Roland*, (1956).
20   Sullerot, *art. cit.*
21   cf. G Kahn, *La femme dans la caricature française*, (1912).
22   Niboyet opposed divorce altogether. See *Le vrai livre des femmes*, p.236ff. Jeanne Deroin idealised the wife and mother: see her pamphlet, *Cours du droit social* (n.d.) and her *Almanach des femmes pour 1854*, (London 1854).
23   E Thomas, *The Women Incendiaries*, (1967), discusses these literary polemics. See also A Perrier, 'Grégoire Champseix et André Léo, *Actualités de l'Histoire*, 30 Jan.-March 1960.
24   O Audouard, *Guerre aux hommes*, (1860). See also L Abensour, *Histoire générale du féminisme des origines à nos jours*, (1921).
25   E Thomas, *Louise Michel*, (1971).
26   Paule Mink, born 1839 at Clermont-Ferrand. Daughter of high Polish nobleman who settled in France and became St Simonian. Author of anti-Second Empire pamphlet, *Les mouches et l'araignée*. Established feminist and revolutionary organisation the *Société fraternelle de l'ouvrière*, (1868). Active *communarde*. Disciple of Blanqui, then of Jules Guesde, then of Vaillant.
27   The republican connection is stressed by P K Bidelman, *The Feminist Movement in France: the Formative Years 1858-1889*, (PhD, Michigan State, 1975).
28   Biographical information on these and other leading feminists is taken, unless otherwise stated, from dossiers in the BMD, Paris.
29   *Congrès international du droit des femmes: ouvert à Paris, le 25 juillet 1878, clos le 9 août suivant. Actes. Compte-rendu des séances pleinières*, (1878).
30   Richer and Deraismes had a temporary disagreement over whether or not to campaign for the female suffrage. Deraismes came round to the view that this should be part of the feminist programme; Richer, as we shall see, was hostile to the idea.
31   For Auclert, in addition to her dossier at the BMD, see APP B/a 885: dossier Auclert: H Auclert, *Le vote des femmes* (1908) and *Les femmes au gouvernail* (1923).
32   *La Citoyenne*, March 1884.
33   APP B/a 885: report 29 April 1880.
34   *Congrès français et international du droit des femmes* (1889).
35   Marya Chéliga-Loevy (1854-1927). Born in Poland, where she was a writer and journalist, and active in feminism. In France she became an associate of Maria Deraismes. Founded the *Union Universelle des femmes* in 1891. In 1900 started a feminist theatre and for two years published an *Almanach Féministe*.
36   Jeanne Schmall (1846-1916). English by birth and retained connections with English feminism (a friend of Sophia Jex-Blake). Difficult to work with, but a major influence on French feminism.
37   Jeanne Oddo-Deflou. Wife of Henri Oddo, a librarian at the Chamber of Deputies. Member of the *Solidarité des Femmes*, before founding her own feminist society. Author of *Le sexualisme* (1906), denouncing the male supremacist type of mentality. See BMD dossier *Le Groupe Français d'Etudes Féministes*.
38   Mme Vincent (1841-1914). One of the earliest feminists. Interested in trade union movement. President of the UFSF. Campaigner against regulated system of prostitution (vice president of the *Association pour la répression de la traite des blanches*).

39   Maria Martin. Born in England. Mother of a large family. As feminist, primarily interested in the suffrage. Pacifist. Involved in adult education (one of the organisers of the *'universités populaires'* in the eighteenth arrondissement of Paris).

40   Eugénie Potonié-Pierre (1844–1898). A close collaborator of her husband, the pacifist Edmond Potonié-Pierre. A delegate to the congress of the Guesdist party 1893.

41   Marguerite Durand (1864–1934). Born Marie Rose de Labriolle, the illegitimate daughter of General Bocher, who did not recognise her. Convent-educated, but at 17 broke with her milieu to become an actress, eventually joining the Comédie Française. After four years, left to marry the brilliant young barrister Georges Laguerre, a protégé of Clemenceau. Their salon was noted for its enthusiastic promotion of General Boulanger. Separated from her husband and became a journalist. After her conversion to feminism, she concentrated on the issues of the female franchise and women's right to work.

42   *Voeux adoptés par le congrès féministe international tenu à Paris en 1896 pendant les journées du 8 au 12 avril.*

43   E Sullerot, *La presse féminine* (1963): Li Dzeh-Djen, *La presse féministe en France de 1869 à 1914* (Paris thesis, 1934).

44   The FFU (initially the *Fédération Féministe Primaire*) was the creation of Marie Guérin, a primary teacher, who in 1903 organised a movement to campaign for equal pay for women teachers. Some of its sections (e.g. that of the Isère, led by Venise Pellat-Finet, and that at Le Havre, led by Pauline Rebour) were militant supporters of women's suffrage. See *L'Action Féminine*, no. 11, Aug. 1910 and *L'Action Féministe*, Aug.-Sept. 1913.

45   Founded by Mme Marbel in 1907.

46   The CNFF was founded as a result of two congresses in 1900. The first, the *Congrès des institutions et des oeuvres féminines* was concerned largely with the organisation of charity. The second, the *Congrès international de la condition et des droits des femmes*, was much more feminist in inspiration (though the question of the franchise was excluded from discussion). Many delegates attended both congresses and a joint committee set up the CNFF. See dossier *Conseil National des Femmes Françaises*, BMD.

47   *La Française*, 7 Feb. 1914.

48   See *Congrès national des droits civils et du suffrage des femmes, 26-28 juin 1908, compte-rendu par Mme Oddo-Deflou*, (1911) and *Dixième congrès international des femmes; oeuvres et institutions féminines. Compte-rendu des travaux par Mme Avril de Sainte-Croix*, (1914).

49   P K Bidelman, 'The Politics of French Feminism: Léon Richer and the *Ligue Française pour le Droit des Femmes*, 1882-1895', *Historical Reflexions*, vol.3, no.1, 1976, pp.93-120.

50   *ibid.*, p.106, (transl. Bidelman).

51   E Brault, *La franc-maçonnerie et l'émancipation des femmes*, (1954).

52   M Pelletier, *La femme en lutte pour ses droits*, (1908), p.162, n.1.

53   M Fletcher, *Christian Feminism: a Charter of Rights and Duties*, (1915).

54   M Turmann, *Initiatives féminines*, (1903), p.18ff.

55   *ibid.*, pp.15-18.

56   One of the most frequently heard claims of the feminists was that the entry of women into politics would inject a new moral element into national life. cf. L Félix-Faure-Goyau, *La femme au foyer et dans la cité*, (1917).

57   See J Guesde and P Lafargue, *Le programme du parti ouvrier*, (1883); H Ghesquière, *La femme et le socialisme*, (Lille 1893).

58   E Thomas, *The Women Incendiaries* and *Louise Michel*. See also the review of the former by R C Cobb in *A Second Identity*, (1969).

59   On Rouzade, see C Sowerwine, *Women and Socialism in France 1871-1921: Socialist*

Notes

207

Women's Groups from Léonie Rouzade to Louise Saumoneau, PhD Wisconsin 1973).

60   *La Femme Socialiste* 1 March 1912. The history of the group is traced by C Sowerwine, 'Le Groupe Féministe Socialiste (1899–1902)', *Le Mouvement Social*, Jan.–March 1975, pp.87–120.
61   Sowerwine, *art. cit.* pp.100–5.
62   C Sowerwine, 'The Organisation of French Socialist Women 1880–1914: a European Perspective for Women's Movements', *Historical Reflexions*, 3, no.2, 1976, p.4, n.2.
63   M Pelletier, *La femme en lutte pour ses droits*, p.60. Aline Valette, secretary of the Guesdist party, was very much an exceptional case.
64   This concept has been developed by W L O'Neill in *Everyone was Brave: The Rise and Fall of Feminism in America*, (1969).
65   R Evans, *The Feminists: Women's Emancipation Movements in Europe, America and Australasia 1840–1920*, (Croom Helm 1977), p.133 is wrong to claim that all the leaders of the women's suffrage in France were Protestants. Jane Misme for example came from a Catholic background.
66   I Bogelot, *Trente ans de solidarisme 1877–1906*, (1908).
67   This theme figures prominently in all mainstream feminist propaganda. See *L'Action Féminine*, the official bulletin of the CNFF, *passim*.
68   BMD dossier, *Conseil National des Femmes Françaises*.
68   F Buisson, *Le vote des femmes*, (1911), p.45 stresses the point, putting the suffrage in the context of the other reforms demanded by the feminists.
69   BMD dossier, *Conseil National des Femmes Françaises*.
70   cf. the motion of Avril de Sainte-Croix at the congress on the condition and rights of women in 1900, (*compte-rendu*, p.111).
71   For an interesting comparison with the social purity campaign in America, see P J Pivar, *Purity Crusade: Sexual Morality and Social Control*, (Conn. 1973).
72   See for example G Greer, *The Female Eunuch*, (MacGibbon and Kee 1970) and J Mitchell, *Woman's Estate*, (Penguin 1971).
73   On Pelletier, see her file at the BMD and the thesis of C Sowerwine.
74   M Pelletier, *L'Admission des femmes dans la franc-maçonnerie*, (1905).
75   M Pelletier, *Mon voyage aventureux en Russie*, (1922).
76   M Pelletier, *La femme en lutte pour ses droits*, (1908).
77   M Pelletier, 'La question du vote des femmes', *La Revue Socialiste*, Sept.–Oct. 1908, pp.193–206.
78   AN F7 12557: reports 11 May; 21 May 1908.
79   M Pelletier, 'La question du vote des femmes' argued that prostitution would disappear once women had the vote.
80   M Pelletier, *L'emancipation sexuelle de la femme*, (1911) and *La désagrégation de la famille*, (n.d.).
81   M Pelletier, *L'amour et la maternité*, (n.d.).
82   M Pelletier, *Le droit à l'avortement*, (2nd edn. 1913).
83   M Pelletier, *La femme en lutte pour ses droits*.
84   M Pelletier, 'Les femmes et le féminisme', *La Revue Socialiste*, Jan. 1906, pp.37–45.
85   For Roussel, see her file at the BMD and her pamphlets, *Trois conférences*, (1930) and *Derniers combats*, (1932).
86   See reports in AN F7 12554. C Sowerwine, thesis, has a chapter on Petit.
87   *Le Droit des Femmes*, April–July 1910.
88   APP B/a 18 1651: Le mouvement féministe (1880–1940) report 6 July 1914.
89   *ibid.*
90   *ibid.*
91   *La Française*, 16 May 1914.
92   *La Française*, 4 April 1914.

93 According to the census of 1891, 17.5 million people – 46% of the population – still made their living from agriculture.
94 Maria Vérone (1874–1938). Born into a free-thinking family. Became a primary teacher but banned from teaching because of radical views expressed in public lectures. Joined *Fronde* as court correspondent, covering the Dreyfus trial. Read for the bar while bringing up two children by her first husband. Made *début* at the bar in 1907, soon became one of its leading figures, specialising in children's cases. Favoured militant tactics to obtain the suffrage.
95 cf. the discussion and vote on *union libre* at the 1900 congress on women's rights (*compte-rendu*, pp.195–205). At the congress of 1908, divorce on the initiative of one party only was decisively rejected (*compte-rendu*, pp.90–2). Clotilde Dissard, 'Féminisme et natalité', *La Revue féministe*, no.4, 20 Nov. 1895, pp.174–81, strongly denied that feminists were the enemies of marriage.
96 *La Française*, 22 Sept. 1907.
97 According to a letter in her file in the BMD written by a certain Marguerite Belmont.
98 *La Suffragiste*, Oct. 1911.
99 *La Suffragiste*, Nov. 1911.
100 IFHS, fonds Hélène Brion, 14 AS (183) 4 f. *Le combat féministe*, July 1914.
101 Pelletier herself took the gun-toting advice seriously (cf. *L'emancipation sexuelle de la femme*, p.9). She was also a friend of Arria-Ly, as is clear from a letter dated 8 Aug. 1925 in the collection of her correspondence in the BMD.
102 See Chapter I.
103 S Grinberg, *Histoire du mouvement suffragiste depuis 1848*, (1926).
104 *L'Action Féminine*, Feb. 1910.
105 Abbé P Naudet, *Pour la femme: études féministes*, (1903).
106 L Félix-Faure-Goyau, *op. cit.*
107 *La Française*, 9 May 1914.
108 cf. *L'Assiette au Beurre*, 6 June 1908.
109 C Turgeon, *Le féminisme français*, 2 vols., (1902).
110 A Lampérière, *Le rôle social de la femme*, (1898).
111 E Faguet, *Le féminisme*, (1907).
112 M-H Z Hocquard, *Féminisme et syndicalisme avant 1914*, (Thèse, 3e cycle, Tours, 1973).
113 *L'Ecole Emancipée*, 4 Feb. 1911; 22 April 1911.
114 *L'Ecole Emancipée*, 19 Nov. 1910.
115 *L'Ecole Emancipée*, 25 Feb. 1911.
116 *L'Ecole Emancipée*, 1 April 1911.
117 *L'Ecole Emancipée*, 17 June 1911.
118 Hocquard, *op. cit.*, p.347ff; BMD, dossier, 'typographes'.
119 Dossier, *Congrès du Travail Féminin*, BMD.
120 See above, chapter II.
121 *La Vie Ouvrière*, 5 July 1913.

Chapter V

1 See P Boulin, *L'organisation du travail dans la région envahie de la France*, (1927); G Gromaire, *L'occupation allemande en France (1914-1918)*, (1925); G Lyon, 'Dans Lille occupée', *Revue des Deux-Mondes*, 1 Feb. 1919, pp.537-66.
2 In addition to the works already cited, see the file on the forced labour of women in the BMD dossier, *Union Française pour le Suffrage de Femmes*.
3 M Donnay, *La Parisienne et la guerre*, (1916), p.26.
4 L Descaves, *La maison anxieuse*, (1916), pp.45-6, 48.
5 M Lesage, *Journal de guerre d'une Française*, (1938), p.25.

6   AN F7 12936: guerre de 1914: rapports de préfets et de commissaires spéciaux sur l'état d'esprit de la population, (1914–18). Report Dec. 1915.

7   *ibid.*, report 13 Aug. 1915.

8   M Vincent, *Memories of Paris 1914-1919*, (n.d.), pp.11–12.

9   G Perreux, *La vie quotidienne des civils pendant la grande guerre*, (1966).

10   APP B/a 1587: Physionomie de Paris (déc 1917-18). Resumée des surveillances exercées par la section spéciale. Report 13 Dec. 1917.

11   M Corday, *The Paris Front: An Unpublished Diary, 1914-1918*, Gollancz 1933, p.24.

12   *ibid.*, p.46.

13   APP B/a 1639: situation morale de la France pendant la guerre, 1914–18. Report 15 Aug. 1917.

14   *ibid.* The same attitudes were to be found in the countryside: cf. Besançon.

15   APP B/a 1587: report 3 Jan. 1918.

16   *ibid.*, report 19 Jan. 1918.

17   AN F7 12936: report Nov. 1915, 12e *arrondissement*.

18   *ibid.*, report 6 Sept. 1915, 4e *arrondissement*.

19   *ibid.*, 15e *arrondissement*; and AN F7 12936 report 13 Aug. 1915, 13e *arrondissement*.

20   AN F7 12936: report 13 Aug. 1915, 19e *arrondissement*.

21   *ibid.*, report 6 Sept. 1915, 19e and 20e *arrondissements*; report Nov. 1915, 10e *arrondisement*.

22   Marguerite Lesage, *op. cit.*, p.27.

23   *ibid.* pp.76, 85.

24   APP B/a 1614: report 20 Oct. 1918.

25   cf. André Ducasse, Jacques Meyer, Gabriel Perreux, *Vie et Mort des Français*, (1962).

26   *ibid.*, p.265.

27   AN F7 12936: report 4 April 1916.

28   Gabriel Perreux, *op. cit.*, pp.328–9.

29   Robert Graves, *Goodbye to All That*, (1929), pp.159, 209.

30   Dr Léon Bizard, *Les Maisons de prostitution de Paris pendant la guerre*, (1922).

31   See for instance *La Française*, 22 May 1915, where Odette Bussard describes the 'Trains Roses' which took spouses to the front 'en contrabande'.

32   Michel Corday, *op. cit.*, p.132.

33   Léon Riotor, *Journal de marche d'un bourgeois de Paris, 1914-1919*, (1934), pp.152-3.

34   APP B/a 1587: report 8 Dec. 1917.

35   *ibid.*, report 9 Dec. 1917.

36   *ibid.*, report 28 Jan. 1918.

37   *ibid.*

38   Ettie Rout, *La Belle Discrétion* (1923).

39   P Masson, *Marseille pendant la guerre*, (1926), p.55.

40   Gabriel Perreux, *op. cit.*, p.126. (March-April 1917: 10,538 cases of syphilis in the Army; July-Aug. 1917: 14,811 cases.)

41   *ibid.*, p.329.

42   Michel Corday, *op. cit.* p.81; cf. entry Oct. 1916: 'But a truer and deeper sign of the times is the unbridled extravagance and the widespread adultery'. (p.203).

43   Léon Riotor, *op. cit.*, p.321.

44   *ibid.*, p.325.

45   *La Française*, 13 Feb. 1915.

46   R Radiguet, *Le diable au corps*, (1923).

47   M van der Meersch, *Invasion 14*, (1935).

48   A Redier, *La Guerre des Femmes*, (1926).

49   *L'Illustration*, 28 June 1919.

50   *ibid.*
51   Marthe Richard, *Mon Destin de Femme*, (1974).
52   Mme Léa Bérard, *Les décorées de la grande guerre*, (2 vol.), (n.d.), who cites other names singled out for praise in the *Livre d'Or du Mérite Civil* and the *Citations de l'ordre du jour de l'Armée*.
53   See Bérard and also Dr Berthem-Bontoux, *Les Françaises et la grande guerre*, (1915).
54   Bérard, *op. cit.*, p.9.
55   Fernand Corcos, *Les femmes en guerre*, (1917), p.112. See also A Capus, *Le personnel féminin des P.T.T. pendant la guerre*, (1915).
56   Dr C Fromaget, *De l'utilisation de la femme comme infirmière en temps de guerre*, (Bordeaux 1916), p.6.
57   M Eydoux-Demains, *Notes d'une infirmière*, (1915).
58   Lucien Descaves, *La Maison anxieuse*, (1916), p.81. Louis Narquet, 'La Française de demain, d'après sa psychologie de guerre', *Revue Bleue*, 21-8 Sept. 1918 and 19-26 Oct. 1918, cf. Jane Misme, 'Le costume des infirmières', *La Française*, 5 Dec. 1914.
59   cf. the testimony of Gabriel Perreux, himself a *grand-blessé*, in Ducasse, Meyer, Perreux, *op. cit.*, p.229.
60   P. Masson, *op. cit.*, p.53.
61   Paul Courteault, *La vie économique à Bordeaux pendant la guerre*, (1925).
62   Henriette de Vismes, *Histoire authentique et touchante des marraines et des filleuls de guerre*, (1918).
63   Vismes, *op. cit.*, p.91.
64   See L Abensour, *Les vaillantes* (1917); Marie de la Hire, *La femme française: son activité pendant la guerre*, (1917).
65   *La Française*, 23 Feb. 1918.
66   Léon Abensour, 'Les femmes et l'action nationale', *Grande Revue*, Dec. 1915, pp.39-54.
67   La Hire, *op. cit.*, p.170.
68   BMD dossier Mme Brunschvicg.
69   *La Française*, 15 Nov. 1914.
70   AN F7 13226: La propagande féminine en faveur de la paix: synthèse d'activités des divers groupements. See also the articles by Mme Brunschvicg in *Jus Suffragii* 1 April 1915 and 1 Oct. 1915.
71   AN F7 13226.
72   *ibid.* and C Sowerwine, *Women and Socialism in France, 1871-1921: Socialist Women's Groups from Léonie Rouzade to Louise Saumoneau*, (PhD, Wisconsin 1973).
73   See A Kriegel, *Aux origines du communisme français, 1914-1920*, (1964), vol.I, p.132.
74   AN F7 13372: Rapport d'ensemble sur la propagande pacifiste en France; and Kriegel, *op. cit.*
75   BMD dossier *Hélène Brion*.
76   Sowerwine, *op. cit.*, pp.352-3.
77   For a stimulating discussion of this difference between 'private' and 'public' calendars, see R C Cobb, *Reactions to the French Revolution*, (OUP 1972).

Chapter VI

1   L Narquet, 'La femme dans la France de demain', *Mercure de France*, 16 July 1917, pp.250-74. See also *id.* 'La Française de demain d'après sa psychologie de guerre', *La Revue Bleue*, 21-8 Sept.; 19-26 Oct. 1918.
2   J Gabelle, 'La place de la femme française après la guerre', *Renaissance Politique*, 17 Feb. 1917.
3   H Robert, 'La femme et la guerre', *La Revue*, May 1917, pp.243-57. cf. Mme T d'Ulmès, 'Les femmes et l'action nationale', *Revue Hebdomadaire*, 7 Aug. 1915,

pp.73–83 and H Spont, *La femme et la guerre*, (1916).

4   BMD: dossier Marguerite Clément.
5   J Misme, 'La guerre et le rôle des femmes', *La Revue de Paris*, 1 Nov. 1916. cf. L A Gayraud, 'L'oeuvre féminine et le féminisme', *Revue Hebdomadaire*, 22 July 1916, pp.525–40.
6   M Lambert, 'La crise du foyer', *Opinion*, 9 Aug. 1919.
7   J Williams, *The Home Fronts*, p.34.
8   J Daric, *L'activité professionnelle des femmes en France*, p.30.
9   J Bordeaux, *Les carrières féminines intellectuelles: guide complet de toutes les situations ouvertes actuellement aux jeunes filles*, (1923); A La Mazière and S Grinberg, *Carrières féminines. Nouvelles écoles, nouveaux métiers, nouvelles professions*, (n.d.).
10 E Charles, 'Pour que les femmes deviennent des commerçantes', *La Renaissance Politique*, 11 and 25 Nov. 1916.
11 BMD dossier, Louise Sanua.
12 A La Mazière and S Grinberg, *op. cit.*
13 Charrier, *op. cit.*
14 A La Mazière and S Grinberg, *op. cit.*
15 N Kaan, 'Les écoles professionnelles et les écoles pratiques de commerce et d'industrie', *Europe Nouvelle*, 9 Feb. 1918.
16 A La Mazière and S Grinberg, *op. cit.*
17 M Facy, 'Les écoles supérieures de commerce', *Europe Nouvelle*, 26 Jan. 1918.
18 R Lagorce, *Carrières et métiers de femmes*, (1929).
19 ibid. cf. S Cordelier, *Femmes au travail: étude pratique sur dix-sept carrières féminines*, (1935).
20 Daric, *op. cit.*, p.39.
21 Mlle L Mauvezin, *Rose des activités féminines pour l'orientation professionnelle des jeunes filles*, (Bordeaux 1925).
22 Cordelier, *op. cit.*
23 Charrier, *op. cit.*
24 E Sullerot, *Woman, Society and Change*, (1971) p.184.
25 La Mazière and Grinberg, *op. cit.*
26 A Lehmann, *Le rôle de la femme française au milieu du XXe siècle*, (2nd edn. 1960).
27 Verdeau, *op. cit.*; Lehmann, *op. cit.*
28 E Morel and A Zegel, *Tous les métiers féminins, les métiers d'avenir, ceux qui meurent, ceux qui demeurent*, (1964).
29 Lehmann, *op. cit.*
30 Lagorce, *op. cit.*, p.21.
31 *Revue de l'enseignement secondaire des jeunes filles*, new series, 1927, No.1.
32 E.g. Mauvezin, *op. cit.*, p.363.
33 Lagorce, *op. cit.*, pp.30–1.
34 H Bureau, *Guide pratique pour le choix des professions féminines*, (1921), p.124.
35 Dr M Lipinska, *Les femmes et le progrès des sciences medicales*, (1930).
36 Morel and Zegel, *op. cit.*
37 Lagorce, *op. cit.*
38 *Revue Universitaire*, Jan. 1917, 63ff.
39 Cordelier, *op. cit.*
40 Lagorce, *op. cit.*; Mauvezin. *op. cit.*; Morel and Zegel, *op. cit.*
41 Morel and Zegel, p.155.
42 Cordelier, *op. cit.*
43 ibid.
44 Mauvezin, *op. cit.* p.290.
45 Morel and Zegel, *op. cit.*
46 S Babled, 'La vie difficile des jeunes "professeures" dans les petites villes', *La*

Française, 19 Aug. 1922.

47   J Misme, 'Hommage aux enseignantes', *La Française*, 10 Feb. 1923.

48   cf. Daric, *op. cit.*

49   Sullerot, *op. cit.*; J Daric, 'La répartition des sexes dans les populations urbaines. Le cas de Paris et du département de la Seine', *Population*, 1952, pp.593-618.

50   *Revue Universitaire*, April 1917, p.245ff.

51   *Revue Universitaire*, May 1917, p.331ff.

52   *Revue Universitaire*, Feb. 1919, pp.126-7.

53   *Revue Universitaire*, March 1919, p.183ff.

54   *Revue Universitaire*, April 1922, p.297ff.

55   F Mayeur, thesis, pp.979-80.

56   *Revue Universitaire*, March 1922, p.219.

57   cf. *Revue Universitaire*, July 1922 and *Quinzaine Universitaire*, 15 Nov. 1922.

58   *Revue Universitaire*, May 1922, p.364ff.

59   *Revue Universitaire*, July 1922.

60   G Coireault, *Les Cinquantes premières années de l'enseignement secondaire féminin 1880-1930*, (Law thesis, Poitiers 1940), pp.110-11.

61   cf. *Revue de l'enseignement des jeunes filles*, 1928, pp.49-55, 257-60.

62   Coireault, *op. cit.*, p.132.

63   E Charrier, *L'évolution intellectuelle féminine*, (1931).

64   Mayeur, thesis.

65   See for example M Rameau, *De la condition sociale des femmes au temps présent*, (1927); G Lombrosa, *La femme dans la société actuelle*, (1929); and E Baudoüin, *Comment envisager le retour de la mère au foyer*, (1933).

66   F Vitry, 'La bourgeoisie française dans la lutte pour la vie', *Renaissance Politique*, 24 and 31 July 1920.

67   A Lichtenberger, 'Le bourgeois', *Revue des Deux-Mondes*, 15 Nov. 1921, pp.338-57.

68   L Berger, *Le vaste champ du célibat féminin* (1936).

69   G Hourdin, *Les femmes célibataires vous parlent*, (1962).

70   M Huber, *La population de la France pendant la guerre*, (1931), p.552.

71   *ibid.*, pp.497-8.

72   G Duplessis-Le Guélinel, *Les mariages en France*, (1954), pp.185-7.

73   L Henry, 'Perturbations de la nuptialité résultant de la guerre, 1914-1918', *Population*, vol.21, 1966, pp.273-332.

74   A Girard, *Le choix d'un conjoint: une enquête psycho-sociologique* en France, (INED 1964).

75   L Chevalier, *Les Parisiens*, (1967).

76   S de Beauvoir, *Mémoires d'une jeune fille rangée*, (1958).

77   Girard, *op. cit.*

78   W D Camp, *Marriage and the Family in France since the Revolution*, (1961), p.66.

79   M Prévost, *Nouvelles lettres à Françoise*, (1925), p.147.

80   J Misme, *art. cit.*

81   *Revue Universitaire*, June 1926.

82   C Dyer, *Population and Society in Twentieth Century France* (Hodder and Stoughton, 1978, p.49.

83   J Cérez, *La condition sociale de la femme de 1804 à l'heure présente. Le problème féministe et la guerre*, (1940), p.253, citing the view of Professor A Bonnecase.

84   J Donzelot, *La police des familles*, (Editions de Minuit 1977).

85   A Isoré, *La guerre et la condition privée de la femme*, (Law thesis, Paris 1919), p.221.

86   *ibid.* pp.117, 221.

87   BMD, dossier *Conseil National des Femmes Françaises: Etats Généraux du féminisme*, 14-16 Feb. 1929, p.142.

88   M Vérone, *La femme et la Loi*, (n.d.).
89   *Etats généraux du féminisme*, pp.143-4.
90   *ibid.*, pp.144-5.
91   J Cérez, *La condition sociale de la femme de 1804 à l'heure présente: le problème féministe et la guerre*, (1940), pp.1-2.
92   Mlle Ballofy, *De l'admission des femmes aux fonctions de tutelle*, (Law thesis, Poitiers 1918), p.124.
93   M Ancel, *Traité de la capacité civile de la femme mariée d'après la loi du 18 février, 1938*.
94   S de Beauvoir, *Mémoires d'une jeune fille rangée*, (1958).
95   H Bordeaux, *Le mariage (hier et aujourd'hui)*, (1921).
96   J Rémy and R Woog, *La Française et l'amour*, (1960).
97   J J Spengler, *France Faces Depopulation*, (1938) and *id.*, 'Birth prevention in France', *Marriage Hygiene*, 3 Aug. 1936, pp.67-76.

Chapter VII

1   J Williams, *The Home Fronts*, p.30.
2   C Duplomb, 'L'Emploi de la femme dans les usines', *Renaissance Politique*, Aug, 1917; A Pawlowski, 'La main d'oeuvre féminine pendant la guerre', *Revue Politique et Parlementaire*, 10 May 1917; Magd-Abril, 'La femme à la conquête de l'usine', 8 June 1918.
3   G d'Avenel, 'Les nouveaux riches', *Revue des Deux-Mondes*, 16 July 1918, pp.378-96.; M Lambert, 'La crise du foyer', *Opinion*, 9 Aug. 1919.
4   See W Oualid, *The Effects of the War upon Labour in France* (New Haven 1923), p.139ff and A Créhange, *Chômage et placement*, (1927), p.74ff. In August 1914, 137,320 women were officially unemployed in Paris out of a total of 162,539 unemployed workers.
5   BMT March-April-May 1916, and H Sellier, A Bruggemann and M Poëte, *Paris pendant la guerre*, (1926).
6   We have no precise figures to measure the extent to which the female labour force expanded. A fairly clear picture of what was taking place, however, can be obtained from the results of surveys carried out by the Ministry of Labour. See BMT, Jan.-Feb. 1918 and BMT Nov.-Dec. 1918 for the statistical details. The findings of these enquiries have been used by A Fontaine, *French Industry during the War*, (New Haven 1926), an invaluable study on which most of this paragraph is based.
7   Sellier, Bruggemann and Poëte, *op. cit.*, p.45.
8   M Deschaud, *Les transports par chemin de fer pendant la guerre*, (1926).
9   M Ferro, *La grande guerre 1914-1918*, (1969), p.292
10   M Dubesset, F Thébaud and C Vincent, *Quand les femmes entrent à l'usine . . . les ouvrières des usines de guerre de la Seine, 1914-1918*, 2 vols. (Maîtrise d'histoire, Université de Paris VII, 1973-4), p.66. See also their article 'Les munitionnettes de la Seine' in P Fridenson (ed), *1914-1918: L'Autre Front*, (Editions Ouvrières, 1977).
11   E Sullerot, *Histoire et sociologie du travail des femmes*, (1968).
12   Ferro, *op. cit.*
13   AN F22 534, where the survey is classified under the unlikely title of *Organisation de crèches*.
14   A Pawlowski, 'La Main d'oeuvre pendant la guerre', *Revue Politique et Parlementaire*, 10 May 1917, pp.248 55.
15   P Hamp, *La France, pays ouvrier*, (1916), cited by Dubesset etc., thesis p.46.
16   BMT Nov.-Dec. 1918, table p.474.
17   *Renaissance Politique*, Aug. 1917.
18   *L'Information Ouvrière et Sociale*, 19 May 1918.

19   BMT Jan.-Feb. 1918.
20   *Union des Métaux*, May-Dec. 1915.
21   cf. the articles by Duplomb and Pawlowski cited above.
22   A Kriegel, *Aux origines du communisme, français 1914-1920*, 2 vols., (1964).
23   *L'information ouvrière et sociale*, 5 May 1918; article by J Servière, 'La peine des femmes'.
24   *L'Information ouvrière et sociale*, 13 June 1918.
25   *Union des Métaux*, May 1916; A Rosmer, *Le Mouvement ouvrier pendant la guerre*, 2 vols. (1936-39), vol.I.
26   Rosmer, *op. cit.*, p.453.
27   E Perrin, 'Bénédicte, ouvrière de guerre', *Revue Hebdomadaire*, 6 July 1918, pp.113-25. cf. J Domergue 'Le sort des femmes après la guerre', *La Réforme Economique*, 21 April 1916.
28   *Union des Métaux*, Aug. 1916.
29   *Union des Métaux*, Sept.-Dec. 1916.
30   *Humanité*, 24 Jan. 1917.
31   Baronne Brincard, 'L'armée féminine de la défense nationale', *Revue Hebdomadaire*, 9 May 1917, pp.339-47.
32   BMT, Sept.-Oct. 1919, pp.383-94.
33   BMT Jan.-Feb. 1919, pp.33-7.
34   *ibid.*
35   AN F22 443: 29 May 1917, Minister of Armaments to Minister of Labour.
36   AN F22 443: 22 April 1916. Division Inspector (Marseilles) to Minister of Labour.
37   BMT April-May-June 1925, p.185.
38   AN F22 538: Note sur les accidents du travail dont sont victimes les femmes occupées dans les usines de guerre. (Sous-sèc d'Etat de l'Artillerie. Comité du travail féminin.)
39   Dubesset, etc. thesis, p.57.
40   'Le mouvement des salaires depuis la guerre', BMT, June-Sept. 1921, pp.268-93.
41   W Oualid and C Picquenard, *Salariés et tarifs. Conventions collectives et grèves*, (1928), p.261.
42   *ibid.*, p.192.
43   Dubesset, etc. thesis, p.73ff.
44   M Guilbert, *Les fonctions des femmes dans l'industrie*, (1966), p.63.
45   L March, *Le Mouvement des prix et des salaires durant la guerre*, (1925), pp.289-90.
46   BMT July-Sept. 1927, pp.287-315; BMT, Oct.-Dec. 1927, pp.429-52.
47   Oualid and Picquenard, *op. cit.*, p.287.
48   J Lupiac, *La loi du 10 juillet 1915 pour la protection des ouvrières dans l'industrie du vêtement*, (Law thesis, Paris 1918). E & F Combat, *Le travail des femmes à domicile. Textes officiels, avec commentaire explicatif et étude générale sur les salaires féminins*, 1916.
49   BMT, July-Sept. 1925, pp.237-54.
50   Oualid & Picquenard, *op. cit.*, p.267.
51   BMT July-Sept. 1925.
52   R Jay, 'Une expérience sociale – le minimum de salaire dans l'industrie du vêtement', *Revue Hebdomadaire*, 17 Feb. 1917, pp.365-72.
53   BMT July-Sept. 1922, pp.79-80.
54   J Bouvier, *op. cit.*, pp.110-1.
55   L March, *op. cit.*, p.244.
56   M Guilbert, *op. cit.*, p.63.
57   E Sullerot, *Woman, Society and Change*, (1971), p.125.
58   Y François, *Des Mesures destinées à améliorer la situation des travailleuses*, (Law thesis,

Paris 1919), p.98ff, P Dumas, 'La semaine anglaise en France', *L'information ouvrière et sociale*, 16 Feb., 2 & 20 March 1919; R Jay, 'La semaine anglaise', *Revue Hebdomadaire*, 12 Jan. 1918, pp.155-62.

59 J Cavaillé, *La journée de huit heures: la loi du 23 avril 1919*, (1919).
60 R Picard, 'La journée de huit heures', *Europe Nouvelle*, 29 March 1919.
61 BMT, Oct.-Dec. 1925, p.399.
62 BMT, July-Sept. 1927, pp.290-2.
63 J Domergue, 'La journée de huit heures', *La Réforme Economique*, 21 Feb. 1919.
64 A Barjot, 'La sécurité sociale', in A Sauvy (ed), *Histoire économique de la France entre les deux guerres*, (Fayard 1972).
65 C-L Brunschvicg, 'Dans les usines de guerre. Les surintendantes d'usines', *L'Information ouvrière et sociale*, 24 March 1918; Magd-Abril, 'Les "surintendantes" dans nos usines de guerre', *La Renaissance Politique*, 22 Dec. 1917.
66 M Frois, *op. cit.*
67 *Humanité*, 10 Nov. 1924.
68 AN F22 439: Infractions à la législation 1894-1931: report of inspector, 3 Dec. 1924.
69 AN F22 443: Correspondence between Division Inspector (Lyons) and Minister of Labour, 9, 18, 25 June 1920.
70 AN F22 443: Division Inspector (Marseilles) to Minister of Labour, 29 Oct. 1920.
71 AN F22 443: Minister of Labour to Division Inspector (Marseilles) 22 Feb. 1919.
72 Dubesset etc. thesis.
73 A Fontaine, *op. cit.*
74 APP B/a 1406: 28 June 1917.
75 *ibid.*
76 *Humanité*, 4 Jan. 1917.
77 *Humanité*, 9 Jan. 1917.
78 *Humanité*, 16 Jan. 1917.
79 *Humanité*, 30 Jan. 1917.
80 *Humanité*, 14 May 1917; L-J Malvy, *Mon crime*, (1921).
81 *Humanité*, 16 May 1917.
82 *Humanité*, 19 May 1917.
83 *Humanité*, 22, 23 May 1917.
84 *Humanité*, 24 May 1917.
85 *ibid.*
86 *Humanité*, 26 May 1917.
87 *ibid.*
88 *Humanité*, 27 May 1917.
89 *ibid.*
90 *ibid.*
91 APP B/a 1376(2): rapports quotidiens d'ensemble, 26 Sept. 1917.
92 *ibid.*
93 *ibid.*
94 *ibid.*
95 *ibid.*
96 APP B/a 1376(2): 28 Sept. 1917.
97 *ibid.*
98 APP B/a 1376(2): 7,9,12,15,19,26 March 1918.
99 APP B/a 1376: (correspondance) Sept. 1918.
100 *L'Information ouvrière et sociale*, 18 Aug. 1918.
101 *ibid.*
102 APP B/a 1376: (correspondance) 18 Aug. 1918.
103 *ibid.*, 13 Sept. 1918.

104   *ibid.*, 15 Sept. 1918.
105   *ibid.*
106   *ibid.*, 24,25 Sept. 1918.
107   *ibid.*, 26, 27 Sept. 1918.
108   *ibid.*
109   *L'Information ouvrière et sociale*, 3 Oct. 1918.
110   APP. B/a 1376 (correspondance) 4 Oct. 1918.
111   *ibid.*, 5 Oct. 1918.
112   *ibid.*, 10 Oct. 1918.
113   *ibid.*, 12 Oct. 1918.
114   *L'Information ouvrière et sociale*, 17, 24 Oct. 1918.
115   Mlle Crabol, 'La presse et les grèves parisiennes de 1917', *Le Mouvement Social*, 53, Oct.-Dec. 1965, from which the quotations are also taken. See also APP B/a 1406, Chef. R G to Prefect of Police, 28 June 1917.
116   cf. *Humanité*, nos. for Dec. 1916 and Jan. 1917.
117   APP B/a 1406: report 28 June 1917: AN F7 13366(1): report 4 June 1917.
118   *ibid.*
119   AN F7 13366(1): report 4 June 1917.
120   APP B/a 1406: Chef. R G to Prefect of Police, 30 May 1917.
121   APP B/a 1406: 'Gérard', 30 May 1917.
122   *ibid.*, 'Debeury'.
123   AN F7 13366 (1): report 1 June 1917.
124   APP B/a 1406: Chef. R G to Prefect of Police, 30 May 1917.
125   *ibid.*
126   *ibid.*
127   APP B/a 1406: 'Guillaume', 31 May 1917.
128   AN F7 13366(1) report 4 June 1917.
129   APP B/a 1406: Chef. R G to Prefect of Police, 28 June 1917.
130   APP B/a 1406: 'Debeury', 30 May 1917.
131   APP B/a 1306: Chef R G to Prefect of Police, 28 June 1917.
132   APP B/a 1406: 'Debeury', 30 May 1917.
133   APP B/a 1406: Chef R G to Prefect of Police, 28 June 1917.
134   APP B/a 1406: 'Debeury', 30 May 1917.
135   *ibid.*
136   *ibid.*
137   Kriegel, I, p.214.
138   *ibid.*, p.213.
139   APP B/a 1376: (correspondance) 28 Sept. 1918.
140   APP B/a 1375 (2): report 22 Sept. 1917.
141   *ibid.*, and report 28 Sept. 1917.
142   *ibid.*, report 23 Nov. 1917.
143   *ibid.*, report 21 Dec. 1917.
144   *ibid.*, report 14 Feb. 1918.
145   *ibid.*, reports 16, 19, 23, 24, 25 March 1918.
146   *ibid.*, report 22 March 1918.
147   *ibid.*, reports 15 and 18 March 1918.
148   *ibid.*, report 15 Feb. 1918.
149   *ibid.*, report 9 March 1918.
150   *ibid.*
151   *ibid.*, report 2 March 1918.
152   *ibid.*, report 5 March 1918.
153   cf. Dubesset etc. thesis p.339ff., who take a different view, stressing the militancy of the women workers in the war factories.

154 APP B/a 1375 (4): report 8 March 1918.
155 Dubesset etc. thesis, p.285.
156 M Guilbert, *Les fonctions des femmes dans l'industrie*, p.64.
157 F Clark, *The Position of Women in Contemporary France*, (1937), p.89.
158 *La vie ouvrière*, 10 July 1919.
159 BMT, Jan.-Feb. 1918 p.3. A Fontaine, *French Industry During the War*, p.43 suggests a coefficient of expansion of 7.5 rather than 9.
160 Daric, *L'Activité professionnelle des femmes en France*, p.31.
161 A Vallentin, 'L'emploi des femmes depuis la guerre', *Revue Internationale du Travail*, April 1932, pp.506-21.
162 Daric, *op. cit.*, p.44.
163 *ibid.*
164 *ibid.*, p.58.
165 *ibid.*
166 *ibid.*
167 BMT, Jan.-Feb. 1918.
168 For a case study of this process in the metal industry, see M Guilbert, *Les fonctions des femmes dans l'industrie*, (1966).
169 Dubesset etc., 'Les munitionnettes', p.218.
170 AN F7 13356(3): Licenciement des ouvrières des usines de guerre.
171 BMT Jan.-March 1919.
172 P Juquelier, 'Le travail féminin dans l'industrie après la guerre', *Chimie et Industrie*, April 1919, pp.482-5; L Abensour, 'Le problème de la démobilisation féminine', *La Grande Revue*, Jan. 1919, pp.506-21.
173 This paragraph is based upon AN F22 534.
174 *L'Information ouvrière et sociale*, 18 July 1918.
175 *ibid.*, 14 July 1918.
176 *ibid.*, 18 July 1918.
177 *ibid.*, 28 Sept. 1918.
178 *Union des Métaux*, July 1918.
179 *ibid.*, Sept. 1918.
180 Guilbert, *Fonctions*, pp.69-70.
181 Anne-Marie Sohn, 'Exemplarité et limites de la participation féminine à la vie syndicale: les institutrices de la CGTU', *Revue d'Histoire Moderne et Contemporaine*, vol.24, July-Sept. 1977, pp.391-414.
182 *L'Information ouvrière et sociale*, 12, 16 Oct. 1918.
183 J Bouvier, *Mes mémoires*, p.93ff.

Chapter VIII

1 F Boucher, *A History of Costume in the West*, (1967).
2 J Pernaud, *Le vote des femmes et la thèse antiféministe*, (1929).
3 M Prévost, *Nouvelles lettres à Françoise ou la jeune fille d'après-guerre*, (1925).
4 Monks of Solesmes (eds), *The Woman in the Modern World*, (1953), p.29.
5 *ibid.*, p.35.
6 R Guyon, *Sex Life and Sex Ethics*, (1933), p.180.
7 Prévost, *op. cit.*, p.37.
8 Dr Toulouse, *La question sexuelle et la femme*, (1918), p.16.
9 *La Voix des Femmes*, 9 Jan. 1918.
10 M de Torina, *Mère sans être épouse*, (1917).
11 V Margueritte, *La Garçonne*, (1922).
12 A M Sohn, 'La garçonne face à l'opinion publique: type littéraire ou type social des années 20', *Le Mouvement Social*, no.80, 1972, pp.3-27.
13 G Guilleminault (ed), *Les années folles 1918-1927*, (1963), p.121.

14   H de Monthérlant, *Pitié pour les femmes*, (1936).
15   The point is made in Lt-Col O Berkley-Hill, 'Some reflections on the part played by inhibitions in the matter of sexual reciprocity', *Marriage Hygiene*, vol.2, 1935–6, pp.145–50.
16   *La Française*, 9 May 1925.
17   *ibid*, 6 May 1922.
18   Dr Alibert, *The Vices of Love: Self-Abuse among Women*, (new edn. 1918).
19   H Ellis, 'Sex in contemporary life', *Marriage Hygiene*, 3, 1937, pp.275–8.
20   Dr Bourgas, *Le droit à l'amour pour la femme*, (1923).
21   Dr Eynon, *Manuel de l'amour conjugal*, (n.d.), p.131.
22   *L'Accord Conjugal (les Cahiers Anonymes)*, (1925).
23   Association du mariage chrétien, *Les initiations nécessaires*, (1922), p.10.
24   Surbled, *op. cit.*, p.97.
25   *ibid.*, p.77.
26   I de Recalde, *Un scandale jésuite. L'Initiation sexuelle*, (1924).
27   Association du mariage chrétien, *op. cit.*
28   Dr H Abrand, *Aux parents et aux éducateurs: éducation de la pureté et preparation au mariage (jeunes filles)*, (2nd edn. 1927).
29   Dr G Surbled, *La vie de jeune fille: ouvrage réservé aux mères de famille*, (new edn. 1935).
30   *ibid.*, p.97.
31   J Veulette, *Pour trouver un fiancé*, (1923), p.19.
32   Veulette, *op. cit.*, p.12.
33   Dr Monin, *L'Hygiène de la beauté* (1922).
34   E Fenouillet, *L'Art de trouver un mari: étude pratique et lumineuse de la plus grande difficulté sentimentale d'après guerre*, (n.d.), p.125.
35   F L Schoell, *La femme française*, (New York 1924).
36   Monin, *op. cit.*
37   E Caustier and Mme Moreau-Bérillon, *Hygiène à l'usage des élèves de quatrième et de cinquième année de l'enseignement secondaire des jeunes filles*, (6th edn. 1924), p.140.
38   *ibid.*, p.141.
39   Guillemineault, *op. cit.*, p.227ff.
40   S de Beauvoir, *La force de l'âge*, (1960).
41   S de Beauvoir, *Mémoires d'une jeune fille rangée*, (1958).
42   *La Française*, 2 April 1923.
43   Dalloz, *Nouveau Répertoire de Droit*, (2nd edn. 1963), under 'filiation'.
44   P B Ghensi, *Cinquante ans de Paris, t. II: leurs femmes. Mémoires d'un témoin, 1889-1938*, (1940).
45   Dr Toulouse, *op. cit.*
46   Dr G Surbled, *La vie à deux: hygiène du mariage*, (new edn. 1925), p.51, cf. Dr R Chable, *Jusqu'au mariage*, (1923).
47   BMD, Jane Misme, correspondence.
48   S de Beauvoir, *Mémoires d'une jeune fille rangée*.
49   cf. R Franck, *L'Infidelité conjugale*, (1969); J Baroche, *Le comportement sexuel de l'homme marié en France*, (1969).
50   Dr L Bizard, *Les maisons de prostitution de Paris pendant la guerre*, (1922).
51   A Villette, *Du troittoir à Saint-Lazare*, (1925).
52   *ibid.*
53   N-M Boiron, *La Prostitution dans l'histoire, devant le droit, devant l'opinion*, (1926), p.243.
54   L Faivre, *Les jeunes filles vagabondes prostituées en prison*, (Medical thesis, Paris 1931).
55   Boiron, *op. cit.*

56   E Rout, *La belle discrétion*, (1923).
57   Villette, *op. cit.*
58   M Rogeat, *Moeurs et prostitution*, (1935), p.59.
59   F Jean-Desthieux, *Scandales et crimes sociaux*, (3rd edn. 1924), p.90. cf.
      G Pomeraud, *Notes sur la prostitution*, (1950).
60   See S Haïdar, *La prostitution et la traite des femmes et des enfants*, (Law thesis, Paris
      1937).
61   P Marcovici, *Au sujet de la prostitution: 'L'Expérience de Grenoble'*, (Medical thesis,
      Paris 1937); Dr Bütterlin, *L'Exemple de Grenoble. 15 années de lutte contre ce fléau
      social: la prostitution*, (1943).
62   P Gemähling and N Strohl, *Un dossier: les maisons publiques, danger public: l'exemple
      de Strasbourg*, (1925).
63   M Gand, *La traite des femmes*, (1927).
64   P Gemähling, M Pinard and Dr Maitry, *Les scandales de la prostitution réglementée*,
      (n.d.); M Legrand-Falco, *Les rouages secrets du système de la prostitution réglementée*,
      (1936).
65   J J Servais and J-P Laurend, *Histoire et dossier de la prostitution*, (1965).
66   P Gemähling and D Parker, *La fin d'un scandale: les maisons publiques seront fermées*,
      (1946).
67   *ibid.* and M Richard, *Mon destin de femme*, (1974).

Chapter IX

1   G Rageot, *La Française dans la guerre*, (n.d.), p.3.
2   Bracke, 'Le suffrage des femmes', *Humanité*, 23 June 1917.
3   *L'Oeuvre*, 2 Feb. 1916.
4   S Grinberg, 'Le suffrage des femmes', *Renaissance Politique*, 19 Jan., 2 Feb. 1918.
5   F Masson, 'Les femmes pendant et après la guerre', *Revue Hebdomadaire*, 3 May
      1917.
6   *Journal Officiel*, (Chambre) séance 8 May 1919.
7   *ibid.*, séance 20 May 1919. cf. S Grinberg, *Histoire du mouvement suffragiste depuis
      1848*, (1926).
8   L Colliard, 'Le suffrage des femmes', *La vie ouvrière*, 11 June 1919.
9   *Journal Officiel*, (sénat) séance 7 Nov. 1922.
10   *Impressions Sénat*, (1919) no. 564.
11   J P Marichy, *La deuxième chambre dans la vie politique française depuis 1875*, (1969).
12   A Marwick, *War and Social Change in the Twentieth Century*, p.77.
13   *Minerva*, 5 July 1925.
14   AN F7 12544: report, 7 Oct. 1904.
15   Quoted by E Sullerot, *La presse féminine*, (1963), p.43.
16   L Weiss, *Années de la lutte pour le droit de suffrage 1934-1939*, (1946), p.22.
17   Lt G Grandjean, *De la déprivation . . . des femmes . . . des décadences!*, (1919).
18   A Leclère, *Le vote des femmes en France: les causes de l'attitude particulière à notre pays*,
      (Law thesis, Paris 1929).
19   L Zanta, *Psychologie du féminisme*, (1922); C Yver, *Dans le jardin du féminisme*,
      (1920); Mme Rachilde, *Pourquoi je ne suis pas féministe*, (1928).
20   J Pernaud, *Le vote des femmes et la thèse antiféministe*, (1929), p.86.
21   The phrase is borrowed from Stanley Hoffmann. See *In Search of France*, (Havard
      UP 1963).
22   *Excelsior*, 3 Dec. 1919.
23   *L'Oeuvre*, 27 Nov. 1919; *La Française*, 29 Nov. 1919.
24   *Le Journal*, 7 Nov. 1922.
25   R Evans, *The Feminists*, p.124.
26   F Goguel, *La politique des partis sous la Troisieme République*, (1958), p.222-3.

220   *Housewife or Harlot*

27   J F McMillan, 'Clericals, Anticlericals and the Women's Movement in France under the Third Republic, to appear in *Historical Journal*, (1981).
28   See H S Paul, *The Second Ralliement: the Rapprochement between Church and State in France in the Twentieth Century* (Catholic University Press, Washington, 1967).
29   P J Larmour, *The French Radical Party in the 1930s*, (Stanford, 1964); F de Tarr, *The French Radical Party from Herriot to Mendes-France*, (1961).
30   *La Française*, 22 Nov. 1927.
31   *ibid.*
32   *Le Journal*, 2 March 1935.
33   *La Française* kept its readers informed of politicians' attitude to the suffrage.
34   M Pugh, 'Politicians and the Women's Vote 1914-1918', *History*, 1974; D Morgan, *Suffragists and Liberals: the Politics of Women's Suffrage in England*, (Oxford 1975).
35   A S Kraditor, *The Ideas of the Woman Suffrage Movement 1890-1920*, (Anchor Books edn. 1971); E Flexner, *Century of Struggle. The Woman's Rights Movement in the United States*, (Cambridge, Mass. 1966).
36   C Sowerwine, *Women and Socialism in France 1871-1921: Socialist Women's Groups from Léonie Rouzade to Louise Saumoneau* (PhD, Wisconsin 1973), p.207. See also the revised version of Dr Sowerwine's thesis, *Les femmes et le socialisme. Un siècle d'histoire*, (Fondation Nationale des Sciences Politiques 1978).
37   M Pelletier, *La femme en lutte pour ses droits*, p.60.
38   Sowerwine thesis, p.207.
39   See chapter V.
40   *La Française*, 15 Nov. 1919.
41   S Desternes, *Trente ans d'efforts au service de la cause féminine*, (Union Nationale pour le Vote des Femmes), (1959).
42   L Sanua, *Figures féminines 1909-1939*, (1942), p.45.
43   BMD, dossier *Conseil National des Femmes Françaises. Etats-Généraux de Féminisme*, 14-16 Feb. 1929.
44   AN F7 13226 (3) 1: report 5 March 1925.
45   *La Française*, 5 May 1923.
46   *La Française*, 3 Feb. 1923.
47   AN F7 13226: UFSF, 1926-1928: report 28 June 1928.
48   AN F7 13226 (2): report 25 Oct. 1928.
49   *ibid.*
50   Article in *L'Oeuvre*, quoted by F Golland, *Les féministes françaises*, (1925), p.177.
51   H Louise, 'Le féminisme dans la rue', *Le Cri des Femmes*, 4 April 1914.
52   APP B/a 1651: (correspondance) 16 March 1918.
53   *La Lutte Féministe*, no.1, 20 Feb. 1919.
54   *La Lutte Féministe*, no.2, 20 March 1919.
55   APP B/a 1651: report 20 June 1920.
56   E.g. two candidates of the PCF were elected at Bobigny and Douarnenez in the municipal elections of 1925. *La Française*, 9 May 1925.
57   APP B/a 1651: report 24 Feb. 1922.

Conclusion

1   See D V Glass, *Population Policies and Movements in Europe*, (1940); and *id.*, 'The Effectiveness of Abortion Legislation in Six Countries', *Modern Law Review*, 1938, pp.96-125.
2   A Sauvy (ed), *Histoire économique de la France entre les deux guerres*, (Fayard 1972), pp.386-8.
3   F Lepelletier, 'La situation de la femme au lendemain de la guerre', *La Réforme Sociale*, March 1919, pp.180-92.

4   H Joly, 'De l'extension du travail des femmes après la guerre', *Le Correspondant*, 10 Jan. 1917, pp.3-34.

5   A de Sainte-Croix, 'Le travail des femmes et le demi-temps', *Musée Social. Mémoires et Documents*, June 1919, pp.171-8.

6   P Juquelier, 'Le travail féminin dans l'industrie après la guerre', *Chimie et Industrie*, April 1919, pp.482-5.

7   Dubesset, etc., 'Les munitionnettes de la Seine' in *L'Autre Front*, p.202ff.

8   Y François, *Des mesures destinées à ameliorer la situation des travailleuses*, (Law thesis, Paris, 1919), p.159ff: Mme P Gemähling, *La maternité ouvrière et sa protection légale en France*, (1915) in AN F22 444: brochures diverses: and P Hamp, 'Le droit de la mère', *L'Information ouvrière et sociale*, 30 May 1918.

9   M Frois, *La santé et le travail des femmes pendant la guerre* (1926), p.119ff: Mme Letellier, *Les chambres d'allaitement dans les établissements industriels et commerciaux*, (1920) in AN F22 444: and Dubesset, etc., 'Les munitionettes' pp.203-9.

10   L Bernard, *La défense de la santé publique pendant la guerre*, (1920) p.294ff: AN F22 534: organisation de crèches 1916-1918: and BMT, Aug.-Sept. 1917, pp.341-53, 'Enquête sur les crèches d'établissement et les chambres d'allaitement'.

11   Cited by Dubesset etc. 'Les munitionnettes', p.208.

Bibliography

1 Unpublished Primary Sources

A) ARCHIVES NATIONALES
1) sous-série F7: Police Générale
  F7: 12522–25: Congrès divers (1878–1914)
       12541–45: Elections législatives (1902–06).
       12553: Notes sur la situation politique (1899–1905).
       12554–59: Rapports quotidiens de la Préfecture de police (1904–1913).
       12560–65: Notes de police (1901–09).
       12652: Publications obscènes: traite des blanches (1910).
       12765: Métallurgie: situation industrielle, questions ouvrières (renseigne-
              ments généraux, congrès et série départementale) (1901–10).
       12766: Industries de verre (1901–10)
       12767: Industries textiles (1901–10).
       12768: Industries diverses (1901–10).
       12773: Grèves: instructions ministérielles: plans de protection: emploi de
              troupes et usage d'armes: dessous politiques: amnesties: état
              chronologique des grèves (1849–1914).
       12936–39: Guerre de 1914: rapports des Préfets et de commissaires spéciaux
              sur l'état d'esprit de la population (1914–18).
       13266: Assemblée Nationale de Versailles.
       (1)   1) Liste des principaux groupements féministes.
             2) La propagande féminine en faveur de la paix.
             3) Activité internationale pour les droits de la femme.
             4) Suffragettes anglaises.
             5) Union Nationale pour le Suffrage des Femmes.
       (2)   1) Notes générales concernant l'agitation féministe dans les divers
                départements (1918–28).
             2) Résultats du scrutin – séance du Sénat, 21 Nov. 1922, sur la proposition
                de loi tendant à accorder aux femmes le droit de vote.
       (3)   1) Rapports et notes concernant l'activité des différents groupements
                féminines (1913–28).
             2) Extraits de presse concernant les revendications féminines et notam-
                ment le suffrage des femmes (1908–28).
       13356: Usines de guerre (1915–19).
       13357–69: Surveillance des usines: activité syndicale: état d'esprit:
              sabotage (1915–19).
         esp. 13366: Seine (1915–17).
              1) Renseignements statistiques.
              2) Accidents.
              3) Licenciements des ouvrières des usines de guerre.
       13370: Propagande pacifiste (1915–19).

13372: Rapport d'ensemble sur la propagande pacifiste en France.
13374: Manifestes et tractes pacifistes (1915-17).
13375: Manifestes et tractes pacifistes (1914-15).
13594-96: Questions ouvrières et revendications syndicales (1909-17).
13819-22: Textile: congrès: activité syndicale. (1909-21).
13882: Habillement (1919-23).
13891: Métaux (1917-18).
13909-10: (includes) Textile (1911-20).
13955: Malthusianisme (1907-25).

2) sous-série F17: Instruction publique
F17: 8753-84: Enseignement secondaire des jeunes filles: lycées et cours secondaires (1867-97).
8754-8756: Dossiers classés par académies (1867-68).
8757-70: id. (1879-86).
8771-78: cours secondaires de jeunes filles transformées ou supprimées (ordre alphabétique des noms de villes) (1881-86).
8779-80: Affaires diverses (1880-85).
8781-83: Etats de traitements (1886-90).
8784: Affaires diverses.
8785-99: Certificat d'aptitude à l'enseignement secondaire des jeunes filles: agrégation dudit enseignement.
8800-07: Diplôme de fin d'études secondaires des jeunes filles (1893-95).
8808-14: Ecole Normale de Sèvres (1882-96).
9398: Articles de journaux (1880-95).
9399: idem (1880-1901).
12440-41: Application de la loi du 16 juin 1881 sur les écoles de jeunes filles.
14187: Ecole Normale de Sèvres.
14201-05: Agrégation et certificat d'aptitude (CAP): procès-verbaux et listes d'admissibles (1894-8).

3) sous-série F22: Travail et prévoyance sociale.
F22: 438-443: Travail des femmes et des enfants (1886-1937).
438: Législation, enquêtes, judgements (1886-1930).
439: Infractions à la législation (1894-1931).
440: Application du décret du 28 déc. 1909 sur les surcharges imposées aux femmes et aux enfants (1910-14).
441: Application des décrets du 13 mai 1893 et 21 mars 1914 (1893-1930).
442-443: Travail de nuit des femmes (1894-1937).
444-48: Protection de la maternité.
444: Brochures diverses (1917-27).
445: Repos des femmes en couche (1893-1923).
446: Crèches et chambres d'allaitement (1907-21).
447: Ouvrières employées dans les usines de guerre (1915-18).
449-50: Salaries des ouvrières à domicile: Protestations contre les tarifs fixés par les comités départementaux (1915-18).
458-61: Travail des femmes et des enfants: commissions départementales du travail et comités de patronage (1872-1938).
462-72: Travail des femmes et des enfants (1898-1922).
491-94: Accidents du travail (1899-1937).
495-500: Prévention des accidents du travail (1888-1936). Securité des travailleurs.
512-14: Hygiène des travailleurs (1902-29).
517-18: Maladies professionnelles. Application de la loi du 25 oct. 1919 (1921-36).

530–39: Usines de guerre (1915–19).

530–31: Enquêtes sur les établissements susceptibles de travailler ou déjà travaillant pour la Défense Nationale, sept. 1915.

534: Organisation de crèches (1916–18).

538–39: Hygiène et sécurité des travailleurs, alcoolisme, travail féminin, accidents du travail (1916–18).

565–574: Inspecteurs du travail: enquêtes diverses (1908–18).

B) ARCHIVES DE LA PRÉFECTURE DE POLICE

B/a 885: dossier Auclert

   1375: Grèves des usines de guerre (sept. 1917–mai 1918).

     1) Missing.

     2) Rapports quotidiens d'ensemble du 11 sept. 1917 au 3 mai 1918.

     3) Rapports des Renseignements Généraux heure par heure des 25-26-27-28-29-30 sept., 26 oct., 18-19-20 nov. 1917.

     4) Compte-rendu des réunions du 13 sept. au 29 avril 1918.

     5) Correspondance du 4 sept. 1917 au 17 avril 1918.

     6) Rapports (sept. 1917).

     7) Télégrammes du 7 sept. 1917 au 29 mars 1918.

   1376: Grève de l'habillement de 1917 à 1918.

   1406: Grèves dans le département de la Seine (1876-99: 1906-20).

   1407: Grèves de sept. 1917. 1 dossier.
      Grèves de mai à juillet 1919. 8 dossiers.

   1423: Chambre syndicale. Habillement. (1909-18).

   1587: Physionomie de Paris (déc. 1917-1918).

   1588:   (jan.-mai 1919).

   1614: Rapports sur l'état d'esprit de la population parisienne (de juin 1918 à mai 1920).

   1639: Situation morale de la France pendant la guerre (1914-18).

   1660: dossier Séverine.

C) ARCHIVES DE LA GUERRE

   16 N 2439-2451: Main d'oeuvre et travailleurs.

D) BIBLIOTHEQUE MARGUERITE DURAND

   1) Papiers de Jane Misme.

   2) Personal dossiers of:

   Hubertine Auclert
   A Blanche-Schweig
   Cécile Brunschvicg
   Isabelle Bogelot
   Marie Bonnevial
   Marcelle Capy
   Marya Chéliga (or Chéliga-Loevy)
   Marguerite Clément
   Maria Deraismes
   Marguerite de Witt-Schlumberger
   Marguerite Durand
   Caroline Kaufmann

Odette Laguerre
Sarah Monod
Madeleine Pelletier
Maria Pognon
Maria Martin
Jane Misme
Jeanne Oddo-Deflou
Eugénie Potonié-Pierre
Mme Remember (Louise Deverly-Dupont)
Nelly Roussel
Jeanne Schmall
Avril de Sainte-Croix
Mme Jules Siegfried
Maria Vérone
Mme Vincent

3) Dossiers classified under Groupements-Femmes:
L'Action des Femmes
L'Action Féminine
Comité de Propagande Féministe
Conseil National des Femmes Françaises
Le Droit des Femmes
Groupe de la Solidarité des Femmes
Groupe Français d'Etudes Féministes
Ligue Française pour le Droit des Femmes: Cinquante ans
de féminisme 1870-1920
Ligue Nationale pour le Vote des Femmes
Union Française pour le Suffrage des Femmes

4) Other dossiers:
Congrès du Travail Féminin
La Femme dans la vie française
Typographes

E) INSTITUT FRANÇAIS D'HISTOIRE SOCIALE
Fonds Hélène Brion: an extraordinary collection of materials amassed by Hélène
Brion with the purpose of bringing out a feminist encyclopaedia.
purpose of bringing out a feminist encyclopaedia.
14 ASP 337 and 14 ASP 338 contain collections of feminist (and other) newspapers:

1871-1914:	L'Action Féministe
	Le Combat Féministe
	L'Equité
	Le Féminisme Intégral
	La Femme Affranchie
	La Femme Socialiste
	La Française
1914-18:	L'Action Féministe
	Le Combat Féministe
	Le Cri Des Femmes
	L'Equité
	Le Féminisme Intégral
	La Femme Socialiste
	La Française
	L'Humantié

Le Journal
Le Journal du Peuple
L'Oeuvre
La Vérité
1918-39:   L'Action Féministe
La Femme Affranchie
La Femme Socialiste
La Française
La Fronde
La Lutte Féministe
Le Rélèvement Social
La République Intégrale
La Tribune des Femmes Socialistes

Index